D1536655

Piloting for
Maximum
Performance

Piloting for Maximum Performance

Lewis Bjork

McGraw-Hill

New York San Francisco Washington, D.C. Auckland Bogotá
Caracas Lisbon London Madrid Mexico City Milan
Montreal New Delhi San Juan Singapore
Sydney Tokyo Toronto

McGraw-Hill

A Division of The McGraw-Hill Companies

pbk   1 2 3 4 5 6 7 8 9 DOC/DOC 9 0 0 9 8 7 6

Library of Congress Cataloging-in-Publication Data
Bjork, Lewis.
    Piloting for maximum performance / by Lewis Bjork.
        p.   cm.
    Includes index.
    ISBN 0-07-005699-4 (pbk.)
    1. Airplanes—Piloting.   I. Title.
TL710.B555   1996
629.132'527—dc20   96-13568
                                                                          CIP

Acquisitions editor: Shelley IC. Chevalier
Editorial team: Lori Flaherty, Executive Editor
                       Charles Spence, Book Editor
                       Susan W. Kagey, Managing Editor
Production team: Katherine G. Brown, Director
                        Ollie Harmon, Coding
                        Donna K. Harlacher, Coding
                        Wanda S. Ditch, Desktop Operator
                        Jennifer M. Secula, Indexer
Design team: Jaclyn J. Boone, Designer   GEN1*/AV
                  Katherine Lukaszewicz, Associate Designer   0056994

To Linda

Disclaimer

As with all flight operations, the surest road to proficiency is practice and experience. This book does not attempt to replace the valuable time spent in the cockpit with a competent flight instructor. Some of the concepts discussed in this text should not be attempted without first achieving flight proficiency under the tutelage of a flight instructor in the airplane to be used. The author of this book makes no claims, expressed, implied, or otherwise, as to the effect this text *alone* might have on the reader's flight proficiency.

Contents

Acknowledgments

It's time to send out the thank-yous and express my appreciation for those who helped make this book possible. First and foremost, I thank my wife, who has worked with me side-by-side on this project from conception to completion: reading, editing, writing, encouraging, organizing, removing distractions, listening to my nonstop talk about airplanes, and so on and so on. It truly was a joint effort. Thanks to Jack Butler for use of his story and photographs; Ron Tew, who photographed the Maule, Dan Sullivan, who photographed the Cricri, and Dick Pratt for the Maule photo in the introduction. Thanks to my friends Maurice Park and Joseph Richardson for their editing and constructive criticism. Dan Vanzeben graciously allowed me to use his beautiful Maule for a photographic and theoretical example throughout the book. My parents generously let me wear out their printer in making numerous hard copies of this text. Paul Smith contributed the computer upon which the book was written and allowed me to work at his home late into the night, on many occasions, to produce the drawings. Obviously, without their assistance this book wouldn't have gone very far. Finally, I thank all those who taught me over the years: my former flight instructors, coworkers, and students, many of whose experiences you will soon be reading about.

Introduction

Whenever pilots boast about their favorite airplane, they always make some claim about its performance. They might contend that one plane takes off from incredibly short runways while another reaches blazing speeds at half throttle. The pilots then attribute the assorted performance highlights to a particular system or feature of the airplane. Huge wings and leading-edge slats, fowler flaps, light weight and high power, all combine to produce a minimal takeoff roll. High speed might stem from smaller airframes with thin, knife-like wings. I heard one pilot of an especially fast experimental plane describe his Ferrari-red speedster as "a huge engine bolted to a little red accessory." All of these characteristics and systems have, of course, direct bearing on the performance of the airplane, but none of these can equal the performance gains possible with a skilled pilot at the controls.

The pilot of an airplane has such a profound effect on the airplane's utility that the features of the airplane's design are secondary. Obviously, even the world's greatest pilot cannot make a Cessna 152 fly as fast as an F-16, nor can a pilot make a Citabria do aerobatics like a Suhkoi, but that is not the point. My points are these: First, every airplane performs better with a skilled pilot at the controls. An Extra 300 does not do flawless eight-point, vertical rolls of its own accord; it takes a skilled pilot to make the plane perform that way. Second, many times an airplane's most amazing capabilities are entirely lost because of improper piloting. For example, I know of one well-educated professional who flies his Cessna 206 as if it were a T-38. He decided that if it is dangerous to stall, then he would stay as far away from the stall speed as possible. He takes off like a top-fuel dragster out of the launch gate. Full throttle and roll and roll and *way* down at the far end of the 9000-foot long runway, tires smoking from the speed, the airplane sort of levitates from the pavement to fly away, already nearly at cruise speed. A Cessna 206 has numerous features that enable a respectably short takeoff roll. When it's lightly loaded, it can fairly leap from the ground. Not so with this pilot at the controls. Improper piloting can void all those design features and negate the short-field utility of a good airplane.

I-1 *Even with a plane like the Pitts Special, the pilot is the key to maneuvering performance.*

This book is an effort to improve the performance capabilities of pilots through education, insight, and practical drills. With a skilled pilot at the controls of the airplane, the machine can safely reach its maximum possible performance. Here are numerous bits of insight, techniques, and practical drills designed to assist in preparing, training, and equipping the pilot for flight at the full capability of the airplane. Piloting for maximum performance means meeting or exceeding the book numbers easily and without significant risk. It means far-greater safety and utility from an airplane than might otherwise be hoped for.

Benefits

Piloting for Maximum Performance is written from an instructor's viewpoint. The intent is for a pilot to *apply* these concepts in an immediate and practical way. Its organization is such that you may easily reference a particular flight procedure and then go practice the skills necessary to master it, a sort of operator's and instruction manual for pilots. Some other benefits include the following:

- Most planes do not perform entirely as advertised, largely because of a lack of pilot skills as compared to the manufacturer's test pilots. This book will teach many techniques to safely duplicate or surpass the performance of those test pilots, realizing personal improvements in runway requirements, speed, and efficiency.

- Because most airplanes are not flown to the full extent of their capabilities, some of their safety features are compromised by a pilot unable to use them. This book will enhance safety by training the pilot to fly the airplane to the full potential of its performance envelope, offering more options in the event of an emergency.

- A pilot able to maximize the landing performance of an airplane has more runways to choose from and the airplane's utility is thus increased, perhaps placing the airplane closer to the intended destination.

- A startling number of general aviation accidents are weather-related. Hearty respect for weather is certainly the healthiest attitude for a pilot, and the principles contained in this book will foster that respect with increased understanding.

- It is often disconcerting for me, as a flight instructor, to find so many experienced pilots that have erroneous, often highly creative, explanations for the physics behind fixed-wing flight. The pilot's understanding of why and how the airplane flies will improve from these pages.

- This book is an excellent source for recurrency and advanced training procedures. The pilot's ability to control the airplane might have a drastic effect on nearly every other aspect of the flight. The pilot will be inspired and challenged to become and remain sharp. The FAA should be overjoyed.

- Many pilots' friends or families do not enjoy flying. The pilot who can deftly demonstrate all the skills and exercises presented in this book will become unusually smooth in the normal flight regime. The enhanced skills of the pilot will be immediately obvious to the passengers in the plane, as evidenced by a smoother and more enjoyable ride.

- Airplanes are notoriously expensive. A careful student of the techniques described in this book should realize fuel savings and shorter block-to-block trip times, both of which reduce the cost of flying.

- Because of better takeoffs and landings, the airplane will experience less wear. Maintenance expenses decrease with fewer replacements of tires, struts, brakes, and less overall wear and tear on the machine.

Structure

This book makes no effort to be specific to any plane except where it uses the examples of a particular airplane's performance. Hopefully, the principles in this book will improve the cockpit performance of any pilot, whether in an ultralight, an F-16, or anything between. General organization roughly follows that of a typical flight, beginning with the preflight decisions and ending with a lovely landing. Some chapters, such as maneuvering and weather, are grouped among the other inflight sections where they seem to logically fit.

Each chapter is further broken into the following sections:

Story

The best way to learn a concept is to experience it. That is somewhat beyond the scope of a book, but a relevant experience related firsthand can provide terrific insight into a topic. All of the stories and anecdotes used in this book are true, unless otherwise indicated.

Background information

It is often difficult to discuss the technical details behind a particular technique or skill without a little background understanding. This section highlights certain technical basics and aerodynamic principles on which to build an understanding of the topic at hand.

Technique

This is the meaty part of each chapter: a detailed discussion of various methods used by pilots to enhance an airplane's performance. It might involve simple things like over- or underinflating tires or the more complex methods of precise glidepath control; a collection of ideas, tricks, and methods, allowing a pilot to pick and choose the best suited for a particular airplane and purpose.

Skills to practice

In some cases, it is possible to develop important skills with the use of a few simple exercises. This section presents several reliable methods of obtaining inflight skills in a particular area, such as slow-flight maneuvering, without undue risk. These methods, for the most part, have been gleaned from numerous flight instructors over a period of several years. This section provides an immediate opportunity for a pilot to practice and develop the skills discussed in this book. Many of the drills can be practiced safely without the services of a flight instructor unless otherwise indicated.

Getting your own figures

This section discusses simple and effective methods of measuring the pilot's personal performance in the cockpit to get the pilot's own figures. Every effort is made to keep the numerical aspects simple. You are certainly welcome to go out and measure specific takeoff performance as viewed from the runway and conduct the same myriad tests previously accomplished by test pilots and aircraft manufacturers, but the purpose of this section is to grade the performance of the pilot alone, as it relates to airplane performance. The measurements create an opportunity for a pilot to learn which specific flying skills work best to maximize performance on an individual, uncharted scale. Often, the only additional help required to conduct these tests is an observer with a stopwatch. Pilots can then find out exactly the performance of which they are capable.

Further reading

This book concentrates on the performance aspect of flying as viewed from the cockpit. The information contained herein has been filtered to the point that the particulars of flying where performance is not a direct factor are dropped. You might want to read further detail elsewhere. For convenience, a few related book titles and publications are included at the end of each chapter.

Individual chapter summaries

Chapter 1—Pilot preflight

Pilot judgment is perhaps the single most important factor in the safety of a flight. This chapter is a preflight analysis of the pilot's ability to make a flight as planned, addressing concerns about the pilot's health, mental state, flying skills, attitudes, and limitations as they relate to flight performance.

Chapter 2—Airplane preflight

The performance potential of an airplane varies somewhat with its physical condition and maintenance. This chapter discusses several conditional factors that determine whether the airplane can safely perform as expected.

Chapter 3—Takeoff

Think in terms of attitude instead of rotation speed for the shortest takeoffs. Learn the pertinent factors affecting takeoff distance that assist the skilled pilot to develop an accurate feel for an airplane's runway requirements. Pilots will make shorter, smoother, and safer departures after applying these principles.

Chapter 4—Climb

Climb is a condition of change. The airplane ascends into different temperatures, wind, and flight conditions. This chapter illustrates the various philosophies behind a maximum-performance climb and helps create an advantageous *climb profile,* as performance interests change from one phase of flight to the next.

Chapter 5—Cruise

During cruise flight, the pilot has a golden opportunity to consider performance options. This chapter explores various methods of trimming, pilot choice of altitude, use of winds, weather, and navigation tools to maximize speed and minimize fuel consumption while the airplane is in transit.

Chapter 6—Weather

Chapter 6 develops a practical and simplified understanding of the physics behind various inflight weather phenomena. It illustrates several ways to recognize and use weather to benefit performance in all phases of flight. An exercise in powered-airplane soaring allows a skilled pilot to experience weather firsthand and presents a way to stay airborne for very low cost.

Chapter 7—Maneuvering

A pilot's ability to finely control the airplane in maneuvering flight will improve with the exercises illustrated in this chapter. It explains the relationship between speed and turn radius, stall speed and load factor, angle of bank, the concept of energy, and much more.

Chapter 8—Approach

Fabulous spot-landings are the goal at the end of a perfect approach. This chapter focuses on airspeed and glidepath control for the purpose of meeting the runway at a predetermined point and energy condition.

Chapter 9—Landing

An accurate landing flare is the capstone to a successful approach. This chapter simplifies the objectives of short-field, soft-field, no-flare, and crosswind landing techniques in the interest of accuracy and minimum energy.

Chapter 10—Emergencies

All inflight emergencies boil down to a serious need to land. This chapter discusses the emergency landing in terms of energy reduction and impact survivability.

Final note

Throughout this book, you will find a great many references to slow-speed flight, maneuvering, and stalls, with numerous exercises that require the pilot to make the airplane dance around at high angles of attack. Of all the regions of the flight envelope, slow flight is perhaps ignored the most. I have yet to meet a pilot who cannot make an airplane fly at cruise. However, very few are effective at the low end of the envelope. Accordingly, the biggest performance improvements available to the typical pilot occur in the slow flight regime.

If you are nervous about stalls, you have all the more reason to practice the skills mentioned in these chapters. Get a talented flight instructor to assist you. Stalls, in themselves, are not dangerous. They are a natural part of fixed-wing flight. It is loss of control that is dangerous. Hitting the ground out of control is deadly. Control is the key. Control the plane well near stalled flight and incredible short-field landings are possible. Slow, survivable emergency landings are another by-product of good control in slow flight. Not to mention, a pilot who is thoroughly versed in stall dynamics will be able to avoid the stall with uncanny dexterity, when it is appropriate to do so. It is my sincere hope that your skills at flying at maximum angles of attack will improve with reading this book and a little inflight practice. When you are done, the cockpit of an airplane will be a far safer

I-2 *The author, left, and his brother enjoy an outing in Southern Utah.*

place with more performance options available to you than you thought possible.

Happy flying.

1

Pilot preflight

Dave looked at the battered Piper Cherokee with the same disdain that he viewed any other fixed-wing airplane. This is not to say that he wouldn't get in it, after all, he did want to obtain his commercial fixed-wing ratings and round out his already impressive list of aviation credentials. It's just that the airplane before him looked, for lack of a better word, frumpy. It had no turbine engine, no armor plating, not even any guns, for crying out loud. It could barely carry four people on a cold day, if they flew with no gas in the tanks and everyone stripped to their underwear to save weight. This was certainly not the kind of airplane to enhance his hairy-chested self-image of a combat helicopter pilot, a decorated veteran of the Vietnam war. It did not fit that image in the least.

Dave had already logged several thousand hours of the most intense, challenging, and satisfying flying of his life, flying his beloved helicopters. Now he stood looking at a rented, somewhat battered Piper Cherokee 140 and listening to his instructor tell him how little the experienced helicopter pilot knew about flying a *real airplane*.

Dave thought it was a little peculiar that *he*, a pilot of such vast experience, was forced to learn from a weeny little instructor who had barely amassed 350 hours. He bit his lip, not wanting to get off to a bad start, but it did smell a little funny. The instructor helped check the oil, verified that fuel was in the tanks, and the two climbed aboard. Dave noted with disgust that the airplane generally felt flimsy, as if he could step in the wrong place and put a hole in the wing. The interior resembled that of a really cheap car with plastic liners and cloth seats. This was the closest thing to a flying Volkswagen Beetle that he had ever seen. "Airplanes," he sighed and shook his head. Fixed-wing pilots, like his instructor, were surely a lower class—couldn't even hover. As they completed the preflight checks and announced readiness for takeoff, Dave wondered why there weren't airplanes in everyone's garage. Surely this airplane fly-ing business is easy enough. Maybe people didn't appreciate the VW image.

Takeoff was nothing more than a fast taxi, at the end of which you get to use your hands and fly. *Fly* was relative. In a helicopter, the con-trols demand constant attention, but this plane would fly itself. Trim it and you're done. The flight instructor was busy giving suggestions, doing his best to match the super-pilot image suggested by his Ray-Bans and leather jacket, but Dave could easily discern the pimple-faced, inexperienced idiot behind the facade. The instructor called for a few turns, and Dave complied; demonstrating the smoothness and accuracy of control for which he was well known in rotary-wing cir-cles. The plane flew easily. It was silly.

Next the instructor asked for a stall. He was sitting comfortably in the right seat, trying to look smugly competent and provide a challenge. Dave was pleased that they were moving on to stalls so quickly. The instructor must be impressed with his natural ability to fly. Maybe the instructor was just trying to frighten him? Either way, he'd faced worse and was pleased to be getting accelerated training. "Just pull the nose up," the instructor said. Dave raised the nose until the in-structor's eyes widened slightly, "Must be high enough," Dave thought and held it there. The plane began to buffet gently, like a car on a gravel road. He'd read about this. No big deal. A stall warning began sounding warily and the nose began to drop, gently turning to the left. Dave moved the control yoke to the right and pulled harder to bring the nose back up. The instructor looked amused. Dave found himself aggressively pulling and turning the controls to keep the plane in position. It wasn't too hard. "Do this in a heli-copter," he thought, "and things happen pretty fas . . . !" At that mo-ment the plane turned upside down, then came upright, then appeared to be going straight down, rolling hard to the left. The stall horn was blaring away and Dave was pulling on the controls for all he was worth. His thoughts raced. "What in the ----- is going on!" The world outside was rotating like a rifle ball. Everything out the front window was blurry except for a distant, looming fencepost in the middle which seemed to mesmerize Dave while the world spun around it.

Dizzy and frightened, Dave looked over at the instructor and was surprised to find him laying on the cabin ceiling, pinned there over the back seat. His face was smashed awkwardly into the headliner with the Ray-Bans wrapped partly around his neck. At the beginning of the flight, Dave hadn't noticed that the instructor had neglected to fasten his seatbelt. The G forces were enough at the moment to throw him out of his seat like limp spaghetti and plaster him to the ceiling. He was desperately trying to influence Dave's flying by screaming unintelligible commands and grasping at Dave's ears and hair and by slapping his head, the only things he could reach from his pinned position. Dave, sweat pouring from his face, struggled on the flight controls with one hand and fought off the instructor with the other while the altimeter unwound like a clock with a broken spring. The frantic instructor screamed obscenities and the din was incredible. The cockpit was a mess. The contents of the ash trays filled their eyes and noses, and everything smelled like cigarettes. The instructor yelled something about spinning and Dave was pretty sure, no, positive, that's what it was. "A spin," he thought. He'd read about this too—this *is* a big deal. To get out, he just had to . . . "Let's see. . . ."

Then the combat pilot in him took over. He ignored the slap-happy idiot instructor, the spin, the noise, and tried to concentrate. Somewhere in the back of his mind he remembered reading that most airplanes are inherently stable, therefore all he had to do was let go of the controls. He did. The airplane stopped turning rather abruptly and stayed there, diving at the ground. The rest of the world came into focus as it stopped rotating. The stall horn no longer sounded, and when Dave began pulling on the controls, the instructor fell across his seat with a thump. The instructor had been yelling non-stop at the top of his lungs, and by this time he was a little hoarse. "I TOLD YOU TO PUSH THE RIGHT RUDDER! RIGHT RUDDER RIGHT RUDDER RIGHT RUDDER! YOU IDIOT! YOU COULD HAVE KILLED US!" He looked red-faced angry, like a swollen tomato about to burst, his mouth open wide and spitting mad, rapid-fire curses. Dave, who is rather large and now also rather miffed, was not about to take abuse from this fool who was too cocky to wear a seatbelt. His response instantly quieted the rabid instructor; he simply told him he would "beat the living ------ out of him" when they land. As they flew back, Dave gained a new respect for this kind of flying machine. "Could have killed us," he thought, even in a Volkswagen. The instructor said little else as they headed for the airport.

When the plane slowed down on the runway, the instructor opened the door, leaped from the still-rolling plane, and ran across the ramp, leaving Dave alone to taxi in. Dave hasn't seen him since—nor does he want to.

Background information

A wise pilot observing these two getting into the Piper could have foreseen a future accident with startling clarity. It would be the same as watching a couple of hormone-riddled teenagers speed off in a fast car. The airplane was obviously not responsible for their aerial mishap.

Aviation accidents

Let's examine the circumstances that led to this near disaster. A Piper Cherokee 140 has extremely gentle stall characteristics. Dave really had to goof up to get it to spin. In light of the fact that such forceful control inputs are required to spin the plane, responsibility for it certainly rested with Dave. He was far too self-assured and above the task at hand and the airplane bit him, like a caged tiger that bit a kid who teased it and got too close.

The instructor was equally at fault. He should have done better. I was about to say that he should have *known* better, but he probably did. He just didn't do anything with his knowledge. Both occupants of the airplane exhibited poor judgment for the flight. Dave is an excellent pilot with superb flying skills. The instructor probably went on to log a great many flying hours. It is hoped both pilots are better off for having survived their brush with poor judgment.

You might wonder why the first discussion in a book about performance is centered upon judgment. First, any plane that crashes and kills the occupants certainly delivers bad performance. To achieve high performance in any flight, the flight must at least end safely. Anything else is failure. Second, the skills that are soon to be presented will quickly kill a pilot who does not apply them correctly or at the proper time. Superb flying skills and poor judgment combine to destroy airplanes and pilots.

The law requires pilots to demonstrate good judgment. Part of the FAA regulations detail specifically who is responsible for a flight. The title, *pilot in command,* along with a certain ego-stimulating re-

1-1 *Sometimes pilots are outperformed by their own egos.*

spect, carries the ultimate responsibility for a safe flight. If anything goes wrong, the pilot in command will often carry the blame. If, for example, a pilot flies a plane in which a mechanic has failed to adequately attach the wings, the pilot might receive blame for the crash. Ultimately, the pilot should not have attempted to fly a plane that was not structurally sound. Bad judgment—pilot error.

Pilot error means the *pilot* is responsible for the vast majority of aircraft accidents. The exact statistics vary with different sources, and I have read figures ranging from 77 to 96 percent. If the law is strictly interpreted, however, the pilot is responsible for *all* aviation accidents. If a crash occurred, it is the pilot's fault—he or she just should not have gone flying. This viewpoint is a little strict, but the ultimate responsibility for a flight, and thus the crash, indeed rests on the shoulders of the pilot in command.

In light of the above facts, the pilot deserves the first and closest scrutiny for the safety of any flight, the airplane second. This chapter concentrates on some judgmental exercises that amount to a few simple questions about the pilot's readiness and capability for a flight. Answer them honestly and poor judgment at this stage can be avoided.[1]

Attitude

Poor attitude control caused Dave's accidental spin. I'm not talking about his failure to control the airplane's attitude. Dave had an attitude of his own that was out of control. He was doing anything but considering his actions in the plane against their possible consequences. How could a Volkswagen bite? He was nearly killed. I'm sure that flying into combat rather forcefully narrows a pilot's viewpoint. Most just want to survive the war so they can go home. Save the bravado and posturing with the girls for later. Dave had certainly flown with *that* attitude before. All flying is a serious and potentially lethal exercise. If the pilot's reasons for being in the cockpit are for anything other than flying the plane, then the pilot shouldn't be flying.

The attitude case goes further than this. A lot of professionals choose to obtain a pilot's license because of the rapid transportation benefits that airplanes offer in commuting or business travel. Fine. However, the professional person in any field who flies to work had better be only a pilot while in the cockpit. I heard of one crash, a Beech Baron, that was scraped from the top few feet of a mountain. The *lawyer in command* was sleeping at the time of impact. During his lengthy business commutes he would commonly adjust the autopilot to maintain a comfortable altitude, one that would guarantee obstacle clearance along the route of flight, set his alarm clock for 15 minutes and go to sleep. Waking 15 minutes later, he would check all the important stuff, set another 15 minutes on the alarm and go back to sleep.

A friend of his described this procedure, saying that it had worked successfully for years. The lawyer claimed that the airplane was his only real opportunity to rest, since there was so much work going on at his thriving law practice. He found it a great time-saver in getting around as well as a nice way to nap. The alarm, as I understand it, was set to go off a few minutes after impact. During those final, fateful minutes of the lawyer's rest, the airplane had traversed more than

1 Chapter 2 will detail an assessment and evaluation of the airplane.

50 miles of countryside and flew into a region of reducing atmospheric pressure. The altimeter interpreted this reduction in barometric pressure as a gradual climb. The dutiful autopilot compensated by flying a gradual descent, maintaining a constant indicated altitude. A couple of hundred feet later and the plane was stopped, crunched like an accordion against cold rock. The lawyer died in his sleep.

The lawyer possessed many of the same attitudes about airplanes as Dave had previous to his eventful flight: "This thing is idiot simple." However, fate didn't give him a second chance. The lawyer in the Baron was not a pilot. Oh, he had a license and the proper ratings, but at the time of the crash he was a sleeping lawyer; a pilot would have been flying the plane. Dave was a helicopter pilot trying to fly a Piper. An airplane pilot wouldn't have fought so hard to spin it. Likewise an aerobatic pilot doing maneuver demonstrations with a Boeing would be a disaster in a gold-striped suit. Each airplane demands that a proper and conscientious pilot be at the controls. Anything less is pilot error.

The proper attitude to have while in command of any flying machine is one of respect for its limitations. An airplane flown within its limits will not break or even wear out prematurely. It will not spontaneously shed its wings or try to spin. When flown within its limitations, every plane will do pretty much what it was designed to do.

The pilot demands respect as well, and I'm not trying to stroke any egos here. Every pilot has limitations, just like the airplane's. Sometimes the airplane's limits exceed those of the pilot, sometimes it goes the other way. Whatever they are, the most conservative limits dictate the nature of the flight. Suppose, for example, a pilot has access to an airplane that is quite capable of performing aerobatic maneuvers. Its operating handbook might even offer a few suggestions of entry speeds and techniques. However, this pilot has never done aerobatics before and while in charge of that plane it will be the pilot's, not the airplane's, limits that will rule. Accordingly, the flight will be straight and level. Reverse the situation, putting Captain Airshow Whirligig in the cockpit of a Cherokee and the result is the same, straight and level flight, this time in accordance with the airplane's structural limitations. It is up to the pilot to determine the safe limitations for the flight and abide by them.

One last aspect of the proper attitude in flight is perhaps the most compelling: THE PENALTY FOR A SERIOUS MISTAKE IN AN AIRPLANE IS *DEATH*.

Physical readiness

The pilot must be physically capable to fly. This seems obvious of course. No alcoholics, drug addicts, or suicidal terrorists belong at the controls of an airplane. To maximize the performance of an airplane, the pilot must be thinking or concentrating accurately at a fast pace. This level of concentration can be tiring to sustain for a whole flight and requires skill to do successfully. If the pilot is a little tired at the beginning of the flight, not feeling sharp and completely ready to fly, fatigue will become powerful by the end, and performance will suffer. If the pilots skills are *average* on a given day, then exceptional performance should not be expected.

Regular exercise, where possible, will do much to improve clarity of mind and physical dexterity. Hair-trigger reflexes are rarely needed in flying, but rapid-fire decision-making skills often are. Being physically active improves both.

Sickness and other maladies must be considered as detriments to pilot, and thus airplane performance. I have often heard pilots blame a poor showing during a checkride on having a cold, being tired, or simply on being sore from a hard game of tennis. In most cases the safety of the flight was not compromised in the least. The pilots were merely explaining that they expected more of themselves or could have done a better job. This is common. The pilot must be careful not to count on a sterling performance in the cockpit when experiencing the effects of a health problem. Good judgment would dictate that pilots avoid situations that demand their best skills when they are not physically feeling up to it, and that can be a difficult assessment to make.

A little preflight planning for the physical demands of a flight can go a long way. Consider my usual spiel to a new aerobatic student in the Pitts: "Come with your stomach half-full of dry, absorbent food. Eat soda crackers, biscuits, bread, anything that you won't mind losing. The absorbency of the food seems to delay the effects of an upset stomach a little longer. Wear soft-soled tennis shoes. The rudder pedals are sensitive and best felt through the soles. Loose-fitting clothing will prevent any constrictions. Bring warm socks. The airplane has no heater. I'll provide a bag for any contingencies." That's it. You can see how a little preparation can dramatically improve the student's performance in the airplane. Forget anything important and performance is reduced because the student can't pay full attention to flying. What if you go on a long, over-water flight and forget about your bladder? I don't want to get into some of the creative solutions I've heard to solve this problem except to say that by the time it's taken care of, you could be lost. That would be a difficult and embarrassing situation to explain to the Flight Service Station.

Combine ego and physical needs and you get a miserable experience. I was flying with a student named Scott one day, teaching the basics of instrument flight. That night the flight rocked about in turbulence. Scott flew under the hood to a little airport for a few touch and goes. As the airplane bounced around the pattern, I felt a little queasy. I dismissed it. I never get sick. It'll go away. A couple of landings later, I was feeling worse. I nonchalantly suggested to Scott that we should be heading back. Tell him why? Of course not. Scott knew and was obviously impressed by the fact that I *never* get sick. I'd be fine. During the 40-mile flight home, it became apparent that I was not going to make it. I needed a bag, and soon. Not wanting Scott to see, I had him again wear the hood. I gave him headings to fly while discretely examining the various pockets behind the seats and elsewhere in the cabin, looking for a barf bag. No luck.

Glancing at Scott, I could see he was still unaware of my plight. Good. I didn't want to tell him, or throw up all over his airplane. There was only one choice left. I loosened my tie and unfastened the top button of my shirt. Taking careful aim, I let 'er rip down my collar, inside my clothing. I was disgusted but relieved. Scott hadn't noticed. Maybe I could hide it. I opened the fresh air vents. He was concentrating pretty well on the flying. A few minutes later I was sick again. I was in the middle of it all, my face down my collar, when Scott happened to look my way. I was mortified. Scott said, "You should have told me, Lewis, I've got a bag right here." Live and learn. I guess I can get sick after all.

Mental/emotional state

While thinking on the stresses of a demanding flight, pilots should evaluate their emotional condition. If the condition is anything but strictly controllable, the flight should be avoided. This one can be a pretty tough check. It's hard to be rational during times of emotional stress. Facing the need for performance in the cockpit, however, it is mandatory that the pilot gain self-control in this area. During an emergency situation, for example, the pilot must control fears and subdue emotions. To lose control and panic quickly brings loss of control of the airplane—pilot error.

Crash statistics indicate that a large majority of serious aircraft accidents are survivable if the pilot maintains control of the airplane all the way through the crash. Those accidents wherein aircraft control is lost are almost always fatal. Aircraft control cannot be sustained by a panicked pilot. When the pilot surrenders to fears of the crash or death, rational judgment is surrendered at that point as well. Of equal importance is the problem of being too relaxed and disregarding indications of serious trouble. Calm attentiveness probably best describes the ideal emotional condition for the pilot. The pilot needs to be aware, alert, attentive, and in rational control at all times while flying the plane. It is no time for temper-tantrums with ATC or fights with passengers. Emotional conflicts of any sort are best left on the ground.

Skills

With the pilot ego being what it is, skill assessment can be one of the most difficult to make. You can see it all over the faces of pilots who say, "I could fly that Learjet if someone would just help me start it." And so on. It seems that most pilots are convinced they are better than they really are. Therefore, perhaps one of the most valuable perspectives to develop is an understanding of the limits of your own pilot skills.

A friend who is a wonderful professional instructor and airline pilot of more than 20,000 hours' experience had this to say about one of the finest pilots he ever saw in action:

> *I was captain of a Boeing 737 for Frontier Airlines. During the course of the day's flying, I like to alternate legs with the first officer. That is to say that I fly one segment of the trip, he flies the other, and so on.*
>
> *It was the last leg of the day and the first officer was flying. We were landing in Billings, Montana, at night. The wind was blowing snow in excess of 30 knots across the runway and the airport was covered with ice. The copilot looked concerned. I*

said, "Just do a normal crosswind landing, plant it solid, and use differential power in the reversers to steer." He thought for a moment, while flying the approach, then looked at me and asked me to make the landing. He said he didn't feel comfortable enough with his skills to safely manage it. So I did. Landed fine. He was the best pilot I ever saw.

What most impressed my friend about the first officer was his ability to assess his skills and make a decision based on them, rather than on his ego; impressive judgment indeed.

Finally, I am reminded of the fable about a couple of hunters enjoying an excursion in the Alaska wilderness. They bagged a moose. When the bush pilot returned to fly them home, he said that the moose was too heavy to go along. "Aw, please," the hunters begged, "the pilot did it last year, and he had a plane just like yours." The pilot did not want to be out-done and accepted the challenge. After loading the two hunters, a week's camping gear, and the 2000-pound moose on board, the airplane was sitting very low in the water. The pilot began to protest a little, "I don't think this is such a good idea." Again came the hunters' plea, and "the pilot did it last year." So the pilot swallowed hard and started the engine. Starting from one end of the lake, he hit the throttle and plowed through the water. The plane accelerated, but slowly, like an oil tanker in the Suez canal. They were barely off the water when they hit the trees at the far end of the lake. Climbing out of the wreckage, the pilot asked the hunters how last year's pilot did it. They said, "Oh, you made it about 100 yards farther than he did. He crashed over there."

Technique

Assessment technique is a simple concept, but in light of the previous story, it is clear that this is something best done in solitude at first, with no one to twist a pilot's ego into doing something stupid. The pilot simply needs to ask and honestly answer a few simple, personal questions before each flight. With practice, this preflight evaluation becomes easy, a matter of habit. If it is done regularly, flight performance will increase before the pilot even leaves the ground.

Please be brutally honest with yourself when answering these and similar questions. Truthful accuracy could be critical to the success of the flight.

1 Are my current skills adequate to safely complete the flight? Any doubts here and the safest move is to stay on the ground and look for more training. Unfortunately many pilots launch into unknown weather or fly difficult terrain with less than adequate skills. Even the appropriate ratings are not in themselves sufficient. The pilot must be practiced, current, and competent.

2 Am I trying to impress anyone by flying the plane? *Showing off* has been responsible for a number of accidents or near disasters. The ego in this case seems to urge the pilot to take unnecessary risks; to get even lower at an airshow, to buzz people to within an inch of their lives, or to demonstrate a really impressive maneuver for the passengers. The solution to this problem is the meat of professionalism in the cockpit: Eliminate the ego.

3 Is there anything on my mind besides flying the airplane? This is an opportunity to evaluate nonflying related stresses and realistically determine if they will adversely affect you as the pilot. If you are too emotionally wound up to honestly consider this question, take a few deep breaths, count to ten, and try again. If you have to go through this process very many times, you probably shouldn't be flying.

4 Am I physically prepared to fly? This category would include everything you can think of about your physical person. Are you drunk? On medication? Are you alert and sharp, or sleepy? Stuffy nose? Are you healthy? The list is a long one, and no one knows the answers better than you. Additional concerns are those of an unexpected landing. Have you brought some survival gear? Speaking of survival, you might include accessories like air-sickness bags and bladder relief as needed.

That's it. Answer the preceding questions truthfully before every flight, act on your answers wisely, and you can be assured of improved pilot performance.

Skills to practice

In this short section, I will discuss ways to improve the pilot's judgment and complete a successful pilot preflight.

Habitual consistency

One of the best rules about flying is that the physics never change. Airplane flight is made possible today based on the same physical laws that made the Wright Brothers successful many years ago, and those same laws will still apply tomorrow. Mess with the laws, and the plane won't fly. Likewise, the safe habits developed today must also be practiced in the future, or they do little to improve safety. It might seem redundant for a pilot to do a self-assessment before every flight, but it is important. Forget many such simple checks and you might one day find yourself blasting off into the unknown, unprepared and vulnerable.

Good judgment is born as much from habit as from wisdom.

Assuming the attitude of a student

It is a good idea from a proficiency standpoint to get a few hours of instruction in the cockpit on a regular basis. Find a good flight instructor who knows something you would like to learn, and go learn it. Nothing moderates an ego like a good critique.

Getting your own figures

Take this little test for the sake of a grade and your own amusement. It is a simple attempt to attach a quantity, or grade, to your readiness for flight. Evaluate yourself against each of the following statements, scoring from 0 to 10 in each. Award yourself a 10 if you are in complete harmony with the statement, 0 if you are completely opposed.

1 My skills are entirely adequate to complete the flight as planned.

2 My ability to cope with emergencies during the flight is finely honed.

3 I have recently practiced and safely demonstrated the skills needed for the flight and any foreseeable emergency.

4 I am familiar with and respectful of the airplane's limitations.

5 I have eliminated my ego while in the cockpit.

6 I am aware and respectful of my own limitations.

7 There are no problems on my mind except those with direct bearing on flying the plane.

8 The safety of the flight takes priority over having to get there.

9 I understand the consequences of a serious mistake.

10 I am healthy and in perfect control of my emotions.

A total score of 100 could indicate that you are 100-percent ready to fly. At what percentage would you *not* fly?

When judgment is truly good

A few sections in this book discuss topics that are difficult to quantify. Judgment is one of those topics. How do you attach a number or a scale to good judgment? Perhaps the simplest indication is a reference to the age and experience of the pilot. You've heard the proverb about the lack of "old, bold pilots." It would seem that to survive in flying for a very long time requires the pilot to possess and demonstrate good judgment. The logbook measure can be inaccurate, however. There are many old pilots who were simply lucky, and they are often the first to admit that they were fortunate to escape some dire circumstances, and experience in itself can be the basis for a swollen ego.

The worst part is that experience of the most instructional and useful nature is usually the direct result of a bad choice. Make a bad decision, survive the consequences, and now you know better. Those pilots who have recorded a great deal of experience might also have made a great many mistakes. It is hoped that those mistakes will bring valuable lessons to bear in future decisions. This is the basis for good judgment. Experience can be a harsh and unforgiving schoolmaster. GOOD JUDGMENT DICTATES THAT PILOTS LEARN FROM THE MISTAKES OF OTHERS.

When you survive your long and exciting adventure in aviation, retiring healthy and happy, looking back on experience aged to a wonderful golden hue, you'll know then that your decisions were adequate, that you have probably used some good judgment. Good luck.

Further reading

Aviation and the Law, Laurence E. Gesell, Coast Aire Publications, 1987
Flying Safely, Richard Collins, Macmillan Publishing Company, 1984
Basic Flight Physiology, Richard O. Reinhart, M.D., McGraw-Hill, 1992

2

Airplane preflight

Max settled into the rich chocolate-brown leather seats of the brand-new company C-T210. The aroma of new plane delighted him; leather mixed with plastic and maybe a hint of the smell of new electronics. Before him was the best instrument panel he could afford, softly humming with electrons; he had carefully selected each piece of avionics after hours of pouring over the sales and options brochures. He had negotiated with the sales people about price, delivery, paint, and other options too numerous to mention. The plane finally arrived and it looked exactly as he had specified: a 1978 Cessna Turbo Centurion, white paint with deep red and black pinstriping, with hardly more than ferry time on the Hobbs meter.

Max went through the starting checklist with ease. This was certainly not the first Centurion he had flown. The company had owned a 210 for the past three years, finally trading the old plane for this one. Most persons in the sales department had pilot licenses. In addition, the company hired Jim, a professional pilot, for those employees who could not fly themselves. As the engine started and fell into the familiar idling cadence of the big Continental, Max was glad that Jim would accompany him for this flight. Jim had more experience than Max and all the other employees combined, and this was a perfect opportunity to brush up on skills and wring out the new plane.

They listened to the ATIS broadcast describing a beautiful spring day as they taxied out to the active runway. The airplane was free of the usual rattling and squeaking that seems to develop in airplanes after regular use. It was tight, quiet, and perfect. Max really enjoyed the preflight inspection. He noticed that even the belly shone, devoid of the usual dark oil smear and exhaust grime streaking back between the main gear. Max could find no scratches in the paint, cracks in the fairings, or even wear on the tires. It was fun to look at a plane so nicely in working order and to know that, at least for now, it was his—the company's, officially, but he owned the company.

Max prided himself on being a careful pilot. He always followed the checklist and completed each item with consistency. He came too far in life to waste it all on a simple mistake like forgetting an item on a checklist. Jim sat there in the right seat, fiddling with the new ARNAV equipment. "Nice," Jim said. He, too, apparently liked this plane.

Max considered the dangers of this flight as they compared to flights in the past. It felt safer than most. A new plane meant that every part was new, every piece in working order. There would be less chance of anything breaking, even minor stuff. Max smiled to himself at his wisdom in paying the extra money for a new plane, instead of buying one from the used market. It made sense from a safety standpoint, not to mention from the standpoint of better performance.

The plane had plenty of oil and fuel. The oil was a golden-brown color. It was straight mineral oil, a brand recommended for breaking in a new engine. The fuel tanks were full. They should be—had better be. Visually checking them presented the only difficulty during the preflight inspection. Fuel tanks are in the wings. The 210 has wings too high to see the tank openings without a small step ladder. The stepladder they had kept in the previous plane somehow was sold with the airplane. Max was unable to check the fuel visually. Jim had offered a boost, but Max declined, besides, the fuel gauges were pegged on full and since the plane was new, they were certainly in working order. Max glanced over at the gauges to check them again. All the engine parameters were in the green, the oil temperature rising, pressures good. The tachometer needle steadied at 900 RPM. The fuel gauges hadn't moved. The tanks were full, Max was sure.

They held short of the active runway and went carefully through the before-takeoff checklist. Controls verified free and correct. As he manipulated the engine during the run-up, Max felt its power every time he adjusted the throttle. Prop cycled beautifully, mags perfect. They completed the checklist and were soon cleared onto the active runway.

As Max advanced the throttle, fuel rushed down the lines through the pump and on to the injectors, air packed into the cylinders, and the whole mixture exploded with power. The engine's sound went from a gentle cadence to a rumble, then to a mighty growl. As the turbo came on line and boosted the manifold pressure to a full 32 inches, the fuel flow increased to stabilize just shy of 27 gallons/hour. The big, three-blade prop bit into the air and produced a healthy pull, pressing the two pilots back firmly into their seats. Max advanced the manifold pressure to redline and smiled as the airplane ripped past 40 knots like a sports car. At 75, he lifted the nose-wheel and the plane shot off the runway like an enthusiastic grasshopper. The plane climbed better than he expected, almost 2000 feet per minute. Max was delighted. He reached down to retract the gear.

As the plane rotated the fuel sloshed rearward in the tanks, at least the small amount of fuel remaining in the tanks. The airplane had been flown extensively the day before. The pilot arrived late that evening, and, tired and anxious to get home, neglected to refuel the plane. The tanks were left virtually empty. Max hadn't noticed that during fuel sampling from the quick drains, the fuel did not gush from the valve as energetically as usual. He also didn't notice that the plane seemed lighter on the wheels in taxi. Finally, he didn't suspect that the wonderful climb rate might be due to a 600-pound lighter takeoff weight. Even Jim attributed the plane's sprightly performance to the fact that it was new. The fuel gauges lied. They were stuck on full and had indicated such for the last six hours of flight. As the plane lifted from the runway, the fuel unported from the pickups, air entered the lines and passed quickly to the pumps, causing them to fail. Fuel pressure as indicated on the gauge fell off sharply, but slipped Max's gaze. He was watching the airspeed and rate of climb. Shortly thereafter, the fuel injectors were starved. Exactly five seconds after liftoff, the engine abruptly stopped.

They were about 150 feet high. Max had his hand on the landing gear lever and was about to retract the wheels when the world took on a different perspective. It rushed upwards towards them with alarming speed. Jim instantly sat bolt upright. His left hand flashed to cover Max's and keep the wheels down and locked, as his right hand suddenly appeared on the control yoke. Max's eyes were so wide he could have read fine print in the dark. An engine failure on takeoff! His beautiful plane undoubtedly would be marred. What could have caused this to happen? Jim pushed the nose down to meet the runway, flared quickly, and landed on the short length of runway still remaining ahead of them. Jim took a deep breath and they coasted onto the last taxiway and stopped. Neither man said a word.

After a few moments the radio came alive. "Cessna _____, tower, are you all right?" "Yes, I think, but we need a tug. We've had an engine failure." The airport authority arrived within a minute. Jim was already outside the plane, looking for damage. He asked for a stepladder. Jim climbed up on the wing and loosened the fuel caps. The tanks were dry. The fuel gauges still indicated full.

Background information

Max was wrong to think that his airplane would perform best when it was new. In several ways, a plane that is well broken-in will perform better than a new one. Max's error was to trust a new airplane as though its systems were infallible because they were unused. He made the mistake before he even got in the plane. The only way to verify the fuel quantity is to fill the tanks and *see* the fuel in there. It seems that fuel gauges, more than any other piece of equipment in an airplane, tend to lie.

There are several reasons why a new plane is not decisively safer than a used one. Many of the components in a new airplane are not really new at all. For instance, the fuel gauges might have been sitting on a shelf at the factory for several months before being installed in the airplane. Worse yet, they might have been moved several times, perhaps shipped from another location, and even experienced some rough handling. Electronic components need to be broken-in, or in their case, burned in, to function reliably. If electrical equipment is going to fail, it will usually happen within the first 100 hours.

The same is true with mechanical equipment. Many mechanical systems, like engines, for example, improve their power and smoothness with a little wear. After several inflight cycles of the metal in an engine block, the temperature changes have a way of *seasoning* the engine, making it well accustomed to normal operation. Again, a new engine often has more opportunity to fail than one already in service. Throughout the plane, there are numerous fasteners, nuts, bolts and other components that will shift slightly as the plane is used. Until they are shifted or vibrated into position and "comfortable," they can never be considered permanently in place. Often a new airplane can be plagued with loose fasteners, nuts and bolts, occupying a mechanic for hours during an annual inspection, just retightening things that have tried to fall off.

The aircraft manufacturers develop flight performance charts based on their airplanes as they roll out the factory door. A new airplane, flown with the same techniques used by the company test pilots, can be expected to perform exactly as the book declares. It is a common misconception to suppose that a used plane is no longer capable of such performance. In this light, we'll examine each of the airplane's components and systems from a performance standpoint as they compare to a factory new plane. It might be surprising to learn that the hammered rental plane available from the local FBO might, in some cases, perform better than one that is factory new.

Engine

Power in an engine is developed through compression. Compression is produced by the combustion of a fuel and air mixture. Increasing compression usually results in better power but also generates greater heat as a by-product. Too much compression can cause an engine to explode. An engine's internal parts and mechanical workings might sap some of the power generated by combustion. An engine literally uses power generated from within itself to make itself work. Like the old saying about money, the same is true with internal combustion: it takes power to make power. The degree of efficiency with which the engine produces thrust necessary to fly will change remarkably throughout the life-span of the engine.

Piston engine

In a piston engine, the combustion is contained within the walls formed by the cylinder, the cylinder head, and the piston. The piston moves as the pressure increases. The moving piston connects to a rod that turns the shaft, and the shaft drives the propeller (Fig. 2-1).

Compression is the key to power. More compression produced means greater power and, hopefully, greater thrust. Invariably, there are internal losses of the power produced with internal combustion. These losses are primarily due to friction and heat. The piston has steel rings that make close, tight contact with the sides of the cylinder to provide the necessary seal and produce compression. Without them, the compressed gasses would simply escape around the piston. These rings produce a great deal of friction. Just try moving the

2-1 *Pistons, rings, valves, rods, bearings, and accessories all produce friction that saps much of the power developed by compression and combustion.*

propeller of an engine with new rings. You'll hear and feel the tight rings as you turn the noticeably stiff prop. The tight rings increase compression by providing a good seal in the combustion area. The tightest seal comes a little after the rings are newly changed, however. When new, there are microscopic differences, or gaps, between the rings and the cylinder walls. As the engine is "broken in," the rings and cylinder walls wear together to form a nearly perfect seal, increasing compression. Therefore, an engine properly broken in will have more compression, and thus more power, than a new one.

A new piston engine will also have tight bearings that cause greater friction and resistance to the engine's operation. Again, with use, the bearings become less tight, reducing friction with the overall effect of better power and smoother operation. Unfortunately, the wear between parts in an engine is continuous. As the engine is used, the rings and cylinder walls erode each other until gaps form in the seal and compression eventually decreases. Bearings might become dangerously loose and allow parts to fly about. Nevertheless, after a few hundred hours of use, a well-treated engine often outperforms a new one.

One of the most powerful configurations occurs when a well-worn engine is given a top overhaul. A top overhaul involves new rings, but not shaft bearings. The old bearings are loose; the new rings are tight. The resulting high compression and low friction combination is a formula for maximum power. This is commonly practiced in racing circles. So the piston engine of a factory-new airplane might actually be a slight detriment to its performance.

Turbine engines

A jet engine also develops power by compression. In this case, the compressor section of the engine packs the air tightly into the combustion section, where it mixes with fuel and is ignited. The combustion increases pressure before the air is allowed to accelerate and pass at high velocity through the turbine blades, which in turn are connected by a shaft to the compressor section. The whole process can be harnessed to develop thrust, as in a turbofan, or geared mechanically to a propeller, as in a turboprop (Fig. 2-2).

The bearings in the main shaft(s) and movement of the air through the engine itself cause the major source of friction in a jet engine. Heat is worse for the turbine than for the piston engine, specifically heat on the turbine blades themselves. The burning fuel and air mixture directly contacts the turbine elements at high velocity. It is as though the delicate, precisely machined turbine blades are exposed to a sort of blowtorch while spinning at 100,000 RPM. If they get too hot, they fly to pieces and the engine fails.

A jet engine has no pistons, cylinders, rods or rings, hardly any of the complexity of the reciprocating engine. Consequently, there is little that would affect the operational condition of the engine with time, reflecting their normally long intervals between overhauls. The primary wear occurs in the *hot section* of the turbine engine, which might require occasional replacement.

A turbine's maximum power output will decline with age, however. High-velocity air and high temperatures cause a fair amount of erosion on the turbine elements and affect the engine's power capacity. Also, carbon build-up within the engine can affect the internal airflow and reduce efficiency, causing the engine to burn more fuel and produce less power. The decline is very slow, but going from a new turbine to an old one, the pilot would definitely notice a difference in power. An old jet engine is pretty much as reliable as a new one, provided all parts and systems are in working order, but,

2-2 *Compressor at one end, turbine at the other; few moving parts, and high power. A jet engine is a delightfully simple concept.*

depending upon its age, it might not be trusted to develop as much power as a new one.

So, there we are doing a preflight on an airplane. We get to the engine and need to know if it will perform as expected. We look under the cowl and check for loose wires, leaking oil, disconnected accessories, and general, overall condition, in addition to the fluid levels themselves. That's it. It's really difficult to inspect an engine thoroughly until you turn it on. We'll get to that in the technique section of this chapter.

Exterior structure

We are moving on to inspect the airplane's exterior structure in relation to performance. I have noticed many pilots complain that since aircraft factories frequently test their planes unpainted, they have an unfair advantage in the performance department. No paint, they say, saves weight. They go on to attribute the poor performance showing of their personal plane as compared to the factory demonstrator to a lovely paint job. Not so. Flight-test aircraft are loaded to gross weight for the purpose of establishing accurate performance figures. Their certificated gross weight is the same for the factory demonstrators and the planes sold out the showroom door. Paint would only contribute an increase to the airplane's empty weight, affecting useful load, but not gross-weight performance.

Radio and electronic apparatus bolted on the airplane's surface might contribute to drag and adversely affect performance. Unfortunately, most operator's manuals don't take this into account. Dirt, grime, oil, frost, and ice might all affect performance. Again, no compensation for these is found in the operator's manual. The *Aeronautical Information Manual* counsels pilots to remove frost and snow from the wings before launching into the wild blue. Many pilots are careful to do so. But many other pilots happily take off and fly airplanes covered with so much dirt that it looks like they were part of an off-road, four-wheel-drive mud rally. Think of dirt the same as frost. If the airplane is extremely dirty, performance will most likely be adversely affected. The dirt, grime, and excess oil deposits also might affect empty weight. Since the pilot refers to weight and balance documents that make no account for dirt, the pilot might inadvertently exceed gross weights by flying a dirty airplane. Under FAR 135 regulations, multi-engine airplanes must be re-weighed every 36 months. The rule is an old one, originating with the fact that the old radial engines would throw a lot of oil, which pools in various cavities within the airplane, changing its weight and balance. The simple solution is to clean the plane. For the most part, however, a plane that is dusty, or a little dull from normal use is not noticeably affected in performance over a clean one. If in doubt and wanting to leave nothing to chance, clean and polish the plane. At least you'll feel better about it.

Most pilots of powered aircraft would do well to visit a soaring competition. Glider pilots arrive early to prepare their ships for flight. They carefully check, clean, and polish every part of the glider's exterior. Using tape, they cover all seams, gaps or any other areas that might produce a whisper of drag. It might seem overkill to the typical pilot, but for a glider, drag reduction is everything. Roy Lopresti once entered the CAFE 400 efficiency race with a stock Mooney 201. He was competing with some highly efficient experimental airplanes, many canards, and a few models designed by the legendary Burt Rutan. Before the flight, he judiciously applied duct tape to various seams and cracks in the airframe, covering vents, and so on, even to the extent of reducing the size of cooling inlets on the cowling, thinking like a glider pilot. During the flight, he used several of the flying techniques later described in this book. He won.

Last, we come to the big, queen mother of exterior inspections. Try to determine if the airplane is broken or if it is about to be. A plane with a broken wing is obviously going to be a lousy performer. The consequences of a structural failure in flight are almost always fatal. You can't be too careful or suspicious here. Most pilots know what to look for: wrinkled skin, loose wings, oil-canning of aluminum skins, loose rivets, missing safety wire, and so on. If you have doubts about a particular problem, feel free to remove access panels, grab a flashlight and look inside. I once took *three days* of poking and prodding during a preflight before I felt comfortable ferrying an old Aero Commander across the country. Pilots should poke, prod, wiggle, and pull on anything that they suspect is amiss. You can't be too careful here. Once you commit to going flying, it's too late to do anything about a problem you should have found on the ground.

Furthermore, a pilot cannot rely solely on the word of a mechanic. If the pilots are at all suspicious, they shouldn't be flying the plane. For example: I attended a company meeting of flight instructors. The boss brought up the topic of a particular Cessna 152 that had been discovered with some slight wrinkling on the bottom of one wing.

The boss mentioned that the mechanic had examined it carefully, declared it airworthy, and said we shouldn't give it a second thought. I said, "Wait a minute. You mean for us to tell the students to look for wrinkles and other signs of damage on the airplane's skin, but that *these* particular wrinkles are okay?" I told him that I would pull my students out of that plane until it was fixed.

The other instructors agreed with my position and said they would do the same. The boss was angry; the mechanic even more so. He came storming into the office the next day to yell at me. He said that when *he* declared an airplane was airworthy, then that was that, and he didn't want any arguments from some peon flight instructor.

Even so, the instructors held their position and the plane didn't fly, so the boss reluctantly grounded it for repairs. As they pulled the first wing skin panel, they found four crushed wing ribs inside. The wing was badly damaged and the instructors were vindicated. Since then, I have been dubious of anything inside the plane that I can't readily see and inspect.

The structure of aluminum airplanes is strong as long as the wings have not been bent. I have had the opportunity to inspect a few light plane wrecks (Fig. 2-3), and in every case the damaged parts could be flexed with one hand, like bending a thick piece of tin foil. Once bent, an aluminum airplane looses much of its structural integrity.

One of the biggest influences on airplane performance is its rigging. This has to do with the way the wings and tail are bolted on. Is the fuselage straight? Is the thrust line properly aligned? Anyone who has built a model airplane should be familiar with a rigging check. Walk to the front of the plane and look at it carefully for anything that appears to be out of alignment. Look at the wings in particular. Does one wing tip appear higher than the other? Does one wing appear thicker than the other one? Is the wing parallel with the horizontal stabilizer (my apologies to Bonanza pilots)?

Check the flaps and see if one or both appear slightly extended when in the up position. Rigging can be adjusted by a mechanic. It is usually done to facilitate trim, but if done incorrectly, the plane will fight itself in flight and a price is paid in performance. Often planes leaving the factory can be improved by better rigging. It takes skill to do it well; call a good mechanic.

2-3 *Once overstressed, an airframe becomes dangerously weak. Would you fly this?*

Factory-tested airplanes are physically sound, checked before and after flight for damage and stress. If we expect similar performance as the test pilots, we should be willing to do the same, that is, pre-flight and *post*flight inspections.

Control system

The control system check is similar in importance to the structural check, because an inflight failure in the control system is probably going to be fatal. The preflight inspection is often the pilot's only opportunity to verify that this system is operable. When the pilot is planning to operate an airplane at the limits of its performance envelope, the control system can be expected to reach its practical limits as well.

Every control surface on the airplane should be tested throughout its full range of movement before the airplane is flown. Failure to do so could bring a surprise at a critical moment in flight.

Chris, a flight instructor, and his student were conducting a lesson in a Cessna 152. They had completed a preflight inspection during which the control surfaces were moved, but not to the limits of their travel. The flight was uneventful except for the final landing.

Chris asked his student to demonstrate a short-field approach and landing. The student configured the airplane with ⅔ flaps and trimmed for an approach speed 10 knots slower than normal. During the landing flare, as the student began raising the nose, the yoke was somehow blocked from behind the panel, preventing the nose from rising farther. Chris became alarmed and began pulling with the student on the yoke. It appeared as though a hard landing on the nose-wheel and possible prop strike would be inevitable. I have always been impressed with Chris's quick thinking at that moment—he extended the flaps fully. In the Cessna, flap extension causes the nose to rise. Chris slapped down the final third, and the flare continued to a beautiful, and rather lucky, landing. The cause of the blockage was a loose transponder mounting bracket behind the panel. It hung down in the path of the control mechanism and prevented the application of full-up elevator.

If full control is not available to the pilot, full performance is not available either. A pilot *must* verify and establish that the control system is working throughout its entire range of operation before committing to flight.

Landing gear

The landing gear is an excellent place to begin enhancing performance, especially performance on the runway, whether taking off or landing. Options available to the pilot in this area are numerous.

Inflation of the tires can have a direct bearing on rolling friction. Less rolling friction translates into better acceleration on the runway and ultimately shortens takeoff roll. If the runway is hard surfaced, higher pressure in the tires should reduce friction. On soft surfaces, however, the footprint of a high-pressure tire might be too small and prone to sinking, or digging in to the terrain. In that case, it might be desirable to somewhat deflate the tires in an effort to increase the wheel footprint and improve *flotation*. This would also have the effect of improving the takeoff roll. However, the improved flotation caused by partially deflated tires will be a detriment on a wet, paved runway, causing longer landing distances.

An alignment check might reveal a potential performance problem. Poor wheel alignment could be responsible for undue rolling friction, unpredictable ground handling, and excessive tire wear. Alignment is quite simple to check, although it might be very difficult to fix. You can bet that the factory verified that wheels were properly aligned when the airplane prototype was flight tested.

Wheel bearings in many airplanes might be unnecessarily tight. As a new flight instructor, I flew with another instructor to a small town in southern Utah to retrieve a Piper Cherokee 180. We test flew the Cherokee around the pattern together. Taxiing out, the plane acted as though it were plowing through heavy mud, such was the high power setting required. During the takeoff roll, I thought the airplane needed an unusually long piece of asphalt to get airborne. Acceleration seemed very slow, enough that several times on the runway I checked to verify that the parking brake was off. Once airborne, the plane seemed normal in every way. I thought perhaps the high field elevation was responsible for the long roll on the runway, but climb rates were actually quite good. Then, in the landing, the instant the tires met the pavement, there was a pronounced screeching of rubber and asphalt, and I felt that the deceleration would nearly pull the hair from my eyebrows. The landing rollout was impressively short, but unintentionally so. I thought that somehow I had landed with the brakes on. It felt exactly like that. I was embarrassed.

At the end of the ferry flight back home, I was sure to verify that all brakes were disengaged. The landing rollout was the same, leaving pronounced skid marks at the point of touchdown. A mechanic put the plane on jacks and examined the brakes. They were fine. When he tried to turn the wheels, however, the bearings were so tight that he could barely get them to budge.

Tight bearings can destroy otherwise good takeoff performance. It is fairly common. One of the best ways to check wheel bearings during preflight is to pull the airplane a little distance on the ramp or out of the hangar. If it rolls easily, as it should, then the bearings are okay. If they are too tight, a mechanic can easily fix the problem.

If the airplane has a retractable undercarriage, the mechanism needs careful scrutiny. Besides looking for obvious signs of damage and leaking fluids, the pilot should periodically arrange for a retraction test. When the plane is up on the jacks and the wheels are in the wells, go around and pull on the gear doors. If they move, the slipstream in flight might also pull them slightly open. This can be a significant source of drag. Another way to verify that the retraction is working properly is to arrange a formation flight to visually check that the wheels are fully retracted and their doors are closed. You can be sure the airplane, when tested by the factory, was fully functional in this area too.

Loading

Loading is an easily manipulated variable that affects performance, and the pilot's only real opportunity to fiddle with it occurs before flight. Heavy gross weights generally degrade performance. This is commonly reflected in the performance charts found in the manual. Most pilots expect reduced performance as the airplane seats and baggage areas become filled. What is not commonly known is that the balancing aspect of the load can also affect performance.

An airplane balanced at its aft limit will perform better than one balanced at the forward limit. The reasons behind this are simple: Loading at the aft limit reduces the overall lift required of the wing, causing a reduction in lift-induced drag.

The horizontal tail of most airplanes produces a downward stabilizing force. That is because many of the most useful airfoils employed by designers in the main wings produce a forward pitching moment. That is to say that they act like water skis that are used upside down. As the airplane flies, this pitching moment must be countered with a downward pull at the tail (Fig. 2-4), or one upward at the nose as in a canard configuration.

The main wing must produce lift to counter this downward pull, in addition to the weight of the airplane. This is one of the main

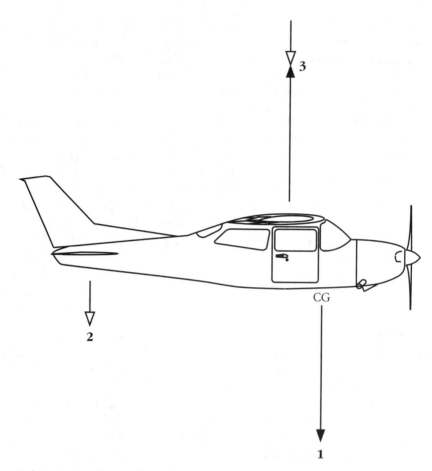

2-4 *Imagine the airplane hanging on the lift vector, or center of lift, as though on a string. With weight (1) acting on the center of gravity, forward of the center of lift, the airplane would hang nose-low unless it is countered by a downward force (2) at the tail. The wing must produce lift (3) totaling the weight of the airplane plus the downward force at the tail. If the center of gravity were located farther aft, closer to the center of lift, the required stabilizing force at the tail would be less, meaning that the wings need produce less overall lift, thereby reducing drag.*

advantages of a canard configuration—the canard does not pull against the main wing, thus providing greater efficiency (Fig. 2-5).

If the airplane were loaded to its aft limit, the load at the tail can be reduced, or in some cases even eliminated. This reduces the overall lift required of the main wing, even though the total weight of the

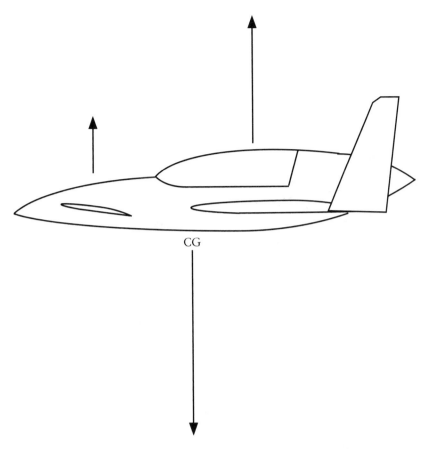

CG

2-5 *A canard planform exhibits positive lift from both wings in op-position to gravity. The tandem-wing arrangement stabilizes forward pitching moments without producing any negative lift or unnecessary drag.*

airplane has not changed. The pilot should expect a few knots faster cruise speed, slightly better climb rates, and a little slower stall speed as a result of aft loading (Fig. 2-6).

Another benefit of aft loading occurs in airplanes with tricycle gear. With the center of gravity more toward the main gear, it becomes easier to lift the nosewheel on takeoff, improving soft-field opera-tions. The opposite occurs with a tailwheel, however. A final bene-fit of a rear load is that it might make the plane more responsive in the landing flare during a slow-speed, short-field landing.

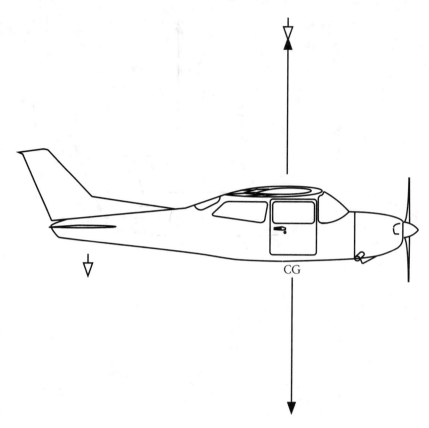

2-6 *Aft center-of-gravity locations require less downward, or negative, lift at the tail to stabilize the airplane. Aft CG also improves elevator effectiveness.*

I have heard many pilots speak fearfully of rearward center of gravity conditions. They claim that the airplane might be uncontrollable or exhibit divergent stability characteristics. I'm not recommending that *any* limits be ignored or exceeded, just that they be utilized to the pilot's advantage. Certificated airplanes are required to meet or exceed FAA-established stability profiles throughout their range of loading; that includes when the center of gravity is at its aft limit.

Technique

Manufacturers of modern airplanes produce flight performance data that is published in detail in the pilot's operating handbook. Many pilots claim this data is overly optimistic and unreachable for the average pilot. This myth hopefully will find its end with this book. The performance achieved by the factory begins with a simple preflight. They created ideal conditions for flight testing their airplane, so can we. The following is a detailed look at certain preflight concerns as they affect the aircraft performance.

Loading

The best published performance figures were probably achieved when the airplane was loaded at or near its aft center of gravity (CG) limit. In an effort to reduce lateral-trim drag, the load would also be configured so as to balance laterally, with careful attention paid to fuel management throughout the test flights to the same end. The effects of center of gravity are not reflected in the published performance charts, however, we can safely assume that the manufacturers all would optimize the load to cause the airplane to perform favorably.

Center of gravity (CG) position is certainly at the discretion of the pilot. The primary benefits of forward CG would be better pitch stability, whereas aft CG tends to make the airplane less stable in this area. Nevertheless, to make performance more closely resemble the factory published figures, passengers and their baggage should be configured so as to balance the airplane near its aft center of gravity limit. The pilot must take care to verify that the consumption of fuel during the flight will not move the CG aft beyond that limit. The method is simple. After computing the weight and balance with passengers, cargo, and required fuel, verifying the CG condition, compute it again with all factors constant and zero fuel. If the airplane is still in balance, then go flying, if not, readjust the load and compute again until you're sure you are within the CG limits with zero fuel. Also, you must take care to ensure uniform lateral balance. If the airplane were loaded heavy to one side or another, constant control pressure or trim is required for level flight, which produces unnecessary drag. Furthermore, an engine failure in a multiengine airplane might become uncontrollable if a significant lateral imbalance exists.

Now, to further manipulate a load and possibly exceed the published performance figures, carry only minimum fuel. Minimum, of course, means enough to get comfortably to your destination(s) plus an *adequate* reserve. Any extra fuel is simply dead weight. It's easy to understand a pilot's desire to have extra fuel aboard, but too much of it can be a hazard; it reduces general flight performance and increases the opportunity for fire after an unfortunate crash landing.

If the pilot carries an extra 50 gallons or so around in flight, that equals roughly 300 unneeded pounds (6 to 6.7 pounds/gallon). The extra weight means that the airplane spends more time climbing to altitude and more time en route due to its reduced cruise speed. Some might call it cheap insurance, but the reserves are already built into your minimum requirement. By the way, pilots may select whatever reserve fuel quantity they desire. FAA requires 30+ minutes; you might need more, depending on circumstances. Anything beyond that is overkill and a safety hazard because of reduced flight performance.

Additionally, because *any* excess weight is a detriment to performance and safety, passengers might be talked into leaving certain nonessential items behind, perhaps to be mailed or shipped ahead.

Exterior

The factory begins with a clean airplane. Their plane is likely to be free of the small dings, nicks, and dents so common to airplanes in regular service. Their propeller is new and free of erosion damage. These advantages might be difficult to duplicate years after the plane rolls out the factory door, but regular maintenance and care will help a great deal in this area.

One of the best ways to preflight an airplane's exterior is to give it a bath. Where it is possible, wax and polish the airplane as well. I know a few pilots who do just this sort of inspection before they buy a used airplane. There is just no better way to find defects in its structure. Any defects, like cracks in the primary skin or structural members, should be cause for grounding and repair. Small anomalies in the skin surfaces might indicate internal damage. If the pilot is dubious about these, then the mechanic should be consulted, and perhaps a more detailed inspection arranged.

The propeller is basically a couple of wings spinning to produce necessary thrust. Thrust is the single motive force in any powered airplane. Improve thrust and performance improves with it. Unfortunately, of all the flight surfaces, propellers are probably the least understood, because of the complexity of their aerodynamics. The least you can do is exactly what the factory did, clean the propeller, front and back, and be sure that the leading edges are smooth. If the prop has a small rock-chip or dent, get the mechanic to bring a file—it's a simple fix.

Tires/landing gear

Here is a great opportunity to beat the factory numbers out of non-paved fields. You can bet that they overinflated the tires.

For hard surface runways, tires should be inflated to their recommended pressures. For soft surfaces, however, you might find performance improvements as tire pressures are slightly reduced. Reduction of pressure enlarges the tires' surface contact with the ground and enhances flotation, working like snowshoes. On a soft surface, the slightly underinflated wheels will be less prone to plowing, digging ruts, and mimicking stilts in quicksand. In the Pitts Special for example, my students seem to prefer a softer tire to enhance their landings. The soft wheels bounce less, even on a hard surface (Fig. 2-7). Exactly how much air pressure to lose requires experimentation and will be discussed in the *getting your own figures* section of this chapter.

2-7 *Low tire pressure might improve "flotation" on soft surfaces.*

Physically pull the airplane out of its hangar or a little forward on the ramp. A pilot accustomed to moving the airplane will instantly know if the tire inflation and wheel bearings are adequate for the flight.

While pulling the plane, listen carefully to the brakes. A rasping sound indicates that the brakes might be partially engaged and perhaps be a hindrance to takeoff acceleration. Many planes that sit idle for long periods might develop rust on the brake disks. This rust expands the disk somewhat and might contact the brake pads. This produces unwanted rolling friction until the rust is worn off.

It is desirable for brakes to work properly for a maximum performance landing. The pilot should check for leaks in the brake system, the condition and thickness of the pads, and the progress of wear on the disks.

Due to mass production, the factory plane might have slight alignment problems and could be improved. Poor alignment produces unwanted rolling friction and rapid wear on tires. To make a simple alignment check, load the plane to a normal takeoff weight and clamp two long straightedges to the inside face of the brake discs. Center them so that the same amount protrudes ahead as behind the wheels. Measuring the distances between the front and rear ends of the straightedges will reveal any alignment problems (Fig. 2-8). If the alignment is out, talk to a mechanic for possible repairs.

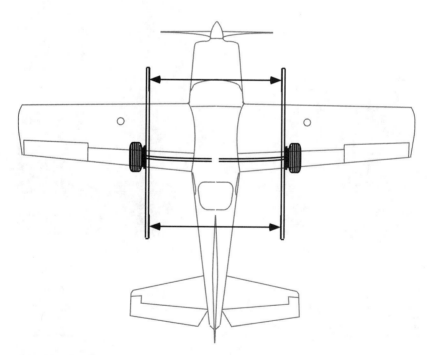

2-8 *Checking wheel alignment with two straightedges against the brake discs.*

Control system

Here is another opportunity to improve on the factory plane because, occasionally, an airplane will leave the factory with poor rigging, a big source of drag.

Move each of the flight controls through their full range of travel. If possible, move them from outside the plane as well as from within the cockpit. Pay careful attention to friction, sloppiness, or unusual sounds within the system as the controls are moved. Check the positions of the flight controls with respect to each other when they are in a neutral position. For example, hold one aileron in alignment with the wing's trailing edge and verify the aileron on the other wing to be the same. Occasionally you will find that when the ailerons are neutral, they are both slightly up or down with respect to the trailing edge. This is a rigging problem and presents certain aerodynamic difficulties as well as a potential penalty in performance. Again, a good mechanic should solve the problem.

Another rigging check involves a long tape measure. Simply check the distances between the trailing edge of the wingtips and the tail cone (Fig. 2-9). If the measurements come up different, then the wing is attached somewhat askew. It might surprise you to find mass-produced airplanes with differences of as much as six inches or more. Crooked wings extract a penalty in the aircraft performance, especially in its behavior near the stall. This one might be much more difficult to fix, but talk to the mechanic anyway.

Be sure to look for signs of damage in the flight control surfaces themselves. Due to their position at the trailing edges of wings and tail surfaces, they tend to be the first point of contact when the plane is pushed back into obstacles like a hangar or parked vehicles. Damaged flight controls can be fatal, let alone hamper flight performance.

The controls should move smoothly. It is difficult to fly an airplane with a high degree of precision when the controls are sticky. It's a little like whittling with a dull knife—everything seems crude and awkward. The smoother the flight controls feel on the ground, the better they will translate the pilot's wishes to motion in the air. Lubricate any areas that squeak, grab, or show any signs of resistance to free movement.

Of course, all hardware and mechanical connections within the system should be carefully inspected for wear, damage, and tightness.

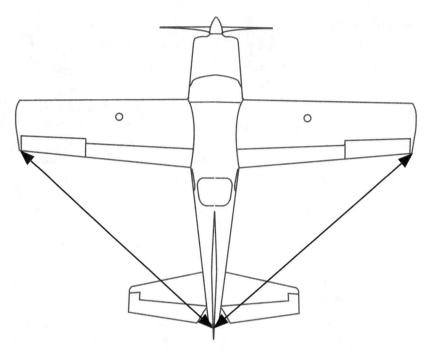

2-9 *One of many simple rigging checks.*

On simple airplanes, the entire control system is easily visible to in-spection; however, complex airplanes might require periodic re-moval of access panels for the pilot's peace of mind. Any frayed connections, loose nuts or hinges, or anything even suspicious in nature should be cause for "no go." Malfunctions in the control sys-tem in flight constitute a *major* problem, one best solved on the ground.

Once the pilot is seated in the cockpit, another careful control check needs to be made throughout the system's full range of movement. You might find that items like hand-held electronic instruments, kneeboards, flight bags, or bulky clothing block the use of the sys-tem at its extremes by physically interfering with the yoke, stick, or rudder pedals. In some cases, an occupant of large girth or stature might limit control. If this is the case, a seat adjustment must be made until the occupant no longer interferes. Loose items in the cockpit should be positioned in such a way that they will not inter-fere with control manipulation. For airplanes with tandem seats and dual controls, that includes things like unused seatbelts as well.

Test flights use numerous data-gathering instruments, some of which normally indicate the flight control positions in flight. The control throws and limit stops are determined based on that data. If you are unable to move the controls freely throughout their intended range, performance, and more importantly, control, will be sacrificed near the limits of the airplane's operating envelope.

Engine/run-up

The factory airplane probably began with a new engine, although by the end of an extensive flight-test program, the engine would be well broken-in. This should offer no significant advantage over the used plane, however.

A properly maintained engine should develop consistent-rated power throughout its recommended time between overhauls (TBO) unless something is seriously amiss. In fact, the best possible procedure to enhance the longevity of the engine is to fly it as often as possible. Regular use improves lubrication, increases overall compression, maintains rubber seals, and improves general internal cleanliness of the engine parts. It also prevents rust and corrosion.

When an engine sits unused for long periods, oil and other lubricants drain away from friction-generating components. Acids might develop from the breakdown of oil and fuel residue. These acids can literally destroy an engine over time, much like a bunch of termites can reduce a tree to a pile of sawdust. Engines with camshafts mounted above the crankcase are especially vulnerable to nonuse. In their cases, the camshaft is one of the first components to dry of lubricant, and the last to get vital lubrication when the engine is started. Excessive wear on the camshaft often occurs just as the engine is started, ultimately reducing valve travel and generally reducing power while causing metal filings to course throughout the system. Be especially cautious when flying an airplane that has not been flown often. The following pretakeoff checks will assist the pilot in verifying full engine power for a reciprocating engine.

When starting the engine, pilots should be keenly aware of abnormalities. Excessive smoke belching at the start might indicate overpriming, too-rich mixture, or oil in the cylinders. Each of these conditions could be normal character of the engine, or a sign of trouble. The pilot must be aware and looking for anything *abnormal*. Observe the oil pressure and take note of any delay in its rise. Check all operating conditions, oil, water (if any), cylinder head, and exhaust gas temperatures, as the engine warms up. Be wary of any unusually slow or fast rates of temperature change. Avoid starting the engine at high power settings. The start is probably the single greatest cause of wear on the engine, due to a combination of cold moving parts and marginal lubrication. High power settings only exacerbate the situation. The pilot should take care to maintain minimal revolutions until lubrication and operating temperatures increase. During taxi, it might be wise to lean the mixture somewhat to prevent plug fouling.

The run-up should be done with equal regard to operating temperatures; high power settings should be avoided until green parameters are reached. In addition to the usual checks recommended in the flight manual, a ground power check will verify that the engine is capable of developing its full rated power. When the engine is known to be functioning well, perform this check to establish a reference. During the run-up, note the manifold pressure at the run-up RPM with the propeller control full forward. The required pressure should remain consistent throughout the life of the engine. Something is wrong if, during later flights, the run-up requires a different manifold pressure to achieve the same RPM. At high elevations, it is best to lean for maximum power before attempting this check. Leaning will reduce required manifold pressure somewhat. The proper procedures for high altitude leaning are readily available in the engine or aircraft operator's manual.

Okay, what if you're flying a plane that does not make use of a constant-speed propeller and has no manifold pressure gauge? Fine, just take the opportunity to check full-throttle RPM as you advance power for takeoff. Again, you should get the same figure throughout the life of the engine. Be sure to get the figure before the airplane gains much speed, before reaching about 10 mph. Faster than that, the prop reacts to the airspeed and will appreciably increase in RPM, invalidating the check. Also, high elevations can be expected to reduce the available power at full throttle, and less static RPM should be expected.

In any case, the pilot should have an RPM figure in mind when the throttle is firewalled. If the pilot observes anything substantially different from that figure, then something is amiss and the takeoff might wisely be aborted. Finally, in no case should the pilot attempt to take off with engine operating parameters not firmly "in the green."

In turbine-powered aircraft the pilot can do much of the pretakeoff checks by simple reference to engine operating gauges. Many airline maintenance programs will take special note of the turbine's internal temperatures during critical phases of the starting cycle because several operational problems manifest themselves at that time. If all is well, they go—easy as that. One airline's procedures with the EMB-120 Brasilia, for example, require the copilot to log the peak internal temperatures each time the engine is started. The data go to the maintenance department for evaluation against the engine's past starting performance, where they graph the results and can make determinations on the operating safety and efficiency of the engines. Also, an inflight trim check is conducted at least once per flying day. The pilots log the indications of each of the engine instruments in addition to airspeed, altitude, ambient temperature and fuel flows. The mechanics then plot the engine's progress on charts and look for abnormalities in power or airplane performance.

Postflight inspection

Aside from military, aerobatic and airline circles, there are few flying environments that promote a detailed post-flight inspection. This is unfortunate because after-flight inspections allow pilots to investigate systems or structures that might have acted peculiar during the flight, while the problem is still fresh in their minds. If the pilot notices any abnormality during the flight, the postflight is the opportunity to find it. If any irregularities are found, written notes should be made so that they can be corrected before flying again.

A routine inspection can be as simple as wiping down the oil from the belly (looking for unusual or new streaks), or cleaning the bugs from the leading edges. More technical operations might involve complete tear-downs and restorations before subsequent flights. The space shuttle and SR-71 spy planes go through exactly that between flights. The manufacturer also would conduct detailed postflight inspections after every test flight, making changes based on the observations and data gathered by the test pilots.

Skills to practice

Familiarity with every part, system, and operational function of the airplane is critical for the pilot to make a valuable preflight assessment. It is especially important to recognize abnormalities. One of the best ways to learn what's normal, as opposed to what needs to be fixed, is to assist the mechanic in performing an annual inspection.

My apologies to mechanics subjected to the ordeal of an owner-assisted annual. I have seen some mechanics post signs indicating a variable pricing scale according to the amount of assistance rendered by the owner or pilot; something like: "$10.00/hour if I do the work, $15.00/hour if you watch, and $30.00/hour if you help." In spite of the problems and perhaps time-consuming teaching that might occur, there is simply no better way to get to know an airplane than to be involved in its repair.

Pilots should take every opportunity to roll up their sleeves, get covered with oil, and pick the mechanic's brain on items relating to aircraft airworthiness. Find out exactly when a given part should be replaced, exactly what too much wear looks like, and how to operate various systems to prevent failures. Who knows? The pilot/owner might gain enough knowledge to actually be of some assistance to the mechanic in the future.

Getting your own figures

Different airplanes might respond in various ways to the same preflight conditions. Dirt for example, might drastically affect the performance of a glider's laminar flow airfoil while being almost unnoticeable on a Piper Cub. The goal of this section is to assist the pilot in establishing what performance-enhancing preflight preparation has greatest value for a particular airplane.

The simplest indicator of overall performance is rate of climb. It is related to weight, drag, glide ratio, excess power and thrust, nearly all of the factors involved in performance calculations. Rate of climb is also conveniently checked by the average pilot without need for a plethora of test equipment and lightning fast reflexes. The only thing that cannot be examined with rate of climb would be the frictional adjustments in the landing gear.

Pick a smooth day for the tests. Thermals, turbulence, and other airborne anomalies could render the most careful test inaccurate. Since you are trying to quantify relative effects and not establish absolute performance figures, the particular altitudes at which you conduct the tests do not matter, just so long as they are consistent with each other. Temperature can skew the test results, so it is wise to conduct the tests during the same time of day in order to provide a nearly constant temperature condition.

You'll need a stopwatch, a pen, paper, and an assistant to take notes. If your plane is single place, get a kneeboard on which to write. Make a table with columns for time, altitude, outside air temperature (OAT), and RPM (Fig. 2-10). To conduct the flight test, establish an appropriate climb speed that you can maintain exactly for at least six minutes. Set the throttle for full power and begin a climb from an altitude far enough below the point where the timing begins to allow at least one minute for climb conditions to stabilize.

As the airplane passes through your target altitude, begin timing with the stopwatch. Have your assistant take exact altitude readings every minute for five minutes, then take steps to repeat the test again in the opposite direction to negate any windshear effects. When the test is complete, land and crunch the figures into an average rate of climb. Then do *one* performance enhancement modification, such as cleaning the propeller or changing center of gravity (CG), and complete the test again. Be sure that the temperature is consistent between checks and that you use the same altimeter setting. Repeat the test as many times as you like while making small adjustments, like those previously suggested, to the airplane's preflight condition.

The test to check improvements in landing gear is like a drag race. Mark the airspeed indicator at the appropriate liftoff speed. Get a stopwatch. Record full-power RPM at the beginning of the takeoff roll and again at liftoff, timing the interval between a standing start and achievement of liftoff speed. Conduct all tests from the same runway, approximately the same time of day, and, most of all, in the same wind. Land, make any changes you like to the gear system and repeat the test. The data should assist in determining the proper landing gear condition for best takeoff acceleration and also give figures for the full static RPM/engine power check.

Good luck and have fun.

Further reading

Flight Testing Homebuilt Aircraft, Vaughan Askue, Iowa State University Press, 1992

"How Good Is Your Engine," Aviation Safety publication, July 1994, article by Bill Kelly

Starting Alt.

CONDITION 1:_____

Time (minutes)	ALT	OAT	RPM
1			
2			
3			
4			
5			

Starting Alt.

CONDITION 2:_____

Time (minutes)	ALT	OAT	RPM
1			
2			
3			
4			
5			

2-10 *A blank sample data sheet for rate of climb comparisons. Be sure that the "starting altitudes" (point where the timing begins) are the same for each test. "Conditions" refer to the enhancements you make. For example, condition one might be a clean propeller; condition two, a change in CG, etc.*

"The Curse of Corrosion," Ibid, article by Clint Lowe

"Keeping Tabs on Maintenance," Ibid, article by Brian Jacobson

Avtest Flight Engineer, Jerry Lawler, Avtest Inc., 1989

Advanced Aircraft Systems, Understanding Your Airplane, David Lombardo,McGraw-Hill, 1993

Standard Aircraft Handbook, Larry Reithmaier, McGraw-Hill, 1991

SR-71 Blackbird in Action, Lou Drendel, Squadron/Signal Publications, 1982

3

Takeoff

I stood in the sand at the west end of Nargana, a small island in the San Blas chain, off the Caribbean coast of Panama. With me were about a dozen native Kuna Indians, and we quietly listened to the morning as we waited for an airplane. A few of the Indian women still wore the traditional gold rings in their noses, as well as the Mola blouse and wrapped skirts. A couple had dark lines painted on their faces. Peculiar that a society as apparently primitive as this one should rely so much on regular air transport.

In the past, we had taken a dugout canoe from our little island to the mainland where the longer runway was cut. LACSA provided the only air transportation available, and because they had no competition they could rudely charge a mint for their lousy service. No one was really sure of the arrival times because the airline reflected the laid-back lifestyle of this place in its operation. Normally we would wait around at the runway all day, swatting the vicious bugs until the company airplane decided finally to rescue us. Sometimes it would come and go unexpectedly at five in the morning, other times in the afternoon, often not at all. But things were about to change with the arrival of a competing airline service that would give LACSA a run for their money.

Among other things, the new company would land at the island runway instead of making passengers travel in their small dugout canoes to the mainland. The runway on Nargana had recently been lengthened as part of an island community work project. As the island was very small, it had to be artificially extended to create a runway nearly 1000-feet long with both ends jutting out into the water. Even at that, it was not much to land on. I wondered what type of plane the new airline would use.

We heard the plane long before it came into view. I finally spotted it, a high-winged speck on a long final approach. Getting closer, and more into focus, the speck developed flaps, fixed gear and a single engine. It eventually took the form of a Cessna 206 making a short-field landing. With nose-up attitude it planted hard on the far end of the runway, carrier style. We could hear the brakes and tires squealing and see the nose strut compress as the pilot rode the plane aggressively to a stop, using the full length of the runway. A blast of power, and it made a one-eighty and taxied back to us at midfield.

A young pilot, about twenty, flashed a toothy grin, and said that I should sit in front to help with weight and balance. I was at least 2 feet taller than the biggest native. The empty plane was then filled with a half-dozen more Indians and a few hundred pounds of mangoes and baggage, packing the cabin and a small, belly-mounted cargo pod. I observed the steel-spring main gear struts squash and spread with the weight. I wondered a little about whether we could take off again, but figured that the pilot must have done this before. After he took his seat, started the engine and blasted the throttle to get moving across the sand and grass toward the concrete runway, he looked at me and jokingly asked if I could swim. I was dead serious when I answered in the affirmative. He had done this before, right?

We moved to the far end of the runway and without so much as a cursory run-up the pilot firewalled the throttle before turning around, the plane still pointed at the ocean about 20 feet ahead. My heart leaped into my throat and I grabbed for a hand-hold, expecting the plane to splash full power into the ocean when the pilot suddenly stomped left rudder and brake to pivot the plane on its left main gear and rocket us out of a 180-degree turn, pointed down the runway and accelerated fast. He used the pivot to gain valuable speed at the beginning of the roll. The pilot lowered the flaps 20 degrees and focused on airspeed.

Looking over the high instrument panel, my chest throbbed and it felt as though my heart stopped beating altogether. Airspeed was building, but it had a long way to go. The end of the runway, on the other hand, was *right there*, approaching fast, and we weren't even to stall speed. I again began to prepare for impact—it would be a bad one—the water at the end of the runway plunged dark and deep. I sat ready to unlatch my seatbelt and thought about kicking off my shoes. We weren't going to make it. I tensed for impact.

Just as the runway disappeared beneath the cowling, the pilot yanked forcefully on the yoke and the nose came up. The plane didn't lift off, however; the runway simply ran out from under the tires. We were just inches above the water. I sat there with a death grip on the upholstery, listening to the stall horn fade away as the plane gathered itself together and began a slow climb. We made it. My breath came in great gulps. I felt as though I had just been jumped from behind in a dark room, and my adrenaline slowly dissipated. The pilot looked unconcerned.

Background information

A great many factors affect the takeoff performance of airplanes. These performance factors can vary significantly from day to day, sometimes with drastically different results. For a pilot to assemble and accurately weigh each of the parameters in a takeoff requires a great deal of experience, and sometimes a little luck. In the case of the Nargana departure, I believe we were very lucky. The first flight of the new airline to Nargana was also its last. The plane never returned for a second flight. That's probably just as well. I, for one, would never volunteer to ride it like that again.

So far we've explored the condition of the airplane and pilot judgment as pertaining to performance, now we have the problem of maximizing a million more factors to get the airplane and pilot off the ground. The object is very simple: accelerate to flight speed as quickly as possible, using the least amount of runway. A pilot well versed in the principles reviewed in this chapter, after gaining experience, should be able to launch into the wild blue without asking the passengers if they know how to swim.

Many of these principles are similar to those behind a top-fuel dragster in the quarter-mile. The drag race attempts to achieve the minimum possible time along a straight, quarter-mile track, at the end of which the cars pop drag chutes and slow down. The drivers' goals are to maximize acceleration and make the most efficient use of power and tires to propel the car down the track. The pilot also attempts to maximize acceleration down a straight track, or runway; except in the case of the airplane, the race ends when flying speed is achieved and the runway is left behind. The pilot should think like a drag race driver and stack the variables favorably.

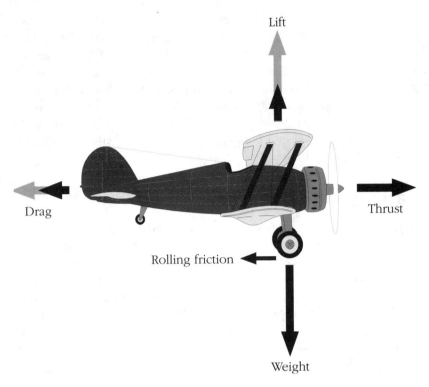

3-1 *Propeller thrust builds quickly during takeoff roll, or remains fairly constant in the case of a jet. Drag begins from zero and builds steadily, then increases dramatically as the airplane rotates to fly. The lift is variable with angle of attack, but its potential grows throughout the takeoff roll and beyond. Weight is constant. Rolling friction is present only while the airplane is in contact with the runway.*

To simplify the complex factors affecting takeoff performance, it is necessary to group them into the basic four forces of flight as they apply (Fig. 3-1).

Anything that will increase thrust will improve takeoff acceleration. A cold, dry day, for example, provides dense air for high compression in the engine, ultimately producing greater thrust. Slight changes in propeller or compressor efficiency might be produced by weather and altitude. Even debris might help, like this example: An acquaintance taxied along a dark tarmac in the winter and hit a small pile of rocks with the propeller. The propeller was sent to a specialty shop, and it returned oddly shaped, with strangely tapered ends. The shop had to file away an enormous amount of metal before the propeller balanced properly. Surprisingly, the plane flew as though it had an extra 20 horsepower. Something in the shape of that prop made more thrust than before, and the plane showed big improvements in takeoff performance.

A runway that slants downhill brings gravity in favor of takeoff acceleration, benefitting the cause of thrust. A headwind provides airspeed before the roll begins and works for the plane like a head start in the race to takeoff.

By improving lift, the necessary flight speed might be reduced to a point where drastic acceleration is hardly needed. Lift-enhancing items run the gamut of air, flaps, angles, and other aerodynamic wizardry. Consider the wings of a Boeing 747 and the cruise missile. The missile is dropped at 600 mph from the wing or belly of a bomber. Its designers hardly intend for it to land gently; it has no wheels. It didn't have to take off. The machine is designed to begin flight at 600 mph and end on target at the same speed. Accordingly, the wing is optimized for 600 mph. Its wings look like thin, spindly toothpicks, and would be lousy tools for lifting a machine the size and weight of a single-place airplane from a runway at anything short of 600 mph. It would be like a drag race. The 747, on the other hand, spends much of its flight time at the same 600 mph and its wings are also relatively small during cruise flight. But seeing them in action during takeoff or landing is like watching George Jetson pull a car out of his briefcase. There are appendages and extensions everywhere. In the few moments before takeoff the wing looses its kinship to the cruise missile and extends in almost every direction, growing and reshaping until it is ready to gently lift an airplane the size of an office building from the runway. Lift-enhancing items like flaps and fancy airfoils literally move the finish line of the drag race. The plane doesn't roll as far down the runway because the needed flight speed is no longer as fast.

Drag is the opposition to thrust. The interesting note is that parasite drag is the only aerodynamic opposition for most of the takeoff roll. It grows from nonexistence when the plane begins the takeoff roll in still air, to an inescapable wall of pressure when the plane reaches its top speed. Induced drag comes into play only when lift begins to develop. In addition to parasite drag, the tires offer some resistance to takeoff acceleration. Rolling friction and inertia are the major resistive factors at the beginning of the takeoff roll. It takes energy to roll the tires. Just try pulling the airplane around on a level ramp and you get the idea. Thrust must pull hard against a lot of resistance to get the plane moving to flight speed. One of the nice things about propeller-generated thrust is that it usually reaches its highest value shortly after the takeoff roll begins. At liftoff, rolling friction is abruptly lost, but induced drag is awake and eager to slow things down. The pilot's objective in the takeoff roll is to minimize drag in every way, making best use of the thrust available.

Weight could be either favorable or detrimental in the takeoff roll, depending upon whether the runway is sloped up or down. A downhill slope brings gravitational acceleration to play favorably in the takeoff. You could leave the engine off if the runway were steep enough. Just push the plane over the edge of a hill and let gravity do the work. Watching hang-glider pilots leap from cliffs wearing flimsy aluminum and fabric butterflies makes me appreciate the effects of gravity. Aim the runway uphill far enough, though, and the plane might begin the takeoff roll backwards. I once taxied a Cessna 172 up a sloping dirt road. I was surprised that it required almost full throttle just to maintain taxi speed. Turning around for takeoff the other way made the plane accelerate quickly. Weight by itself is certainly an adverse factor on level ground as a heavy airplane (or dragster) of limited power has greater resistance to acceleration because of its high inertia. Weight increases rolling friction. Weight also increases the speed required to fly. In the same way that flaps will reduce the necessary liftoff speed, weight will increase it. A heavy airplane has two strikes against it for takeoff performance: higher inertia to overcome in the takeoff acceleration, and the need to get to a higher flight speed.

Basically, considering takeoff performance, anything that increases thrust and lift, or decreases drag and weight, will serve to shorten the required takeoff roll. The following are several critical factors that a pilot might examine when considering a maximum-performance departure. Collecting actual data for performance calculations is, for lack of a better word, approximate. Performance is the art of maximization, not exact figures. The pilot plays the variables in a practical sense to achieve the best, if not the most accurate, performance.

Density altitude

Density refers to the weight of a given volume of air. The higher the weight of the air, the better the performance of the airplane. Higher-density air means better compression in the engine, and thus more power. It improves the efficiency of the wings and propulsive surfaces, and enhances both lift and thrust.[1] All in all, the airplane will accelerate to flight speed much faster in thicker air.

The term *density altitude* comes from the nature of the atmosphere. With higher altitudes the air naturally becomes thinner, a cubic foot of air at 30,000 feet, for instance, is less dense than one at sea level. A *high-density altitude* refers to air density that resembles that of high-altitude air.

Another factor that strongly affects air density is temperature. Air expands and becomes less dense with heat. Its density and physical properties at high temperatures again resemble air at high altitudes, thus the term *density altitude* applies. The interesting fact is that the pressure of the air at a given altitude might be constant as it undergoes a temperature change. Suppose you go camping in the middle of Death Valley. You wake up early in the morning to chilled desert air. Your canteen is nearly frozen and your barometer, which you always carry, is steady at 30.3 inches. Air density is high, due to the cold temperatures and low elevation, and you observe the vultures leaping into the air with wild abandon and climbing like hummingbirds without even breathing hard. Density altitude is low.

By noon, the temperature has risen to nearly 120 degrees. As you sit under an umbrella, sipping hot water from your canteen, you notice that the buzzards have to run for half a mile just to take off. Excited, you run in a sweat to your barometer and read, believe it or not, the same 30.3 inches as before. Density altitude is high, about 8000 feet. The buzzards' performance has deteriorated to that of a comparable buzzard at 8000 feet, but the pressure has remained the same.

A basic aircraft altimeter reads pressure, not density. The rate of pressure decline with height is constant enough to be translated into a fairly reliable indication of altitude. In order to determine the density of the air, on the other hand, it is necessary to look at both pressure and temperature together (Fig. 3-2).

Once having used a chart like this to arrive at a density altitude adjustment, now what? The key to understanding this is that airplane performance is first and foremost directly related to the *density* of the air. When you talk about the service ceiling of your airplane, its

---

1 Propeller, compressor blades, etc.

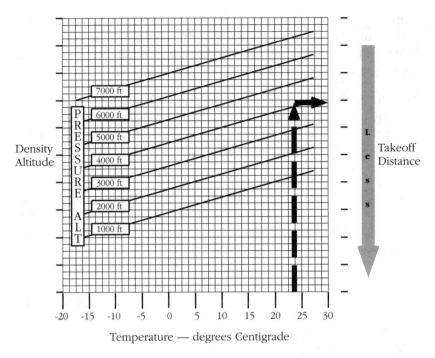

Density
Altitude

Takeoff
Distance

Temperature — degrees Centigrade

3-2 *Density altitude portion of a generic takeoff chart.*

optimum cruise altitude, and any other altitude as related to performance, it is density altitude that you are referring to. If density altitude is high, then the airplane will perform as though it were at high
altitude. You will notice that every aircraft performance chart will, at
the very beginning, make some reference to temperature and pressure altitude in an effort to compute density.

High altitude and hot weather combine to reduce the performance
of airplanes. Hence, a pilot who is in need of the shortest takeoff
might opt to leave at night or very early in the morning, taking advantage of cooler, and thus thicker, air.

Humidity

The word *humidity* refers to the amount of gaseous water in the air
we breathe. Humidity is detrimental to aircraft performance because
it *reduces* air density. The problem that most people have with this
concept is that water *looks* heavier than air. How can something so
relatively heavy cause the air to become thin? The fact is, humidity
refers to water as a *gas*. In its gaseous state water is pretty light. Fill

a balloon full of steam, and it will float away. Essentially, water diffuses into, or dilutes, the air. The amount of water vapor in the air depends on the air's temperature and the amount of liquid water available.

The weather services report humidity in a percentage of saturation. One hundred percent humidity would describe air that is totally saturated with water vapor. Hot air can retain more water vapor than cold air can. Consequently, the driest air in the world would be found at the earth's poles, where temperatures are too cold to permit evaporation. Humidity, when given as a percentage, indicates the air's level of saturation with respect to its capacity to hold water. One hundred percent humidity at the poles will be much drier than say 30 percent humidity in Hawaii. Hawaii's warm air can simply retain much more water.

Another more common way of expressing humidity is with temperature and dewpoint. *Dewpoint* is the temperature at which the air would be saturated with its existing water content. You remember that the air's capacity to hold water is related to its temperature. If the temperature in Hawaii is 80 degrees and the dewpoint is 70 degrees, the air would be saturated if it were cooled to 70 degrees. When the air is saturated it will admit no more gaseous water, it's full. Evaporation will stop. You could pour a bucket of water on the sidewalk in those conditions and it would never dry. If the air is cooled to a temperature lower than the dewpoint, some of the water vapor will condense from its gaseous state and become liquid again. A cloud forms. At that point, the water is visible, and rather dense. If temperatures continue to cool, it might even rain.

Lower air density caused by humidity affects engine compression and causes a reduction of power. On the other hand, *liquid* water, when introduced into the internal workings of an engine might actually enhance performance. The liquid can explode into gas, or steam, and increase compression. You can actually increase the power of a jet engine by spraying water into the intake from a garden hose. Do not confuse this effect with humidity, however. In humid conditions, the water is already a gas and no further expansion will occur. Worse yet, water vapor could hamper the internal combustion because it does not burn, and so it might cause the engine to run excessively rich.

Weight

Weight is the second variable in the typical aircraft performance chart (Fig. 3-3). The effects of weight are two-fold. First, the greater mass of a heavy airplane means greater resistance to acceleration. This resistance lies in the inertia of the heavy airplane and the higher rolling friction in the landing gear. The second detrimental effect of weight is that higher speeds are required to fly. Overall, the difference in takeoff distance between a heavily loaded airplane versus a light one, with all other factors equal, might exceed 50 percent.

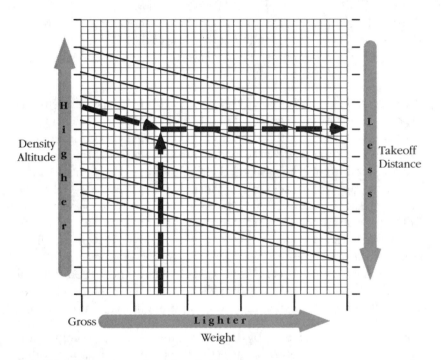

3-3 *Weight portion of a takeoff chart.*

Unfortunately, there is little that the pilot can do to compensate for higher weights, short of maximizing atmospheric conditions. Maximum available power for takeoff is pretty much constant, and the extra weight is simply another stone to carry.

Wind

Wind can translate into free airspeed and reduce the takeoff roll as long as the plane takes off *into* the wind. I'm hoping that most pilots

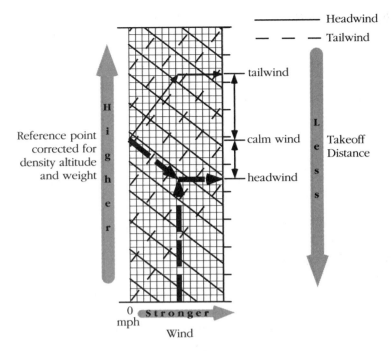

3-4 *Wind portion of a takeoff chart.*

understand this feature. A headwind can significantly reduce takeoff distance and a tailwind can disastrously lengthen it. Notice in Fig. 3-4 that the detrimental effects of a tailwind are slightly worse than the beneficial effects of a headwind.

Crosswind can affect takeoff distance. When the airplane accelerates down the runway, steering must be adjusted to compensate for the crosswind. Because the wheels are somewhat askew with the airplane's direction of travel in this case, rolling friction is increased. Also, aerodynamic controls must be positioned to compensate for the wind. Because the airplane is accelerating with deflected controls, a drag penalty is exacted. The end result is a slightly longer takeoff roll, which is rarely addressed in the average takeoff chart.

Since wind affects the takeoff roll, it is important to estimate its speed and direction. Numerous small wind indicators are available for sale, and some are highly accurate and portable, but useless when the plane is airborne. With the pilot alone, however, the best estimates of wind come from observation and experience.

Some natural wind indicators are smoke, leaves, grass, flags, wind-socks, dust, loose papers, wires, trees, water, hair, and clothing. All of these will respond to wind in some form or another. The pilot merely has to observe carefully and make a best guess. You'll find that with conscientious practice you can be very accurate whether on the ground or in flight.

Runway

The runway can play a dramatic role in takeoff performance. The critical factors from a runway standpoint are its length, surface, temperature, slope, and position.

Runway length should be as long as the pilot can make it. That might sound funny, but many pilots refuse to make use of a runway's full length by taxiing to its end, opting for an intersection take-off somewhere midfield. If high takeoff performance is required of the airplane, the full runway length should be used. This includes taxiing onto the runway at its very end, perhaps with the tail of the airplane hanging out over the weeds. The runway length ahead of the airplane in that position is usually beyond the control of the pi-lot, obviously, the longer the better. I'm not saying that the pilot should force the airplane to *roll* down the entire length of the run-way on takeoff, only that the full runway length should be *available* when the pilot is attempting a high-performance departure. The air-plane should be made to leave the runway behind and fly away as soon as it is able.

Runway surface is critical to acceleration performance. Hard, smooth surfaces are the best. Thick, sloppy quicksand or mud runways are the worst. If the runway surface is soft, the plane's tires tend to sink, causing a great deal of rolling friction and extending the takeoff roll. In some cases, snow or mud might prevent the airplane from ever achieving flight speed. Soft-field technique will be discussed soon, but know for now that it is important for the pilot to look for a hard, smooth surface on which to conduct the takeoff roll. I heard of one pilot who made a successful takeoff from a snow-covered field by taxiing back and forth several times down the length of the run-way—making tracks—and finally taking off by staying in the ruts left by the wheels.

Another aspect of runway surface is its effects on temperature. This has to do mostly with the paved runways at large airports. Because of the nature of the pavement, the air temperature immediately above the runway might be significantly hotter than elsewhere around the airport. As a result, performance might fall below your expectations based upon temperatures measured elsewhere on the field.

Runway slope might be uphill, downhill or sideways. An uphill runway causes the aircraft weight to work against acceleration. Often, it is better to accept a tailwind and take off downhill when the runway has a slope and the winds are unfavorable. It takes a strong headwind to compensate for taking off on an uphill runway. An uphill slope of only six percent is roughly equivalent to taking off with an 18-knot tailwind. Worse yet, most runways that have a slope usually run up the side of a mountain or canyon. Should the plane become airborne going uphill, it might be faced with the task of out-climbing the mountain slope or canyon floor. Because of this, most runways that have a significant incline are "one way in, one way out" affairs. A sidesloped runway presents difficulties akin to a crosswind landing. The airplane will be operating in a slip to maintain directional control while on the ground. Because of this, takeoff roll will be extended somewhat.

Runway position refers to the placement of the runway in relation to its geographic surroundings. This might include any obstacles off the departure end of the runway, prevailing wind, and common thermals. Noise abatement procedures due to local population areas might also play a factor in the pilot's planning and execution of the takeoff.

Lift

Lift production is the goal at the end of the takeoff roll. The airplane needs only the time on the runway that is required to achieve a comfortable liftoff speed. Any time longer than that exposes the aircraft and occupants to all the dangers of low flying, not to mention damage and wear to the tires and landing gear.

The amount of lift required to fly is directly related to the airplane's weight. Since lift is a function of speed, the speed required to fly is also related to weight. This is probably the single biggest takeoff error made by pilots of light aircraft: they stay on the runway too long. I have observed several pilots read a rotation speed from an airplane manual and stubbornly hold the airplane to the runway until that speed is attained. The plane generally becomes skittish and tries to fly substantially below this speed with the pilot tearing down the runway on just the nose wheel as though racing a wheel barrow.

Most of the performance figures contained in a light-aircraft manual are over-simplified and contain general figures for gross weight. The reason why the airplane in the previous example wanted to fly early is because the plane is operating at less than gross weight. Airline pilots routinely consult graphs and tables to compute an applicable rotation speed for their takeoff weight. Since the operator's manuals for light aircraft certificated under FAR part 23 usually give a rotation speed based upon gross weight.[2] However, the pilot is left to estimate the proper rotation speed for lighter weights. That is just as well, because it can be estimated with proper attitude positioning more accurately than it can be calculated.

Angle of attack

One of the few constants in a takeoff procedure is the angle of attack required to fly. Every airplane wing has an angle of attack range within which it produces useful lift. The speeds for liftoff and best angle of climb correspond to an optimum angle of attack. With changes in takeoff weights, that angle of attack remains constant while the correct liftoff speed is allowed to vary.

The secret to exact liftoff/rotation speeds is for the pilot to memorize the proper angle of attack. This angle of attack corresponds to the aircraft's attitude when it is climbing at best angle of climb speed (Vx). Rotation to this same attitude while rolling down the runway allows the airplane to accelerate to the exact flight speed and transition into the air so smoothly that the exact point of liftoff is difficult to ascertain. The airplane will not remain on the runway for even an instant longer than the time required.

The concept of rotation speed (Vr)

Rotation speed (Vr) is a calculated figure designed to allow the airplane to accelerate in its most streamlined condition—that is a level

---

2 Part 23 governs certification of aircraft designed for personal or business transportation— "general aviation." Air transport category, airline and public use aircraft certification is found in part 25. Part 25 rules are far more stringent and require that highly detailed performance data be generated by a manufacturer and minimum flight performance criteria be achieved by the airplane before it is allowed to enter service.

attitude—until the point at which control effectiveness and speed are sufficient to lift the nose to climb attitude just as liftoff speed is reached. It's a nifty idea, and works pretty well for airline operations, where it is sometimes associated with a decision speed, or V1.[3] Transport category airplanes have this and many more performance stipulations required of them by law. If the FAA were to catch an airline flight crew departing without first calculating things like V1, Vr and V2, for example, the crew could be grounded and the company fined.

For small, nontransport airplanes certificated under FAR part 23, rotation speed is academically the point at which the pilot pulls on the controls and transitions to flight. Since it is not a legal performance stipulation for these airplanes, the rotation figures in the average flight manual are somewhat improper; they are usually given as a general range of speeds where the airplanes will probably fly. For example, the manual of a Cessna 152 says to rotate when the airplane reaches approximately 50-60 knots, hardly the specific figure that is required for maximum performance. Experimental airplanes often come with no manual and no idea of proper speeds on takeoff (or anything else, for that matter), leaving the challenge of flight test and actual performance validation to the pilot. That's why they're called experimental.

During the takeoff acceleration, the basic requirement for rotation is that the rudder and elevator controls be effective. Control effectiveness depends upon speed. When the pilot feels that sufficient speed has been attained, the airplane should be positioned to the proper climb attitude and held there until the plane lifts off. If that sounds simple, it is. Pilots should be cautioned, however, that lifting the nosewheel or tailwheel before adequate rudder control is available might send the plane off the runway before the takeoff roll is complete.

Ground effect

Ground effect is a huge reduction in lift-induced drag when the wing flies in close proximity to the ground. It is very noticeable on airplanes with particularly low wings and short landing gear, such as

3 V1 speed is a point of no abort on the runway. If an emergency or abnormality occurs prior to reaching V1, the decision to abort the takeoff is cut and dry simple. An emergency after V1—even if the wheels are still rolling on the ground—is considered to be in-flight, because at that point the airplane and crew are committed to fly.

Pipers and Mooneys. To the pilot, ground effect feels like an abundance of lift, almost like the proverbial *air cushion* by which it is erroneously described. This phenomenon might cause the airplane to become airborne during the takeoff roll at a speed that will seem alarmingly premature.

If the airplane is held consistently at the proper climb attitude, it will not climb out of ground effect until the appropriate climb speed is achieved. A premature *unstick* is actually beneficial to the takeoff roll because when the airplane has left the runway and lost the rolling friction of the tires it will accelerate faster. The rolling friction is traded for lift-induced drag at liftoff, but while the plane is in ground effect, induced drag is at a minimum. The pilot has only to maintain attitude and smile inwardly as the plane gathers itself together and rockets from the runway.

Takeoff performance chart

We finally get to put the three previous charts together and come up with a required takeoff distance. As you look at Fig. 3-5, notice that first is a density altitude calculation, followed by an adjustment for weight, and finally compensation for wind. The ultimate figure should be the required takeoff roll. "Fine," you say, and proceed to add 50 or 100 percent to that figure to account for your "old" airplane and the hairy-chested-factory-test-pilot's legendary skills.

Of course your plane is older than a new plane from the factory, but its performance will really not differ that much from what is published in the operator's manual. From the foregoing discussion you know that many other factors besides the plane and pilot can affect the takeoff roll. Nevertheless, pilot technique has probably the greatest opportunity for error. Ever wonder how the test pilot can break ground at exactly 51 knots and cross the 50-foot mark at exactly 56 knots in the climb?[4] Such accuracy is unattainable, you say? Not so. The test pilot is simply rotating to an attitude and holding it, all the way through 50 feet (Fig. 3-6). The airspeeds are observed as a result of the airplane's acceleration in a constant attitude, not the hair-trigger reflexes of the test pilot.

Keep in mind that the adjustments for runway surface and slope are not complete in the takeoff charts. There are literally a million or

4 As described in the short-field departure procedure for a Cessna 172.

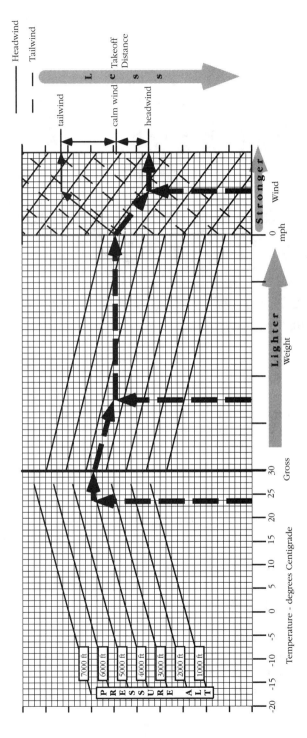

3-5 *A sample takeoff chart. There are many factors in every takeoff that are addressed here.*

3-6 *Rotating to a Vx attitude in a short-field takeoff.*

more factors involved in the takeoff. The chart is at best an edu-
cated, and perhaps over-simplified, guess. When you try it yourself,
you might find that the actual speeds are somewhat slower than
stated in your performance charts, largely because of your plane's
less-than-gross weight. But you'll probably do very close to, or even
better the book figures, if your technique is good.

Technique

If we look back at the C-206 out of Nargana, there were a few tricks
the pilot used that perhaps made the difference between flying and
swimming for the passengers. His pivoting start at the beginning of
the takeoff roll was certainly responsible for about 3–5 knots extra
speed at the critical beginning of the roll. On the downside, he
wasted a good 20 feet of runway at the start by not taxiing to the
very end of the strip. The pilot also made no account for the extreme
humidity and might have benefitted from an engine check and pretakeoff leaning to maximize power. The pilot assumed that 1000 feet
of runway would be plenty for a C-206 and discounted other, very
serious factors, like attempting to carry all the island produce and

half its population at once. The following are some techniques that could have helped get the plane in the air sooner.

Holding brakes

Establishing full power before brake release is thought to measurably shorten the takeoff roll. This procedure is most effective in turbine-powered airplanes that require a few moments to "spool up" to full thrust. Releasing the brakes at that point would maximize acceleration. For the typical reciprocating engine, however, the time required to go from idle to full power is relatively quick and holding brakes for this purpose alone would be of only slight consequence.

The real benefit to establishing maximum power before brake release lies in the fact that the pilot can verify that full power is available before committing to the takeoff roll. Once the plane actually begins moving down the runway and the pilot's attention is focused on steering, flight controls and airspeed, it is more difficult at that time to accurately verify the engine power output. Having established full power before brake release allows the pilot to concentrate on the takeoff itself without the distraction of a detailed engine check.

On the other hand, if the runway surface is contaminated with loose gravel, rocks, other hard foreign objects, or water, full power against brakes could potentially destroy the propeller and tail surfaces of the airplane. Unfortunately, runways like this are usually the very types for which a short-field procedure is needed. The damage is caused when propellers or intakes suck foreign particles from the ground and bring them in contact with spinning machinery. Thirty seconds on a gravel runway with full throttle and locked brakes could render an airplane unflyable. The suction generated by propulsive mechanisms actually forms a little tornado that touches the ground ahead of the blades. If the plane remains still, the vortex acts just like a vacuum cleaner and might suck the runway surface clean.

Just like the whirlpool that might form above the drain in the kitchen sink, the vortex in front of the engines requires a few moments in still conditions to form. The key to preventing propeller or compressor damage is to prevent formation of this little tornado. This is done by not allowing the conditions ahead of the plane to be still for any length of time. A slow forward taxi is usually sufficient to prevent vortex formation from occurring and to prevent the majority of damage from foreign objects. In this case, the plane would taxi slowly to the beginning of the runway, at which point the pilot advances power against enough braking to allow a slow forward creep. When the pilot is satisfied that takeoff power is being developed then full brake release occurs and the acceleration to flight speed begins.

Pivoting on a main wheel

A 180-degree turn at the start of the takeoff might prevent foreign object damage and help takeoff acceleration at the same time. This is most convenient when back-taxiing to reach the end of the runway. Any preflight run-ups or power checks must be completed before beginning this maneuver. When the airplane reaches the end of the runway and is still pointed away from the direction of departure, the pilot sets max power and brakes on one of the main gear. The airplane will pivot rather energetically and accelerate as it completes the turn. When the plane's heading lines up with the runway, the pilot releases the brake and continues the takeoff roll. This technique develops angular velocity in the turn and converts that to forward speed when the brake is released. The couple of extra knots it provides occur at a critical point in the takeoff roll when inertia and rolling friction rule. It works like a sprinter's use of starting blocks. A slight advantage in the beginning of the takeoff translates into a big win at the finish line. It takes practice to do well, but works a little better than holding brakes and adding power.

The danger of this maneuver is that significant side loads might be developed on the landing gear and cause an inadvertent collapse. If the gear is suspected to be susceptible to failure, power and speed could be moderated through the turn to keep the side loads light. Another problem is that of directional control in a plane that uses differential braking to steer. In that case the procedure requires practice on the part of the pilot to prevent turning through the runway heading. Lastly, the pilot must be conscious of the turn radius of wingtips and tail components. Your flying budget will take a beating if you enthusiastically begin a hard turn only to put the wing or tail through a fencepost or runway light.

The power-turn technique is quite effective in shortening a takeoff roll, but requires practice. In some cases it might reduce takeoff distances by as much as 10 percent.

Use of flaps

There is a little argument in the pilot community about whether or not to delay the application of flaps to shorten the takeoff roll. It is thought that the flaps being already down might increase the drag on the airplane and prolong the acceleration to flight speed. This is probably true if the airplane is equipped with very large flaps. But both parasite and induced drag are practically zero at the beginning of the takeoff roll. They build progressively throughout the takeoff. Even so, there is probably some advantage in drag reduction by keeping everything folded away until the right moment. It would be unwise to use this procedure if the plane had electric or hydraulically operated flap systems. These systems often work slowly and could be difficult to reverse in the event of a problem. Mechanical flaps of the hand-lever operated variety seem to be the best for the procedure, because they are inherently fast.

Begin the takeoff roll with the wing in the clean configuration and apply flaps at or near liftoff, just before the airplane wants to fly. The Maule MX7-235 bush-plane is one example of an airplane in which delayed flaps on takeoff provides some benefit if the pilot's sense of timing is good. It has large, lever operated mechanical flaps. The process goes something like this in the Maule: full power, release brakes, raise the tail when control authority is achieved. At about 40-50 mph (the actual speed is determined by the stiffness felt by the pilot in the elevator controls), pull on full flaps and pull back on the yoke at the same time. The tail will usually bounce again on the ground as the mains lift off smartly and you're suddenly airborne. Once established in the climb, begin a careful retraction of flaps while simultaneously raising the nose to begin a normal climb. This method can knock a good 50 feet from the takeoff roll of an airplane that needs less than 300 feet in the first place, a savings of 16 percent or more.

The pilot using this delayed-flap technique must be prepared for any number of flap malfunctions while very low to the ground. If the flap doesn't work properly, a crash is almost inevitable. Suppose the pilot accelerates to flight speed and pulls hard on the flap handle and only one flap comes down? The plane would probably do a quick half roll and land on its back at full throttle. What if the pilot selects partial flaps on an electric switch and they come fully down? The plane could easily jump into ground effect and then be unable to continue a climb. There are several nasty possibilities. Nevertheless, the procedure does, in fact, significantly shorten the takeoff roll in some airplanes. Whether or not to use it depends on the pilot's needs, experience level, the particular airplane and the situation. The airlines, for example, would never use this procedure in their airplanes.

Inflation of tires

When takeoff performance is really needed the pilot should check the tire pressure before flight is attempted.[5] Most airplane tires are composed of rubber compounds that differ slightly from that in automobiles so that they can tolerate the harsh abrasive treatment of landings and very high speeds. These compounds are actually slightly porous and tend to breathe. The typical airplane tire will lose up to five percent of its recommended pressure within the first 24 hours after inflation. The rate of air pressure loss after that point declines somewhat.

The point is that the tire pressure on the airplane is probably not what the pilot thinks it is, if the pilot has not checked it recently. As far as favorably stacking variables in the takeoff roll is concerned, this one is easy. Again, high pressure tires are best on hard surfaces, and soft tires might be best when taking off from soft fields.

Rotation attitude

The single biggest reason why airplanes do not seem to perform as advertised in the takeoff department is that the pilots are simply driving them down the runway too far. Proper speed at liftoff is critical to achieving maximum takeoff and climb performance. Proper rotation is vital for establishing the correct speed. Since the correct speed is variable with weight, but angle of attack is not, the pilot should memorize the correct angle of attack (AoA) that produces best angle of climb speed (Vx). This angle of attack might be judged quite accurately by referencing the aircraft attitude with the horizon. With practice, a skilled pilot could learn to reference attitude with direction of flight and determine angle of attack with precision at variable altitudes and power settings. Either way, as the airplane accelerates for takeoff, the pilot should rotate its attitude to match that of Vx.

5 See tire inflation discussion in Chapter 2.

Exactly when to rotate the plane is somewhat nebulous and requires a practice to be efficient. Ideally, the airplane should be rotated at a point such that Vx attitude is established just as proper liftoff speed is attained. The airplane should rotate into Vx attitude and become airborne all in one smooth motion. Delaying rotation until the last moment minimizes the aerodynamic drag on the craft as it accelerates. As soon as the plane establishes an angle of attack, even on the runway, drag increases rather quickly. Pilots of the MiG 15 fighter plane, for example, are cautioned to avoid over-rotation while on the runway. The induced drag increase at an AoA too high for that airplane with its swept wing is sufficient to prevent liftoff and climb from happening at all.

In the real world, and until the pilot becomes experienced with the characteristics of the airplane at a given weight, rotation speed can be difficult to guess with any precision. The practical compromise is to establish the Vx attitude shortly after control effectiveness occurs. This is easily done. Control pressures change with increasing airspeed. When the pilot feels that adequate control authority is available for rotation, the elevator control should be "loaded," or pressured to its approximate control position at Vx speed. Normally, the pilot will feel the control pressures increase slightly as the airplane gains speed. If the control inputs are correct, the plane will automatically begin the rotation rather close to the proper speed. The pilot should allow the rotation to progress until Vx attitude is achieved and adjust control pressures to maintain it. The plane will continue accelerating until, at exactly the right speed, it will lift off of its own accord and accelerate to Vx speed as the climb begins.

This method of takeoff rotation is perhaps the most satisfying and ego-pleasing way of leaving the ground. If it is done correctly, the airplane will leave the runway so smoothly that the passengers will often question the pilot if the airplane has actually begun flying. Another benefit of this procedure is that, once the proper attitude is well memorized and applied, correct speeds for liftoff and climb are automatic. The airplane will not remain on the runway for an instant longer than is necessary.

If the pilot feels that the best angle of climb speed (Vx) attitude is too steep for passenger comfort and a short-field climb is not necessary, the best rate of climb (Vy) attitude works nicely. Now that you understand that if you allow it to, a plane will lift off safely at precisely the correct speed and of its own accord, your takeoff distances should improve remarkably.

Use of ground effect

Ground effect might be a valuable and necessary part of the takeoff acceleration. The pilot should consider it a natural step in the plane's progression to climb speed. Unfortunately, many pilots figure that once the wheels are off the runway, the plane is airborne and should climb away freely. This can be dangerous, as illustrated by the pilot of a Piper Lance when he attempted a takeoff from Bullfrog, Utah, on a hot summer day.

Bullfrog is a 3500-foot strip near Lake Powell in the southern Utah desert. On this particular day, the temperature on the runway was close to 120 degrees F. The pilot was alone in the plane and felt that the runway would be plenty long for takeoff. Besides, he had flown out of this field many times before while carrying a load. Just to be safe, and for the sheer fun of it, he selected flaps for a short-field takeoff and applied power while holding the brakes. He loved the way the plane climbed with a light load and was in the mood to enjoy it. He released the brakes and the plane began to roll. Sadly, due to the hot weather and corresponding 9000-foot density altitude, the plane did not have its usual pep. The pilot pressed the throttle forward hard, just to make sure it was all in there, and then resigned himself to the sluggish acceleration. By this time, the runway was looking a little short. The pilot rotated the nose up steeply and found that the plane willingly lifted off from the runway, then settled back down and appeared almost ready to land again. The pilot pulled on the yoke a little harder, and again the plane climbed for a moment, then settled back to within a few feet of the ground. The plane did not climb above a few feet for the rest of the flight. The pilot continued to force the plane out of ground effect before it had sufficient speed, and the plane went on settling back down until it plowed through the barbed-wire fence at the end of the runway. The pilot survived and mistakenly thought something was wrong with the engine.

If the pilot had allowed the airplane to accelerate in the low-drag condition of ground effect rather than stubbornly insisting that the plane climb, it could have easily achieved a suitable climb speed and made a safe departure. You recall that ground effect is a condition of reduced aerodynamic drag while the airplane is close to the ground.

Most planes are happy to lift off in ground effect at rather slow airspeeds. But if a pilot insists that they climb above ground effect, induced drag increases heavily and might prevent the airplane from climbing at all.

Again, the key to effective use of ground effect is to maintain a constant attitude for climb speed and hold it until the airplane actually begins the climb. Proper rotation attitude on the runway basically continues through ground effect and into the climb phase of flight. Properly done, the pilot will observe the airplane lift off early, hesitate for a moment just above the runway while it accelerates, and then smoothly start climbing as speed is attained. There is normally no need to lower the nose, the rest is automatic. Because of ground effect, most airplanes will be gaining the last several knots of speed when they are already off the ground.

When to reconfigure

Short-field takeoff procedures usually require the use of flaps. If the plane has a retractable gear, the gear is obviously down for the takeoff. This configuration is subject to change as the plane begins to climb. There is much debate over exactly when to raise flaps and landing gear after the takeoff roll is completed. The answer has to do with the climb speeds at which the plane is flown. Basically, when the pilot is through with Vx, has cleared obstacles and begun accelerating to Vy, the configuration is no longer valid and should be changed appropriately.

Landing gear is the soft spot with most pilots. I know several who lovingly flip the switch to raise the gear when the tires have barely broken ground. True, it does look neat when the gear retracts from under the plane just as it leaves the runway, but the practice is dangerous. In the case of the short-field departure, some pilots will argue that getting the gear up is necessary to reduce drag and improve the climb angle. It sounds good, but for many airplanes, the process of raising the landing gear might substantially increase drag for several critical seconds.

In many planes, raising the gear requires that the wheel-bay doors open first to put the gear away. Often, the cavity that opens in the belly or wings of airplanes is huge, and represents a large increase in drag until the gear is tucked in and the doors are again closed. On airplanes that first open large gear doors as part of the retraction sequence in this manner, raising the gear to enhance initial obstacle clearance might plant pilot and airplane squarely into the trees at the end of the runway. On the other hand, simple systems that have open wheel bays might benefit from tucking the wheels in for reduced drag. In that case, there are no doors to open, no bays uncovered that weren't there already, and putting the wheels where they belong can only help. The procedural differences will often be stated in the pilot's operating handbook under short-field procedure. If nothing is mentioned there, you'll have to do a little experimenting.

Use of wind

Taking off into the wind enhances performance by shortening the ground roll and improving the climb gradient. There is less actual ground speed required to fly, which corresponds to less wear and tear on the tires and undercarriage. Overall, the benefits are too numerous to overlook and the potential improvements to performance are staggering. Nevertheless, pilots every year seem to forget these benefits, instead preferring to run off the end of runways and plow through stationary objects.

Typically, a pilot will taxi to the end of a runway without checking the wind, or not notice that the wind changed during the taxi. The pilot then faces a downwind takeoff or a long taxi to the other end of the runway. They hesitate for a minute, then decide to go for it. What's a little wind, anyway? Most will do that only once. If they don't crash, they learn a great respect for the dangers of downwind takeoffs by making a pale-skinned, cold-sweat, white-knuckled departure in a fast plane that doesn't want to lift off or climb. Needless to say, this is an opportunity for a pilot to dramatically enhance performance, or to totally destroy it.

Wind and sloped runways

A sloped runway presents certain challenging decisions to the pilot. Chiefly, how much headwind is required to outweigh the advantages of a downhill takeoff? Most runways that slope significantly are that way because of mountains or difficult surrounding terrain. The majority of them require one-way operations. If the wind is unfavorable for takeoff, the pilot must make an interesting decision. If the pilot elects to take off into the wind, but uphill on the runway, the wind must be quite substantial to justify tackling even a moderate runway gradient.

Runway slope in percent is the difference in altitude between the two ends of the runway, divided by the runway length. For example a 5000-foot runway with a 100-foot height difference between the runway ends has a slope of 100/5000, or 2 percent. Taking off up a 2-percent slope would be equivalent to departing with a 7-mph tailwind. An uphill slope of 8 percent would be the equivalent of a 24-mph tailwind, and probably a crash. Therefore, the pilot must balance the headwind carefully, in order to justify departing uphill. If the pilot were departing up an 8-percent grade, for example, a headwind of at least 24 mph would be required just to break even on the takeoff roll. Conversely, a downhill takeoff with no wind on the same 8 percent gradient would provide the equivalent performance advantages of a 24-mph headwind.

A general rule of thumb to figure the amount of wind needed to tackle an uphill takeoff is to take the runway gradient in percent and triple it. A 6-percent grade would equal a wind of 18 mph, for example. Wind also has a related effect on the airplane's inflight climb and descent gradient, but that will be discussed in the next chapter.

Short-field technique

A short-field takeoff technique involves most, if not all, of the previously discussed items. In the Maule it is quite an affair. After applying full throttle, checking the power and releasing the brakes, the engine strains, the propwash beats the sides of the fuselage and the airplane trundles forward as if being dragged by a large and powerful fish. The airplane then rocks lightly on its main gear and points skyward, rolling the tailwheel a little further before dragging itself noisily upward at a ridiculous angle. If the flight manual suggests a short-field technique, it is wise to begin by following that.

In the Maule's case, the airplane was originally certificated so long ago that its manufacturer was not required to produce a detailed operator's manual. Now that certification laws require published performance information for new airplanes, the Maule is "grand-fathered" and can stick to the old regulation. Company lawyers advise that the factory volunteer practically no information about the short-field operational characteristics of the airplane for fear of the liability risks that might result. Short-field procedures in the Maule, as a result, have to be discovered by experimentation, trial and error.

Most short-field procedures suggest a flapped configuration, holding brakes for power application and then a speed resembling Vx for the rotation and climb. Occasionally, an airplane manual will identify only the Vx speed for the airplane in the clean configuration. If that is the case, the pilot must experiment with the airplane to determine best angle climb in the short-field takeoff configuration for maximum obstacle clearance. The section on getting your own figures discusses a method to use for identifying procedures that work best for maximizing takeoff performance. Considering the items previously discussed, the general concepts should now be pretty simple to understand.

Soft-field technique

Soft-field takeoffs have a little different philosophy than a short-field procedure. The problem is the sticky runway surface. The rolling friction alone can be enough to prevent the airplane from attaining normal flying speed. In that case, the airplane must be made to fly at a slower speed, literally unsticking the plane from the ground and permitting the balance of acceleration to occur while airborne.

High power is generally required to taxi on soft terrain and the airplane should not be allowed to stop. The danger is the same as for your car on the beach. If you stop, it might sink. Airplane tires for the average light plane are smaller than car tires, so the risk of the airplane becoming a plow is greater. The pilot must be careful to maintain some forward speed in the taxi throughout the pretakeoff checks and run-up. At the end of the runway, full power application in a 180-degree turn is a great way to maintain forward motion into the takeoff roll, but you must be careful to prevent the inside main wheel from digging a posthole.

When power is fully applied and the plane is lined up with the runway, the pilot should make every effort to raise the nose wheel or tail wheel from the runway as soon as possible. The problem of three tires in the mud is lessened this way because now there are only two and acceleration should improve. The pilot maintains maximum angle of attack to lift off at the minimum possible speed. Once airborne, the pilot carefully adjusts the plane's attitude to permit acceleration in ground effect until reaching the proper climb attitude. During this acceleration period, the airplane should not be allowed to contact the ground again or the sticky runway surface might grab the tires and flip the plane over.

When the plane lifts off, its angle of attack is near stall. From that point, attitude is reduced to permit acceleration to climb speed. The pilot must lessen the pitch attitude as the acceleration occurs, or the airplane will soon be well above the ground and lose the benefits of ground effect. Flying out of ground effect too early can place the airplane squarely behind the power curve and prevent further climb, as happened in the crash of the Lance in southern Utah.

Curved runways

A curved or circling takeoff path is nothing new to seaplane pilots, who often use the perimeters of small round lakes to gain flying speed. For the pilot of a landplane, however, a curved runway presents a rather challenging departure. An airplane does not possess the handling characteristics of the typical sport car and will not naturally stick to the runway in a hard turn. The plane must be flown through turns even though the wheels might yet be on the ground. If the pilot neglects to properly manipulate the flight controls as the plane rounds a corner on the runway, it could easily drag a wing tip and cartwheel.

Needless to say, curved runways demand a lot of skill from pilots who use them and should not be attempted by the inexperienced. Many experienced and highly skilled pilots will not tackle a difficult mountain runway without first getting some dual instruction from someone familiar with it.

Skills to practice

The particulars required to truly maximize the takeoff performance of a given airplane are very specific to that plane and do not transfer well to other types. This refers to particular attitudes, configurations and the airplane's response to ground effect. On the plus side, the skills are rather easy for a pilot to master, and can be developed in a new plane with just a couple of hours practice.

Vx attitude

Consult the manual to determine the takeoff configuration for your plane. While airborne and at gross weight, set the takeoff configuration and establish a climb that stabilizes at the published Vx airspeed. Once airspeed has been established, take careful mental note of the airplane's attitude with respect to the horizon and gyroscopic instruments. When you have it nailed, level the plane, accelerate, and then duplicate the *attitude* again. Check to see that the airspeed stabilizes again at Vx.

Back on the runway, practice rotating to this same attitude during the takeoff roll. Take notes of the speeds when the airplane breaks ground, leaves ground effect, and the final speed that stabilizes in the climb (Fig. 3-7). Attempt to rotate to the Vx attitude just as elevator effectiveness is gained. Again note the speed at which the plane breaks ground contact. Practice this until the rotation attitude is burned into your memory. You should be able to do it day, night or IFR.

3-7 *Acceleration and climb with a constant attitude.*

180-degree turn

Begin by taxiing slowly through a tight 180-degree turn. Take note of the wing tip and tail swing throughout the turn. When you're comfortable with the dimensions required to complete the maneuver, try it again at a higher power setting. Eventually, you're working toward a smooth application to full power as the turn is commenced. Be careful not to allow the airplane to turn through the runway heading. It should feel as though the airplane is accelerating in a sling shot.

Be protective of your landing gear in this exercise. If the airplane has fixed gear, you have little to worry about, but a retractable might be less tolerant of high side loads and could require that you be less aggressive with power, speeds, and turn radius.

Use of flaps

If you plan to make use of a technique requiring delayed flap application, some practice is necessary. Due to the aft position of the wing flaps in most airplanes, there is generally an effect on pitch attitude as they are applied. This effect might cancel out your rotation to Vx attitude, or cause the propeller to strike the runway. In some cases, it could even cause an over-rotation and potential stall.

Begin by paying attention to the pitch changes that occur when you apply flaps in flight. Back on the runway, cautiously apply flaps and stand ready to secure a desired attitude with the elevator control. Lift and pitch will both change quite rapidly as the flaps are extended, and you might find yourself airborne before you know it. No problem, just set the attitude properly and fly away.

One common mishap with flaps of the hand-lever operated variety is a pilot-induced flap retraction. This is caused by the pilot habitually pushing the lock release button at the end of the flap handle when the lever is pulled on. Having the button pushed causes the flaps not to lock into position, and they subsequently retract when you let go of the handle. This could be disastrous. As a precaution, do not let go of the flap handle until you are certain that the flaps are locked in position.

Recognition and use of ground effect

Exaggerate the normal soft-field procedure by staying a few feet above the runway on takeoff until well above normal climb speed. Take note of the large reduction of angle of attack that is required with the increased airspeed. Essentially you are attempting to buzz the runway at low altitude while airspeed increases.

When you are comfortable flying down the runway in ground effect, do it again and lower the attitude only to the point at which it matches the Vx climb attitude. The plane will climb away and you will have executed a beautiful soft-field departure procedure.

Getting your own figures

This section will take a different approach to quantifying performance than what you're used to. Instead of raw data and a performance number per se for the airplane, we will concentrate on maximizing your skills as a pilot and identifying procedural techniques that actually work. Actual takeoff distance is not particularly relevant as a numerical quantity in this case. We will concentrate on simply bettering a previous timing mark until your personal performance is optimal. You will need the help of a friend and a stopwatch. Be ready to take notes.

Drag racers and sprinters regularly make use of a stopwatch to see who is the fastest. The principle might well be applied to your airplane with you at the controls. The object will be to shorten the time from brake release to 50 feet above ground level (agl), to a bare minimum. *Note:* Brake release in the 180-degree turn occurs just as the turn is completed, and the plane begins to roll down the runway. The method you use to achieve minimum time should also result in the shortest possible takeoff distance. Since we are concentrating on technique and not distance, the factors of wind, humidity, density altitude and so forth are irrelevant with regard to your personal performance, as long as the timed tests are conducted in the same conditions. We are simply minimizing a time. Once the correct procedure is well understood and practiced, achieving or exceeding the *book* numbers under specified ambient conditions should be relatively simple.

Place a mark on your altimeter at 50 feet above your airport elevation. Your assistant will stand by to time the interval from brake release, until the altitude passes through that mark. If you attempt to "zoom" the airplane through 50 feet agl to minimize the time, your assistant will watch closely for any post-climb sink. If the airplane sinks back through 50 feet agl, the time will be void and the flight considered a crash.

Begin with the published short-field procedure for your airplane, if there is one. From there, modify the technique one item at a time, as described in the technique section of this chapter, isolating the methods that work vs. those that don't for your particular situation. When you have optimized the procedural aspects of the takeoff such that you are consistently matching your best time to 50 feet, you might wish to note the conditions, consult the takeoff charts and compare the distances you achieve with those claimed by the manufacturer (if you have them).

Consistency in a takeoff procedure is critical to safety. When you think that you have the procedure down, practice until you can achieve roughly the same time interval every time you take off in similar conditions. In doing so, your ability to estimate runway length requirements against aircraft performance will improve immensely. Your eyeball will become trained, so to speak. Again, this might sound approximate, but in practical application of your airplane's abilities, you will actually be able to "eyeball" your plane's departure point and climb requirements more accurately than the charts will.

Further reading

The Proficient Pilot, Barry Schiff, Aircraft Owners and Pilots Association, 1980

Aerodynamics for Naval Aviators, H. H. Hurt, Jr., University of Southern California, NAVWEPS 00-80T-80, 1965

A Gift of Wings, Richard Bach, Dell Publishing Company, 1974

Bush Flying, O'Meara, McGraw-Hill, 1990

Good Takeoffs and Good Landings, Christy/George, McGraw-Hill, 1991

4

Climb

Opening the cockpit window in flight sounded like a waterfall coming full blast in my face. Papers and dust in the cabin blew around as though caught in a miniature tornado. I fumbled with the coil of steel cable on my lap. It was carefully wound, ending in a three-pronged grappling hook. The other end was attached to the tail of the airplane. Making sure that the little grappling hook wouldn't catch on anything, I carefully tossed the whole mess out the window. It uncoiled quickly and snapped into position behind the plane. It was difficult to tell exactly where the hook dangled back there, so I felt a little nervous about getting too low to the ground on the first pass. Turning final, I caught sight of the two poles and their orange pennants standing like goalposts in the field next to the runway. I aimed for the hook to pass right between them.

The idea, like an Olympic challenge, was for the hook to catch a rope stretched between the poles. When the rope was snagged, I had to make the airplane climb away steeply to avoid dragging the rope and its large banner through the weeds. It was a political campaign ad, another part of the endless banner blitz in a local, hard-fought, mud-slinging, election-time war. Somebody was running for Congress this year and please can she have your vote? The lengthy slogan dripped with promise about as substantial as the hot wind that made the flags flutter like lips speaking nonsensical phrases.

The radio came alive.

"I need you lower."

"Roger."

I had been plenty lower than this before, but the hook and cable dangling back there made me worry. Suppose it were to snag in the dirt, hook a bush of some kind, and rip the plane's tail off? That shouldn't happen, the cable had weak points that were guaranteed to break before anything in the airplane did, but that sounded suspiciously like another campaign promise. I'd just make sure it didn't snag anything solid.

"Lower." Greg stood near the flags, giving instructions with a hand-held radio. They were getting closer. I inched the plane down. It looked just like the dry practice runs, moments before.

"Perfect. You're hooked."

I smashed the throttle forward and began a steep climb. The tow rope payed out rapidly, as though I'd snagged a big fish. Then suddenly the rope went tight and the plane responded like it flew into Jell-O. The RPM sagged and the rate of climb fell to zero. It felt like flying into a spider's web; an invisible grip held the plane in an empty sky. I lowered the nose quickly to maintain speed. The banner's speed limit was 75 mph. Faster than that, and the political promise would be tattered to shreds. Climb speed was 72 mph, but the plane would not go faster than 68 mph without a dive. The vertical speed was nearly imperceptible, but climbing.

All I had to do at this point was fly around the patch and drop it when we were done. "Piece of cake," I thought, but the plane struggled to climb a dismal 50 feet per minute. Airspeed held steady just below 70, and the airport boundary rolled away beneath the nose. The plane was 200 feet high. The banner trailed somewhere unseen back there, much lower. We flew across the road at the runway's end, then over a cool, green alfalfa field. Vertical speed softly faded to zero.

Behind me, at the airport, Greg noticed that the plane seemed to descend over the field. I noticed, too. I watched anxiously as the airspeed slowly fell away. I held my breath, hoping that the sink would be momentary, perhaps due to local air patterns over the field. Down to 150 feet and falling agonizingly slow, like a powered feather pulling lightly at a ship's anchor. I wanted to turn, but the headwind was substantial and turning away from it would decrease the angle of climb. The plane finally held steady at 60 mph, but it wasn't climbing; it was too slow, and I couldn't make it go any faster.

If I couldn't make the plane get to Vy with this thing in tow, then perhaps I could move Vy to the plane. I lowered the flaps slightly, hoping to adjust the lift curve in my favor. The plane responded with a sound 25-feet per minute climb. I could hold that at 60 mph. There were powerlines ahead. I felt like a fly struggling wretchedly in a room full of spiders. The plane would clear the powerlines, but what about the banner? I turned slightly to parallel the course of those lines, giving up some of my headwind. The plane was stuck interminably at 150 feet. I had no idea how high the banner was. Should it come in contact with anything on the ground, it might catch and pull the airplane down with it—a political catastrophe. Climb! More power! I pressed the throttle to the wall, hard, just to make sure it was all there. Mixture had already been leaned for best power, carburetor heat verified off, the window closed. What else could I do? I concentrated on the rudder ball. I saw more powerlines ahead, crossing the path of the ones to my left. Boxed in by electric steel, netted like a fly, the plane wasn't climbing fast enough.

To simply pull back further would invite an excursion behind the power curve and pile drag on the plane sufficient to bring it down. The spider was waiting out there. Powerlines are real. Only one option left. The banner had to go, and better here over a field than in the wires. I pulled the release handle and the banner stopped and fell to the weeds like an election-day promise. The airplane, free at last, behaved like something shot from a rubber band. It gained 300 feet in an instant.

I circled the banner where it lay, rumpled and dead in the field, directing the ground crew to pick it up. I wondered why the plane would not climb for me, when Greg had towed the same banner around just an hour before. True, Greg weighs 50 pounds less than me, but in a plane like this Cessna 172, what difference could that make?

Background information

Climbing to altitude in an airplane, as in politics, is a matter of excess. The airplane needs excess power to move up. The plane must meet the drag expenses already incurred by its speed, weight and flight condition, just to stay airborne. If power is left over, then a climb is possible. If drag is increased by pulling a large banner around, for example, then the power available might be insufficient to handle it and still produce a surplus. In my case, on a windy, hot summer day, the plane was pooped—its power account was maxed.

Ironically, in spite of this ad failure, the politician who commissioned the banner won the election. I guess she had excess money to spend.

The drag curve

The total drag affecting an airplane is the sum of two sources, namely, induced and parasite drag. These normally are depicted with a drag curve, representing the amount of drag affecting an airplane at any speed throughout its operating envelope.

Induced drag gets its name from the fact that it is lift induced. It is directly related to angle of attack and a major contributor to the total drag when the airplane is flown at low speeds, with the corresponding high angles of attack. Induced drag drops sharply at angles of attack higher than stall, in proportion to the decline of lift at that point. At lesser angles of attack with their coinciding high speeds, induced drag fades to the point of becoming almost insignificant in unaccelerated flight.

Parasite drag is aptly named to reflect its characteristic tenacity. It is always present like an unwanted parasite and impossible to shake completely without bringing everything to a complete stop. This drag is proportional to airspeed, beginning gently at zero velocity and growing exponentially as the airplane accelerates. At high speeds, parasite drag makes up the bulk of the total resistance to the plane's forward motion. The intensity of parasite drag at a given speed is also related to the physical shape and surface, including such drag sources as landing gear, cooling vents, door handles, rivets, dirt, and anything else that interferes with the smooth flow of air around the airplane.

For any given speed, the airplane's forward motion is resisted by the sum of these two types of drag. The bold curve in Fig. 4-1 represents that total drag through a range of speeds. The figure also depicts the individual curves for induced and parasite drag, although for practical considerations we will primarily consider only the total drag curve in future discussions.

Notice that the total amount of drag acting on an airplane begins rather high, then actually *decreases* as the airplane gains speed, until the point at which induced and parasite drag are equal. Beyond that point, parasite drag builds aggressively as induced drag falls away, increasing the total drag as the airplane gains speed.

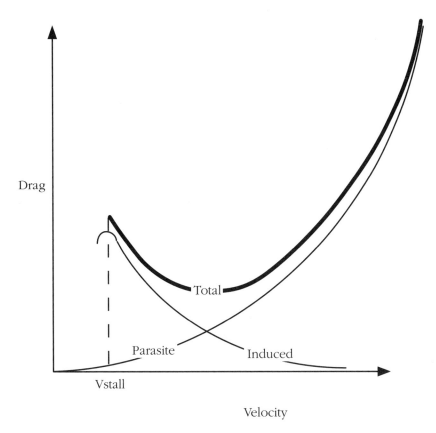

4-1 *A generic drag curve, showing the influences of parasite and induced drag.*

Drag curve and angle of attack

Notice that the same drag curve used previously can also be depicted with reference to angle of attack in place of speed (Fig. 4-2). This is the most consistent and accurate way to portray the drag curve because it does not change with weight. The ideal angles of attack for stall, climb, minimum drag, and cruise are always constant. Since few straight-wing light aircraft are equipped with angle of attack indicators, the airspeed indicator can be used instead. In doing so, the pilot must consider the need to make corrections for the changing conditions of weight, altitude, configuration, and power.

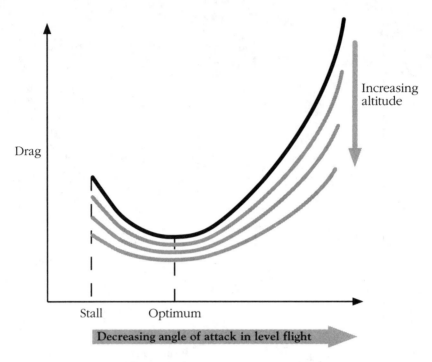

4-2 *Drag curve and angle of attack.*

The drag curve and weight

Weight affects the amount of lift required of the wings, which causes the induced drag portion of the curve to shift up and to the right. The overall effect is generally to tighten the "U" shaped appearance of the drag curve, by shifting the low-speed envelope to the right, as depicted in Fig. 4-3.

Placing the CG (center of gravity) at the aft limit will moderate the effects of weight somewhat. Aft CG reduces the overall lift requirement of the wings, which minimizes the shift in the drag curve.[1]

Aircraft configuration might also shift the drag curve around. During my experience towing the banner, I used flaps to shift the drag curve to the left, hoping to place the airplane in a condition of lower drag for a given speed, as illustrated by Fig. 4-4.

1 Aft CG was discussed in Chapter 2.

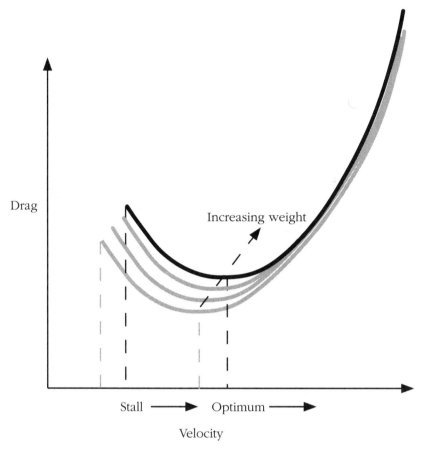

Stall ⟶ Optimum ⟶

Velocity

4-3 *Drag curve and weight.*

Drag and power

The drag curve may be approached from the viewpoint of drag representing the power required to sustain the airplane in level flight at a given speed. Since the forces acting on an airplane to produce unaccelerated flight must be in equilibrium, the drag acting on an airplane must be effectively balanced by thrust. Thrust is produced by some sort of powerplant within the airplane, whether reciprocating, turbine, rocket, or gravity (as with a sailplane). Viewing the drag curve in this manner indicates how much drag exists at a given speed that needs to be countered by thrust. In fact, the curve is often depicted in terms of thrust, or power, required as noted on the left side of the chart. Notice that the thrust requirements are high at

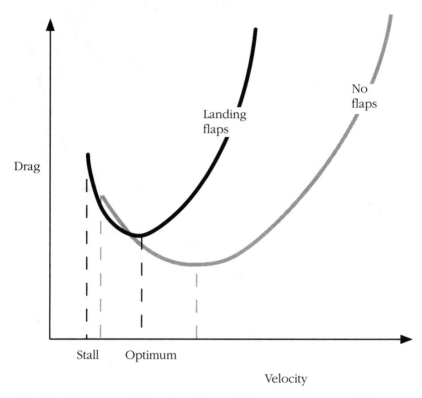

4-4 *Drag curve with a configuration change.*

both the low and high speed extremes, while the middle range needs are relatively slight.

The thrust curve

Combining a depiction of the thrust available from the airplane's powerplant with the airframe's drag curve makes a useful presentation (Fig. 4-5). It is here that the major differences between prop-driven and turbojet-powered airplanes become apparent. The propeller produces large amounts of thrust at slow speeds, decreasing rapidly as speed increases and the propeller loses efficiency. This high thrust at low speeds is in part responsible for the comparatively short takeoff rolls of propeller-driven airplanes. The turbine engine, on the other hand, produces thrust rather consistently throughout its speed range.

Thrust is the ultimate factor in producing a steep climb angle. The Apollo moon rockets had plenty of thrust—point them at the moon,

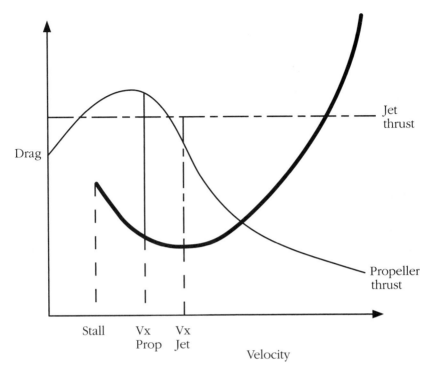

Drag

Jet
thrust

Propeller
thrust

Stall   Vx   Vx
          Prop Jet

Velocity

4-5 *Drag curve and thrust.*

light the fuse, and away they go. Short of rocket planes, and those of very high thrust-to-weight ratios, though, most airplanes are another story. Since thrust is generally less than the aircraft weight, the point-and-shoot method of best angle climb is moderated by the price of gravity. The pilot finds maximum climb angle where the propeller or jet engine develops best thrust over and above the airframe generated drag, generally producing some angle less than vertical.

For the propeller, the speed at which maximum excess thrust occurs is rather slow, often quite near the stall speed. This speed is Vx. Having the speed so close to stall also works in favor of the propeller in the case of a short runway and close obstacles, because the airplane might begin a climb quickly, without wasting much runway for continued acceleration. For the jet, Vx occurs exactly at the point of minimum airframe drag, which corresponds conveniently with best-glide speed. Best-glide speed for the jet might be remarkably fast, exacerbating the problem of a short-field departure. The time spent accelerating to an efficient climb speed might best be spent clearing the obstacles at the end of the runway. In the case of the short-field problem, the jet demands a myriad of techniques, involving things like a rapid pull-up from slow speed, or accelerating in ground effect and zooming for altitude. The only consistency in this case is to consult the manual and do what the designers and test pilots determined to be most effective.

Excess power

The power curve for a propeller increases slightly at the speeds at which the engine/propeller combination is most efficient. It is not entirely related to thrust, but rather to the power that the engine can deliver to the propulsive mechanism. For the turbine engine, increased speed means increased power in a fairly linear fashion, right up to redline. The point above the drag curve at which maximum excess power occurs corresponds to the speed for best *rate* of climb, or Vy (Fig. 4-6).[2]

For the propeller, this speed is often slightly faster than best L/D (best-glide speed, or lift to drag). For the jet, Vy might occur at a speed very near cruise.

It is possible to approximate the excess power of an airplane for a given speed with the help of a simple formula and some known values. Take a Cessna 152, for example. This airplane climbs at about 500 feet per minute at 65 knots, at 5000 feet msl (mean sea level). A full load puts the airplane's gross weight at 1670 pounds. The formula for rate of climb looks like Fig. 4-7.

Since we already know the values of all the variables except excess power, we re-arrange the formula to look like Fig. 4-8.

The 33,000 is just a constant to convert horsepower to feet per minute. If we plug in the known figures, we get 500 feet/minute times 1670 pounds, divided by 33,000, or 25.3 horsepower. A little surprising, isn't it? Of the original 115 hp, almost 90 hp has been lost to cooling, density altitude, lift, and drag—just keeping the plane airborne.

If there were a way to increase excess power without a weight penalty, even a modest improvement like 10 hp could make a dra-

---

2 From this (see Fig. 4-6), it is easy to determine the airplane's normal performance envelope as that area bounded by the drag curve on the bottom, the thrust curve on the top, and the points where the curves meet at each end.

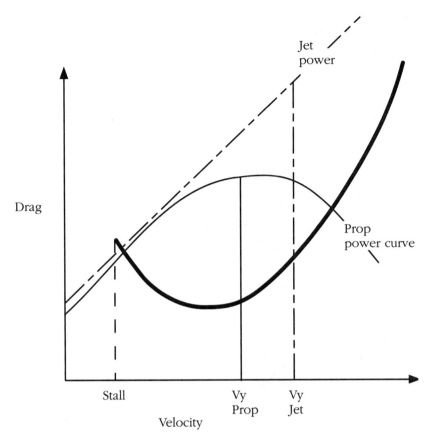

4-6 *Drag curve and power.*

$$\text{Rate of climb} = 33,000 \ \frac{\text{Excess power}}{\text{Weight}}$$

4-7 *Rate of climb formula (piston).*

$$\frac{(\text{Rate of climb})(\text{Weight})}{33,000} = \text{Excess power}$$

4-8 *Rate of climb rearranged for excess power.*

matic improvement to the climb rate. Ten hp would increase the excess power by almost 50 percent. The climb rate should improve accordingly—we would expect around 700 to 750 feet/minute. As it turns out, this is exactly what happens with the popular Sparrowhawk conversion for the C-152. The plane is given a power increase of 10 horsepower, and the climb rate jumps 50 percent—because it all goes to excess (Fig. 4-9).

4-9 *Much of the horsepower generated in a typical engine goes to cooling, lift, and drag. Just keeping the airplane airborne might use enormous quantities. Whatever is left over may be used to climb.*

Behind the power curve

For many airplanes, regardless of their power, it is possible to fly the airplane at a speed for which there is insufficient power to produce a climb. This is what is meant by operating behind the power curve.

The chart in Fig. 4-10 depicts an airplane with a power curve that cannot match the drag quantity when the plane is flown near stall speed. The airplane would be perfectly controllable at that speed—that is to say, when it is not stalled—but it would be impossible to maintain a steady altitude. Full power is simply not enough to match the drag produced by the airframe. The airplane in such a condition cannot climb unless it accelerates to a speed that produces less drag and a surplus of power. The only way to produce that acceleration is for the pilot to accept more altitude loss in a dive until the plane gains sufficient speed and sheds enough drag to allow a climb. Needless to say, to be caught in this position when the plane is close to the ground is to court disaster.

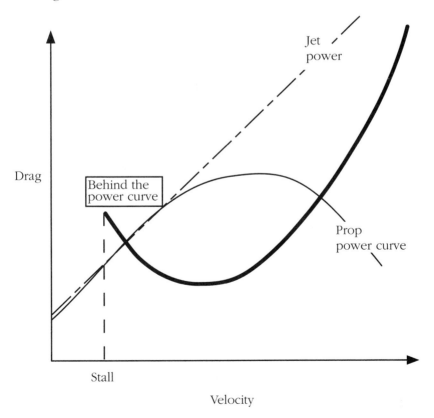

4-10 *The back side of the power curve.*

A closer look at Vx and Vy

Ever wonder why the speeds for best angle of climb (Vx) and best rate of climb (Vy) are not marked clearly on the airspeed indicator? The answer lies in the fact that these speeds are quite variable. We know that Vx and Vy are both slower when the plane is flown at light weights, different when flaps are down, and are even changed a little with center of gravity locations. Perhaps the greatest reason why pilots are often unable to make their airplanes perform as advertised in the climb department, is that they are climbing at improper speeds. The correct speed to fly, considering all of the factors, might vary substantially with each situation. The proper climb speed will also change slightly during the climb itself.

We will discuss each of these factors in detail in this section, followed by methods of actually determining proper speed in the technique section of this chapter.

Vx, Vy, and altitude

Engine power, thrust, and even drag diminish with higher density altitudes, changing the speeds that would be appropriate for best angle and rate of climb. Climb performance, of course, also diminishes greatly with increasing altitude (Fig. 4-11).

Observe the points of Vx and Vy as available power diminishes with increasing altitude. They gradually approach best L/D speed at the bottom of the curve. The incident with the banner in tow was related to this phenomenon, except that instead of lowering the available power, the drag curve was raised to the point that significant excess power could not be generated (Fig. 4-12).

At altitudes ranging between sea level and the airplane's maximum ceiling, the pilot should make a careful approximation of the best climb speed for maximum performance. Take, for example, the Cessna 152 again. The sea level values for Vx and Vy are 54 kts and 67 kts, respectively. At 5000 feet we use the appropriate speeds of 55 kts and 65 kts. At 10,000 feet, I would use speeds quite close to the best L/D speed of 60 kts because, at that point, the airplane is not far from its ceiling.

A detailed climb schedule may be worked out in advance. In the EMB-120 Brasilia, for example, the flight director and autopilot are preprogrammed with a speed schedule to optimize climb perfor-

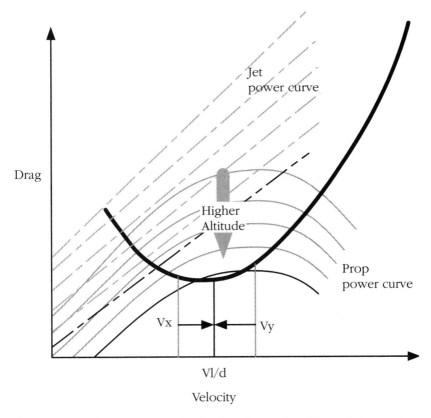

Drag

Jet
power curve

Higher
Altitude

Prop
power curve

Vx

Vy

Vl/d

Velocity

4-11 *Diminishing power at high altitudes pushes Vx and Vy together.*

mance and bring the airplane quickly to more fuel-efficient altitudes. Beginning at 170 knots at sea level, the computer will gradually decrease indicated airspeed to 155 knots by 20,000 feet, then maintain that speed until cruising altitude is attained. The details of working out your own climb schedule will be discussed in the "getting your own figures" section of this chapter.

You might think that the subtle variations in climb speed are too slight to be worth the bother, but when faced with the prospects of flying over the tall trees at the not-so-far end of the runway, or thousands of dollars in fuel savings over a year's operations, every little advantage is help indeed.

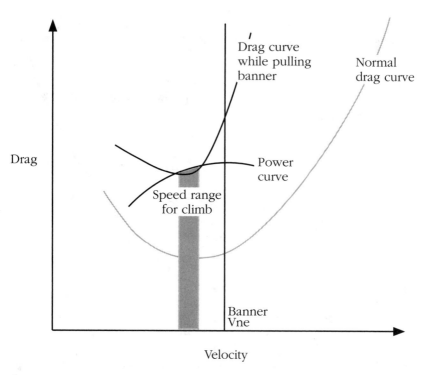

4-12 *Drag curve while pulling a banner.*

Single-engine climb for multiengine airplanes

Consider a light multiengine airplane. Suppose we fly one that weighs 3800 pounds and climbs 1200 feet/minute with both 180 hp engines running (Fig. 4-13):

$$\frac{(1200)(3800)}{33,000} \;=\; 138.2 \text{ excess horsepower}$$

4-13 *Excess power for a generic light twin.*

Of the 360 total horsepower available, 222 hp is required just to make the plane fly. If the airplane were to lose one of those precious 180-hp engines, there would be no excess horsepower and the airplane would be in a precarious situation indeed. In order for such a plane to have acceptable single-engine performance, the engines would have to be of sufficient power to produce an excess with only one of them operative. The excess, or climb power, available with both engines running would be great, as is typical of a good twin.

Cruise climb and cooling

The cooling needs of internal-combustion powerplants often limit the time that may be spent at high angles of attack and slow airspeeds. Since most reciprocating engines in aircraft applications are air-cooled, the limited airflow during optimal angle climbs might create an engine cooling problem. For this reason, maximum angle climbs are used primarily for short durations and obstacle clearance, or until engine temperature limits are reached. Beyond that, angle of attack must be reduced, with a corresponding increase in airspeed to facilitate adequate cooling. Furthermore, in the challenge of getting efficiently from A to B, a maximum-performance climb to cruise altitude might be detrimental. This is especially so when the climb speed is substantially slower than cruise. The most efficient climb might involve a speed only slightly less than cruise speed, as slow a climb as is practicable and a power setting sufficiently low to permit leaning. In this manner, no time is wasted in slow flight during the climb segment. That is the concept of cruise climb: better engine cooling, lower fuel consumption, and reduced block to block times.

Wind and climb angle

Imagine an airplane that is climbing into a headwind that exactly matches its forward airspeed. As seen from the ground, the climb angle would be just like an Apollo rocket. Now suppose the airplane were to turn 180 degrees and climb with the tailwind. The climb angle would be horribly diminished. In both cases, however, the *rate* of climb would be unchanged.

Wind, as we think of it, affects airplane groundspeed, not airspeed nor rate of climb. If the plane's climb rate is constant and the forward groundspeed reduced to zero, the plane will appear to ascend vertically. If the airplane's groundspeed were doubled by a tailwind and the climb rate remain constant, the climb angle will be half what it was. As you can see, wind can have an outrageous effect on the airplane's climb performance when obstacle clearance is required.

Ceiling

When the airplane is at its maximum altitude, the pilot will have applied full throttle and fixed the airplane at best L/D speed, but it climbs no further. The plane will be far from stalling. To fly faster or slower than best L/D speed places the airplane behind the power curve. If the pilot slows the airplane, the increased induced drag would bring it down. Should the airplane be allowed to accelerate, the increased parasite drag would also cause a descent. Often, the airspeed tolerance when the plane reaches its ceiling can be so tight that a single knot in either direction might require a descent.

Such are the conditions for pilots of the famous U-2 spy plane, for example, during its high-altitude cruise. The pilot balances the airplane precariously between stall speed and the speed of sound. At extreme altitudes, the speed of sound slows down remarkably. If we suppose that the clean stall speed of the U-2 is 100 knots, the pilot may ascend only so high that the speed of sound reduces to about 107 knots. That is the flight envelope for the plane at high altitude cruise—7 knots. Go too slow and the plane stalls; too fast and it becomes supersonic debris. (The U-2 cannot tolerate supersonic flight.) As the airplane burns off fuel and becomes lighter, its stall speed decreases. This widens the margin between stall and Mach 1, allowing the pilot to fly higher, where the speed of sound is slower yet, maintaining the 7-knot stall/Mach-1 spread.

The typical light airplane does not often cavort with the speed of sound and live to tell about it. A more common, although less glamorous, scenario is the delicate balance of climb speeds that occurs when the airplane nears its maximum ceiling—or when it pulls a banner. In the same way as the U-2, light weights make the speeds a little slower, reduce drag, and enable a plane to fly a little higher.

Technique

Many of the techniques described in this section have different, even opposing, purposes. For the maximum performance climb, the object is to reach a target altitude as quickly as possible. Best-angle climb devotes all energy to maximizing climb in minimum distance. Cruise climb, on the other hand, is more concerned with fuel conservation, cooling, and shortening block times on a trip. Every technique has a specific purpose. Often, a pilot will use all of these methods in a single flight: best angle of climb to clear the trees on takeoff, followed by best-climb rate to a minimum safe altitude while maneuvering to a course heading, followed at last by a cruise climb on course. The description of the optimum application of climb technique is often called the *climb profile*.

For transport category airplanes, a legal climb profile is stipulated in detail. From brake release to decision speed, termed V1, the airplane is not committed to fly. Any emergency prior to reaching that speed could be cause for an automatic decision to abort the takeoff. Once accelerated past V1, the decision has been made to fly. Rotation speed follows, at which the airplane is pitched to an attitude such that it will reach V2 prior to an altitude of 35 feet.[3,4] Landing gear is retracted when the climb begins, and the pilots establish an attitude to give a speed slightly above V2, until the airplane reaches 400 feet agl.[5]

This initial dash for altitude is meant to shorten the time that the airplane and occupants might be exposed to an emergency at low altitude. At 400 feet the airplane is allowed to accelerate until flap retraction may occur and climb resumes at Vy until it reaches at least 1500 feet agl. Beyond that altitude, the pilots may begin a cruise climb profile.

Believe it or not, climb profiles such as this are mandatory in airline operations, and can be the cause for a pilot's failure of a checkride if flown improperly. Although this might again seem like a lot of overkill, the concept in terms of safety is a sound one. It minimizes the airplane's exposure to the dangers of low altitude.

Climb chart

A detailed operator's manual might contain climb information for your airplane. Figure 4-14 shows charts derived from the manuals of a Beech Sundowner and a Cessna 206.

Notice that many of the figures on these charts are useful for information and planning only, such as predicted outside-air temperature and expected fuel consumption—even the predicted rate of climb itself is of little use to the pilot, beyond facilitating flight planning. From a piloting standpoint, the charts may be reduced dramatically.

As a general rule of thumb, observe that climb speed is reduced by 1 knot for each 100 pounds below gross weight, and about 1 percent

3 Takeoff safety speed, determined to be Vxse (Vx with an engine out).

4 The actual altitude varies with operators, country and the particular plane, but 35 feet is a common choice.

5 V2 plus 10 knots in the EMB-120 Brasilia. V2 plus 10, in this case, corresponds to Vx speed with all engines operative.

Associated conditions:

Power   Full throttle
Mixture   lean to max RPM and then
               enrich slightly
Flaps   up

NOTE: High humidity and use of rich mixture
       has been found to result in approximately.
       70 fpm loss in rate of climb from that shown.

       Any area with low clouds or a dewpoint
       temperature of 60F or higher is an area of
       high humidity.

Weight	Sea level OAT F	C	R/C ft/min	IAS kts/mph	4000 FEET OAT F	C	R/C ft/min	IAS kts/mph	8000 FEET OAT F	C	R/C ft/min	IAS kts/mph	12,000 FEET OAT F	C	R/C ft/min	IAS kts/mph
2450	23	-5	841		9	-13	621		-6	-21	389		-20	-29	167	
	41	5	816		27	-3	596		13	-11	362		-2	-19	141	
	59	15	792	78/90	45	7	572	78/87	31	-1	338	74/85	16	-9	117	74/85
	77	25	769		63	17	549		49	9	315		34	1	94	
	95	55	747		81	27	527		67	19	293		52	11	72	
2200	23	-5	1047		9	-13	812		-6	-21	567		-20	-29	327	
	41	5	1021		27	-3	787		13	-11	539		-2	-19	302	
	59	15	997	76/88	45	7	763	74/85	31	-1	515	72/83	16	-9	277	72/83
	77	25	974		63	17	740		49	9	492		34	1	254	
	95	55	951		81	27	718		67	19	469		52	11	232	
2000	23	-5	1243		9	-13	994		-6	-21	735		-20	-29	478	
	41	5	1217		27	-3	969		13	-11	707		-2	-19	453	
	59	15	1193	75/86	45	7	945	72/83	31	-1	682	70/81	16	-9	428	70/81
	77	25	1169		63	17	922		49	9	659		34	1	405	
	95	55	1147		81	27	900		67	19	636		52	11	383	

Cessna 206

Weight	Sea level 59 F			5000 ft 41 F			10,000 ft 23 F			15,000 ft 5 F			20,000 ft −12 F		
3600	100	920	2	96	640	4.3	93	360	7.6	90	90	15.1	-	-	-
3100	95	1190	2	91	890	3.7	87	585	5.9	83	280	9.3	-	-	-
2600	90	1560	2	85	1205	3.3	81	855	4.8	77	515	6.9	71	150	10.9
	IAS	ft/min	GAL	IAS	ft/min	GAL	IAS	ft/min	GAL	IAS	ft/min	GAL	IAS	ft/min	GAL

NOTES: 1. Power set full throttle and 2700 RPM.
         2. Mixture set per recommended leaning schedule (climb rate increased by 30 ft/min)
         3. Fuel used includes warm-up and takeoff estimates.
         4. Decrease climb rate 30 ft./min for each 10 degrees F above standard.
         5. Climb performance decreases by 45 ft/min with cargo pack.

4-14 *Climb-performance charts for a Beechcraft Sundowner and a Cessna 206.* Beechcraft and Cessna Aircraft Companies

for each 1000 feet of climb. As I said, this is only a rule of thumb and is prone to certain inaccuracies. The proper thing to do is produce your own graph, the details of which will be discussed in the "getting your own figures" section of this chapter.

Climb schedule

With a little homework, the aircraft climb charts can be reduced to a simple table of speeds to use for best rate of climb as the airplane makes its way to altitude. From Fig. 4-14, I developed these sample charts (Fig. 4-15) by dropping everything but climb speeds, altitudes, and standard temperatures.

BEECHCRAFT Sundowner 180

	S.L. 15 C	4000 7 C	8000 -1 C	12,000 -9 C
2450	78	78	74	74
2200	76	74	72	72
2000	75	72	70	70

CESSNA 206

	S.L. 15 C	5000 5C	10,000 -5C	15,000 -15C	20,000 -25C
3600	100	96	93	90	-
3100	95	91	87	93	-
2600	90	85	81	77	71

4-15 *Climb-performance charts reduced for practicality in the cockpit.*

These charts could easily be posted in the cockpit to assist the pilot in determining correct Vy at anytime during the climb. Tables like this are commonly known as *climb speed schedules.*

Keep in mind that the airplane responds to air density, not so much to pressure altitude. The ceiling of the airplane will be a figure of density altitude, meaning that actual ceiling possible as viewed on the altimeter will be a function of temperature. With that in mind, the altitude used for selection of Vy should properly be density altitude. The pilot will have to approximate this with a simple rule of thumb. For every 1 degree Celsius above standard temperature, use the climb speed for 100 feet above what you see on the altimeter. You might want to more accurately approximate pressure altitude by setting your altimeter to 29.92 inches Hg while in the climb. If the temperature is below standard, the same rule works in reverse, that is, every 1 degree below standard temperature means a climb speed appropriate for 100 feet below your pressure altitude. One hundred feet per degree might not sound like much, but it is common in dry regions for temperatures to differ from standard by 20 degrees or more, in either direction, requiring 2000-feet adjustments to your climb speed.

Use of wind to improve climb angle

Suppose you are taking off to fly a left-hand pattern, but the runway has a right crosswind. Obstacle clearance will be enhanced if you first turn into the wind on the initial climb. A headwind has the effect of increasing the airplane's climb angle with respect to the ground. Where obstacle clearance could be a problem, the pilot should use the wind for maximum advantage.

Again, wind does not affect climb *rate*, it affects groundspeed. The reason why climb angle is enhanced in wind is that the wind reduces groundspeed while climb rate is unchanged. If groundspeed were reduced to nil during the climb, the angle would duplicate that of an elevator, which also has no groundspeed.

Use of terrain for obstacle clearance

Believe it or not, the easiest way to improve obstacle clearance on takeoff is to pick low obstacles. That might sound obvious, but you'd be surprised by the number of accidents caused by a pilot attempting to out-climb an uphill slope. With a little course planning, the moments immediately after takeoff might be startlingly effective in distancing the aircraft from the ground. If the runway is built on a slope, the pilot should turn downhill. In this manner, with the ground falling away as the airplane climbs, the departure heading can drastically affect the critical climb gradient, or angle, at which the flight path diverges from the surface. In other words, if obstacle clearance is a potential hazard, pick the flight path over the shortest obstacle.

Trimming for climb

Control pressures are much easier to manage when the airplane is correctly trimmed. In fact, on large aircraft, the control pressures for a given speed and configuration might be so great that they overpower the pilot(s). Nevertheless, deflected trim tabs do incur a drag penalty, and the airplane would theoretically be cleaner if all trim devices were set flush to the trailing edges of the control surfaces, but for most airplanes, this procedure would not only be impractical, it would be very tiring, and the amount of benefit to be derived would be minuscule at best.

Of greater benefit to the plane and ease for the pilot is rudder coordination during the climb. Far too many pilots fly around with their feet flat on the floor. For propellers, the turning tendencies produced at high angles of attack require rudder input from the pilot. If the pilot does not coordinate the airplane properly, the plane will be climbing in a side-slip condition, producing unnecessary drag. The amount of drag produced by a side-slip varies with the amount of rudder input required, but it can be substantial, and is too easily corrected to be ignored.

Pilots seem to become especially forgetful of their feet when flying jets or multiengine airplanes whose engines counterrotate. Even though these planes are not plagued as severely with the coordination idiosyncrasies of a propeller, side-slip drag can be produced in them by imbalanced fuel loads, poor coordination in turns, and asymmetrical power settings. For all airplanes, the pilot must be careful to assure that everything is trimmed and centered to produce minimum drag, especially where big climb performance is desired.

Partial flaps in cruise climb

If your airplane has a high limiting flap speed, slight flap extension during cruise climb might actually reduce drag. This is because the angle of incidence between the wing and fuselage for most airplanes is optimized for minimum drag during cruise flight and cruise configuration. When the airplane is flown at higher angles of attack, such as during a climb, the fuselage might produce relatively high drag as compared to cruise because the incidence is not optimized for a climb (Fig. 4-16). That leaves it up to the pilot.

A partial extension of flaps increases the wings' incidence with the fuselage, allowing the wings to be at an optimum climb angle, while the fuselage may be trimmed for cruise. This also improves the view over the nose by lowering the deck angle and helps engine cooling. Of course, flaps increase drag on the wing, but at light flap settings the drag increase might be minimal when compared to the drag decrease found at the fuselage. The actual benefit depends upon the particular airplane. It will be subject to your own experimentation, but this procedure could enhance cruise climb efficiency significantly.

The pilot must exercise caution during this procedure that design flap speeds are not exceeded.

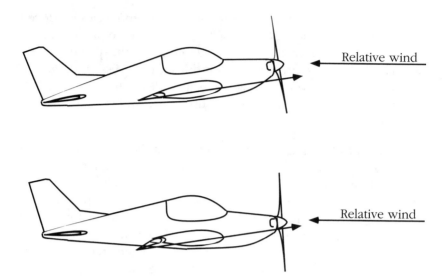

4-16 *Both planes are climbing with identical angles of attack, but the bottom one has the flaps slightly extended to optimize the wing/fuselage incidence for minimum drag.*

Skills to practice

Most of the drills discussed in this section center on improving the pilot's ability to accurately control airspeed. Since the climb portion of a flight usually requires the airplane to spend time at high angles of attack while near the ground, it is also appropriate to become proficient in stall recoveries from the climb condition.

Maneuvering at Vx and Vy

Begin by noting the speeds for Vx, Vy, and Vglide for a given altitude and your current weight. Once established at that target altitude, stabilize a full-power climb at exactly Vy. Trim the airplane and center the ball. Then reduce power gradually and allow the airspeed to bleed to Vglide. Stabilize a descent at Vglide. Practice turns from 0- to 60-degrees bank in both directions, while maintaining Vglide. Increase power smoothly and move the airspeed to Vx. Concentrate on rudder coordination and airspeed control throughout the power change. Climb at Vx, while turning each direction, back to your starting altitude. Repeat the maneuver until you can maintain airspeed within 1 mph of your target, with the rudder ball constantly centered. Your ability to control the airplane in this manner will greatly improve your safety in an emergency.[6]

Flying at a constant angle of attack

Power changes should not require changes in angle of attack if airspeed is maintained constant. The reason the pilot must adjust pitch attitude with power changes (giving the appearance of a change in angle of attack) relates to changes in the aircraft flight path (Fig. 4-17).

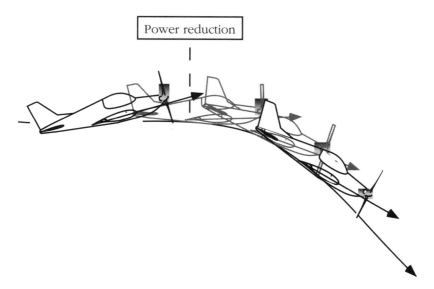

Power reduction

4-17 *The pilot must adjust pitch attitude to maintain a constant angle of attack during flightpath changes.*

Power changes cause the plane to climb or descend. The pilot must therefore adjust the pitch attitude to maintain constant angle of attack. This is equally true, but happens much more gradually, when power diminishes as the airplane gains altitude.

Related stall practice

Other than the generic approach and departure stalls learned in primary flight training, the average pilot is exposed to little in the way of critical angle of attack. The following variations on the stall will

6 Discussed in Chapter 10.

improve safety and the pilot's ability to control the airplane. Since these procedures might be unusual, bring a good flight instructor along for the ride and discuss your intentions for the flight.

Departure stall

- Set Vx attitude and full-power climb.
- Reduce power to idle, simulating an engine failure.
- Maintain Vx climb attitude with respect to the horizon until stall occurs.
- Recover by lowering the nose to Vglide attitude—do not add power.

Departure stall II

- Set Vx attitude and full-power climb.
- Raise pitch attitude to stall.
- Recover without loss of altitude, by lowering the nose no farther than Vx attitude, or as necessary to regain flight speed.

Departure stall III (trim stall)

- Establish Vglide, power off, and trim.
- Advance to full power, allow pitch attitude to rise according to trim, until stall occurs.
- At stall, reduce attitude to Vx for recovery, and retrim.

Power loss on departure

- Establish full power, Vy climb.
- Reduce power to idle, simulating an engine failure.
- Adjust pitch attitude such that airspeed is not allowed to decrease below Vx. (If necessary, do zero G pushover.)
- Pitch for Vglide and trim.

Stalls at aft CG

Since one of the techniques for improving rate of climb involves loading to aft CG, pilots who use this procedure should learn their airplane's stall characteristics with aft loading. Generally, recoveries are more difficult as the airplane becomes progressively tail-heavy; however, as long as balance limits are not exceeded, they can be safely managed. Nevertheless, a good CFI who has experience with aft-CG stalls should be consulted for this type of practice. Simply adjust weight and balance carefully, loading the airplane progressively farther aft, and practice the foregoing maneuvers. Please use caution, and work one step at a time.

Getting your own figures

Climb speeds can be initially determined from the safety of your own home. You'll make a chart of climb speeds for different weights and altitudes. All you need is the airplane operator's manual, a ruler, and some graph paper.

Consult the manual to determine Vx, Vy, and Vglide at sea-level on a standard day. Check the manual again to determine the aircraft ceiling. Plot the climb speeds along the bottom of the graph paper, with altitude up the side as shown in Fig. 4-18.

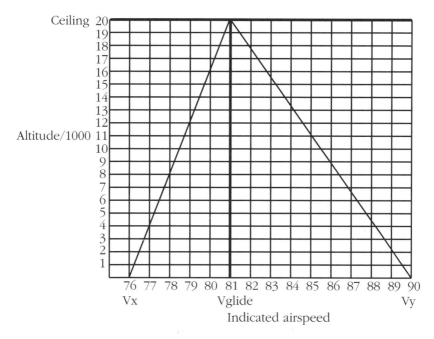

4-18 *Climb speed/altitude plot. Vx and Vy come together at the plane's ceiling.*

Draw a vertical line up from Vglide speed and a horizontal one corresponding to the aircraft ceiling. Use the rule to draw lines from Vx and Vy, respectively, to the point where Vglide intersects with the ceiling, as shown. Make a table to show proper speeds at each altitude, like the one in Fig. 4-19, with standard temperature for each altitude running up the side.

Alt.	Vx	Vy	T.
20	81	81	-25
19	80.5	81.5	-23
18	80.5	82	-21
17	80	82.5	-19
16	80	83	-17
15	79.5	83	-15
14	79.5	83.5	-13
13	79	84	-11
12	79	84.5	-9
11	78.5	85	-7
10	78.5	85.5	-5
9	78	86	-3
8	78	86.5	-1
7	77.5	87	1
6	77.5	87	3
5	77	87.5	5
4	77	88	7
3	76.5	88.5	9
2	76.5	89	11
1	76	89.5	13

4-19

Homemade speed/altitude table. Altitude running up the left side, standard temperature on the right.

Now reduce climb speeds 1 percent for every 4 percent below gross weight. For the typical light aircraft, this means 1 percent speed reduction for every 100 pounds below gross.

Post the table in the cockpit where you can easily reference it. Remember that the altitudes as they apply to your table are *density* altitudes. Set the altimeter momentarily (if it's not there already) to

29.92 so you read pressure altitude. Take what you see on the altimeter, add 1000 feet for every 10 degrees centigrade above standard temperature (or, subtract 1000 feet for every 10 degrees below standard), and use that altitude to determine your climb speed, as shown in Fig. 4-20.

It's really not very hard.

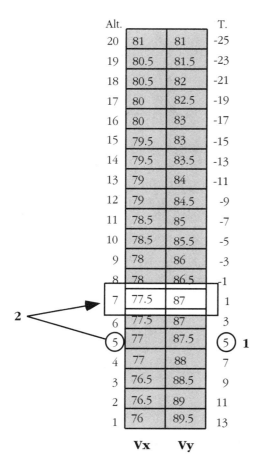

4-20
Pressure altitude is 5000 feet. Outside air temperature is 25 degrees centigrade, 20 degrees above standard (1). Using rule of 100 feet higher density altitude for every 1 degree above standard temperature, density altitude is 7000 feet. In this case, the pilot would use a climb speed (2) for the 7000-foot density altitude, about 1/2 knot difference.

The search for constant angle of attack

Lacking an angle of attack indicator that goes beyond the more rudimentary functions of the stall-warning system, the pilot can closely approximate angle of attack by marking elevator position and using trim. Angle of attack is set and maintained by the position of the elevator in relation to the wings. There will be variations of this position with changes in center of gravity, of course, due to variable down-loads required at the tail. All of this aside, however, the pilot should be able to judge the angle of attack for a given loading with an item as simple as a string in the cockpit.

When the airplane is trimmed for a known best-climb speed when climb begins, the elevator position should remain fairly constant as the plane climbs to altitude, requiring no further adjustment. Angle of attack would in this manner be held constant. Airspeed should automatically change in the fashion predicted by the charts. All that is required of the pilot is to set the trim and monitor the speed and situation as the climb progresses.

To verify this, attach a string to a fixed point in the cockpit, forward of the elevator control stick or yoke. Tie one end to the instrument panel or something immovable. When you have trimmed the air-plane at the climb speed of your choice, pull the string taut like a tape measure and mark it where it passes the elevator control posi-tion (Fig. 4-21). You've just established a rudimentary angle of attack indicator.[7] Referencing the mark on the string with position of the yoke or stick, you have a fairly accurate idea of angle of attack as long as the CG is not changed.

Now conduct the experiment of a long climb-to-cruise altitude while monitoring angle of attack and airspeed. Keep the angle of attack constant and note the airspeed indications at 1000-foot intervals. See how closely the figures you get match those of the charts. You might want to mark the elevator control in a way that indicates climb AoA for a range of CG locations. This could be as simple as a colored band around the yoke torque tube, or a mark on the trim position indicator.

Accurate data

You might try experimenting with various techniques to improve rate of climb. In doing so, you need a method to determine which techniques are actually helpful. As long as you don't have the bene-fit of expensive flight performance data recorders, the best thing you

---

7 There will be some error near the plane's ceiling. Thrust over the horizontal stabilizer might diminish rapidly at higher altitudes, reducing elevator authority and ultimately causing a gradual and undesired change in angle of attack. Jets, airplanes with "pusher" propellers, some twins and T-tail configurations will generally not be susceptible to this error.

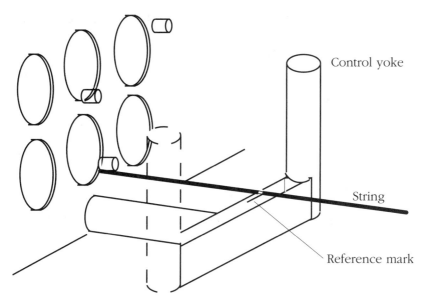

Control yoke

String

Reference mark

4-21 *Mickey Mouse angle of attack indicator: attach a string to the instrument panel and pull it like a tape measure across the yoke or stick.*

can do is produce a performance comparison with your own experimentation. You need an average day, smooth air, an assistant, and a little time.

Turbulence can destroy any accuracy to the information you seek. Pick a smooth, stable day to conduct your experiment. Next, use a climb procedure that you are comfortable with and can duplicate accurately every time to establish a constant. Your assistant is there to record results while you concentrate on the flying. The "little time" is in the form of a stopwatch. The clock and altimeter are far more accurate than any vertical speed indicator. Your assistant should record temperature, speed, altitude and time at 1000-foot intervals during your climb.

The temperature recording is to verify that the conditions for the climb are similar. You have no way of accurately compensating for humidity, so it is best to conduct these tests at nearly the same time of day, in the same weather. To prevent the error caused by a running start uphill, do not begin recording data until the desired airspeed and attitudes have been established for at least one minute.

Select a climb procedure from among the many discussed in this chapter and compare results with the procedures you normally use. If you find a procedure that works better, use it.

Further reading

Aerodynamics, Aeronautics and Flight Mechanics, Barnes W. Mc-Cormick, John Wiley and Sons, 1979

The Proficient Pilot, Barry Schiff, Aircraft Owners and Pilots Association, 1980

Illustrated Guide to Aerodynamics, Hubert "Skip" Smith, McGraw-Hill, 1992

Improve Your Flying Skills: Tips from a Pro, Clausing, McGraw-Hill, 1990

5

Cruise

Jack strained to see the ground. Nothing. Smoky-gray murk blotted out earth, sun and sky. Although the airspeed indicator presented ample evidence of the airplane's 240-knot cruise speed, the featureless smoke of numerous forest fires below disguised any motion. It felt as though the plane stood still, suspended like a model in a giant, muddy paperweight; the cockpit like a dim, noisy closet. The engine was normal, altitude level at 12,000 feet, no ice, outside air temperature cold enough to freeze dry skin in a few minutes. The sky had blocked out everything since their departure from Yellowknife, Canada, more than an hour before.

Kay might have wondered what could bring him 3000 miles from home, to accompany Jack as copilot and photographer for this insane trip over the magnetic north pole in an experimental airplane. Jack said that insanity runs in his family—he got it all. In fact, the two people Jack asked previously to come responded with simply, "I'm not that crazy." Kay was more willing. Maybe he was a little crazy, too. They certainly weren't the first to try this, what the Canadian MOT (Ministry of Transportation) called a "damn-fool, idiot thing to do." Yet, here they were. They were prepared, they thought.

The three GPS receivers in the airplane kept perfect synchronization like electronic prima donnas, flashing the miles, ticking numbers in silent unison. They gave the only indication of the passing of the 67th parallel—the arctic circle. Jack looked for signs on the ground and couldn't see a thing. Kay sat there quietly in the right seat. Nothing to photograph. Hard to call him a true photographer, anyway; he had shown up for the trip with a cardboard, disposable camera.

Gradually and subtly, their gray world seemed to lighten. Then, as if with a flash photo, white-hot and sudden, they were blinded by the view. The motionless sensation instantly shattered as the little plane streaked out of the smoke like a crimson missile. They reacted as though suddenly splashed, headfirst, with ice-water—a quick intake of breath and blinking surprise. The world below was so radically different from the one they had left behind in the smoke that it seemed like another planet. The ice flashed the color of a blue diamond. Endless. They sat dumbfounded—wordless—in awe at the unexpected sight. Equally surprising was the sensation of being very alone, as if they were the last human beings on earth. It was truly the most awesome sight they had ever seen—a flat, frozen desert.

They contacted flight service 80 miles from their intermediate stop in Cambridge Bay; this after a lengthy, 300-mile stretch of radio silence. Jack felt relieved to have made human contact and also to know that they weren't in some kind of trouble for being overdue because of headwinds. No sooner had they finished talking on the radio, however, when it came alive again, this time air-to-air from a DeHaviland Dash Eight. "What kind of *homebuilt* is that thing, anyway? We've been trying to catch you for 120 miles, and you're pulling away." The airliner pilot continued, "Do us a favor, will ya? We've got a full load of people and cargo, and it will take us a while to turn around. Do you mind throttling back, so we can pass you and land first? Then, if you don't mind, we'd like to come over and have a look at that thing after you land." Jack was delighted. He pulled back to 16 inches, then 12. He couldn't reduce power further for fear of shock-cooling the engine. The airliner barely caught them in time.

From Cambridge Bay, Jack called for a weather report at Resolute, the next and final stop before reaching the magnetic north pole. Thick fog, impenetrable as a wall of ice, held Resolute, 400 nautical miles away, in an icy grip. Ceiling, zero; visibility, zero. Tomorrow, conditions expected to improve. Jack and Kay decided to wait in Cambridge Bay until morning.

The next day, the weather in Resolute improved—½ mile visibility and 200-foot ceiling—enough to use their ILS approach. They departed Cambridge Bay with their plane loaded with survival gear, and climbed into the overcast. This leg of the flight contained a critical "point of no return," since Resolute was the only possible stop in an endless sea of ice and the plane simply did not carry enough fuel to fly round trip. If the plane couldn't land there, it wouldn't have enough fuel to make it back to Cambridge Bay and no alternate runways existed anywhere. A forced landing on the ice would be fatal. They could probably survive the landing, of course, but extreme cold and exposure would kill them within a few days. They had a little food, but rescue could take weeks.

Jack enjoyed a calculated risk; it was something to keep the adrenaline pumping, the mind sharp. Fly to the magnetic north pole in a single-engine, homebuilt airplane? It was a little like exploring the center of the earth with one flashlight and a couple of extra batteries. Get lost, lose an engine, forced to divert with no alternates because of weather, and you die—frozen food for polar bears. The risk was balanced by a well-made airplane. Sure, it had only one engine, but they just outran an airliner, for pete sake! The plane had taken years to build, and Jack had flown it in airshows all over the United States. In a dive, it could push 400 mph.

There was enough fuel to fly to Resolute and about two thirds of the way back to Cambridge Bay. Plenty of reserve, by normal standards, but Resolute was the *only* possible stop for 400 miles. Getting lost was really not an issue; GPS receivers took care of that. The satellite receivers could predict their time of arrival to within a few seconds and measure their course with outrageous accuracy. The trouble was that weather in Resolute could change, quite literally, in an instant. Leave the final approach fix inbound to land with the runway in sight and like the snap of your fingers, ice fog could reduce the visibility conditions to zero.

They checked the weather almost constantly during the flight. In theory, they could fly about three-fourths of the way and still be able to make the return flight to Cambridge Bay. If they committed beyond that point and the weather in Resolute went sour, they were hosed. Once again, this time at the three-quarter mark, Jack checked the weather, "Ceiling still 200, visibility improving, showing better than ½," came the voice over the radio. It was enough. They held their breath and pressed on. If the weather worsened in Resolute now, the best they could do would be hold for a break in the weather until they ran out of fuel, then maybe a no-visibility crash landing somewhere close enough for rescue.

Fortunately, the fog continued to lift as the red SX-300 neared the outpost and they were able to land safely. From Resolute, the pole would be a relatively quick round-robin flight. Both Jack and Kay thrilled at the thought of being so near their destination. Nothing could stop them now, they thought, for all they needed was a quick refueling and they would be on their way.

"Where's your 100 low-lead?" Jack asked.

"We haven't sold any of that for 10 years. Nothing but jet fuel here."

Jack frantically pointed out that the literature for the airport indicated the presence and availability of 100-octane fuel.

"Sorry, literature's wrong. If you want, we can have a few barrels flown up here."

"Will it get here by tomorrow?"

"No. Maybe next month."

One of the natives mentioned that he'd seen a couple of barrels of gas "way down there in yonder shed." Another, pointing in a different direction, said a distant building might also contain fuel. Jack looked at Kay and said simply, "You go that way, I'll go this way." They followed the natives in opposite directions. A man named Dave, who seemed to be in charge, accompanied Jack to the shed. The wind howled like an arctic wolf around its thin walls. Dave poked around in the back, looking behind trash that surely hadn't moved since the ice age. When he came back out, his expression was blank.

"Well?" said Jack.

"I found two 55 gallon drums of old fuel back there, but you're not going to like the price. Have you got a screen?"

"No."

"Funnel?"

"No."

"Hand pump?"

"No."

Dave looked at Jack with an expression of contempt. After a long moment, he spoke: "Well, bud, you're on top of the world up here, and I think you're very poorly prepared."

Jack sheepishly asked if Dave had any of the necessary equipment. Dave quietly shook his head and took a good 30 seconds to respond. "Yeah. I got all that."

"How much you want for the gas?" Jack queried.

"Three hundred sixty-five, American, for both."

Jack was delighted. For being so far north, he was prepared to pay much more. A price of $3.32 per gallon seemed mighty reasonable. They moved back to the airplane and began to gas up. Kay came running in a few moments.

"Stop everything, I found some fuel! Two 55 gallon drums. I bought it all," he said.

"What'd you pay?" Jack queried.

"Only $1800."

After the refueling, Dave gave them the coordinates for the most recently surveyed position of the magnetic north pole, which moves about slightly (Fig. 5-1).

5-1
Current coordinates for the magnetic north pole in Dave's handwriting. Jack stuck it on the panel's glareshield for navigational reference in the plane's final dash over the pole. The note came all the way back home.

With the figures entered into the GPS units, and Dave's written coordinates stuck on the glareshield, Jack concentrated on maintaining a perfect course to the pole. Kay was ready with the camera as the last mile ticked by. With one-tenth remaining, Jack pitched the plane up, leaned hard on the ailerons, and rolled the plane. They arrived at the top of the world, upside-down (Fig. 5-2).

They climbed to 14,000 feet for the 237-nautical mile return to Resolute. The winds were on their tail, making groundspeeds in excess of 300 knots. They landed at Resolute in no time at all, tanked up with all they could carry of Kay's $16.36 per gallon fuel, and landed

5-2 *Upside down at the top of the world. Notice the figures indicated on the GPS as compared to Dave's note, the high momentary rate of climb and the inverted attitude indicator almost hidden behind the GPS antenna.*

in Cambridge Bay before bedtime (Fig. 5-3). The rest, as they say, is history.

Background information

As far as the airplane is concerned, the cruise condition is almost a constant, whether the pilot is flying a local round-robin or a daring trip over the north pole. The only real changes happen slowly, as fuel is burned away. Very little in the way of control manipulation is required from the pilot. The pilot trims the plane in cruise, monitors systems, and simply waits for the world to roll by. While the airplane's cruise condition remains relatively constant during the cross-country flight, the pilot is faced with a myriad of choices. This is a golden opportunity to consider options and weigh costs and benefits of small conditional changes. Jack and Kay made several adjustments to their cruise condition as they progressed toward their goal at the top of the world. They changed altitude numerous times, attempting to minimize the headwinds; they considered rest and fuel stops (although, perhaps not very well) and, of course, made the

5-3 *Jack, right, and Kay about to depart on their fearless (insane?) polar flight.*

risky decision to pass a point of no return in difficult, unpredictable weather. For the sake of survival, they had to maximize the performance of their airplane.

In terms of performance, there are two schools of thought. Make the airplane get there in minimum time, or arrive with the least expenditure of money. Better if you can do both. The philosophies behind these two objectives often conflict, and they must always be balanced against safety. Speed is often a function of how much fuel the pilot is willing to burn. Economy often results from the crew's willingness to slow down. In either of these areas, the pilots must work within the performance limits of the airplane. Occasionally, an airplane will be designed for a specific flight profile in which speed and economy are carefully balanced. Anything different from the design profile would miss the mark at both ends of the spectrum; that is, a flight would take longer and cost more money. Examples of this would be the space shuttle and the Concorde. In either case, the flight profile must be strictly adhered to. If the Concorde pilots, for example, choose to fly to Europe at low altitude and enjoy a high-speed buzz job of the ocean-liners along the way, the plane would quickly run out of fuel and splash them in the drink, leaving them to thumb a ride from an angry ship captain. Fuel burn *and* speed would be compromised. The plane is not as fast at low altitude as it is at 50,000 feet, and the fuel burn is so high that the tanks would go dry about half-way across the ocean.

A skilled pilot will not be able to significantly affect the design cruise speed of the airplane itself. Putting a fighter pilot in charge of an ultralight will not suddenly make the ultralight go supersonic. However, significant gains in performance, economy, and safety are possible if the pilot uses the situation well. Here, manipulation of the situation is key, not manipulation of the airplane itself. Changes in altitude, course, power setting, and weather may be played like moves in a chess game to maximize the airplane's performance as it moves from A to B. Each of these factors will hardly affect the indicated airspeed or normal fuel burn in the airplane, but might greatly influence the outcome of the trip in block time or expenses.

Atmospheric pressure, temperature, and density

A basic understanding of the atmosphere in which the plane flies is critical to good performance en route. In the example of Jack's trip, the air at the north pole was very cold and dense. Although not often flown over the poles, most airplanes do commonly ascend into extremely low temperatures. Beginning at the average of 15 degrees centigrade at sea level, air temperature normally decreases about 2 degrees for every 1000 foot increase in elevation. At that rate the temperature is normally a frigid −44 degrees centigrade by 30,000 feet, cooling to −56 by 36,000 feet. Above that point the temperature stays relatively constant until about 80,000 feet, above which the temperatures actually increase a couple of degrees until reaching altitudes where the air becomes too thin to be called "air" anymore. The specific nature of the atmosphere will be covered in some detail in Chapter 6, but for now, please understand that, to a point, the air gets colder with height.

The next important feature of the atmosphere involves static, or barometric, pressure. Barometric pressure decreases at a predictable rate as elevation increases. Every 1000-foot increase in elevation causes a 1-inch drop in a mercury barometer. This can be calibrated into a good estimate of altitude and is the principle behind the aircraft's altimeter. The altimeter is simply a barometer of sorts that translates atmospheric pressure into an indication of altitude in feet. Lower atmospheric pressures cause the altimeter to read higher elevations. Unfortunately, this method of estimating altitude becomes inaccurate at elevations above approximately 18,000 feet msl because the normal rate of pressure decline changes rather dramatically above this level, thus making simple altimeters rather prone to error at high altitudes. This is why the airspace system uses the concept of "flight level" instead of "altitude" above 18,000 feet.

Next, air becomes thinner, or less dense, as the airplane ascends. The pressure reductions and temperature changes that occur with altitudes cause corresponding reductions in air density. Colder temperatures do much to moderate the reduction of air density with altitude, however. Conversely, hotter temperatures accelerate the reduction of air density with increased altitudes, causing the airplane to behave as if it is flying much higher than what is displayed on the altimeter. As air thins for whatever reason (high water vapor content, high temperatures and/or high altitudes), its ability to sustain an airplane diminishes.

Finally, a given airplane design will cruise most efficiently at a specific density altitude, for a given power setting. Jack's SX-300, for example, has an optimal cruise density altitude of 8000 feet. However, from what we've learned about density altitude we know that it varies, depending on the temperature and other atmospheric conditions in the area and accordingly might not match pressure altitude as indicated on the altimeter. Consequently, an optimal cruise density altitude of 8000 feet might be found at pressure altitudes ranging from 4000 to 12,000 feet—the latter in very cold temperatures like those encountered when flying over the pole. The pilot seeking the greatest speed for the dollar first consults charts to determine optimum density altitude and power setting for cruise, then checks temperature and chooses a pressure altitude, as indicated on the altimeter, that equals the desired density altitude for cruise.

Dynamic pressure and indicated airspeed

When the wind blows, it exerts a force upon any object in its path. It might fill the sails of a boat, knock down the walls of a building, or lift the weight of an airplane. This pressure, caused by the motion of the air, is called *dynamic pressure*. It is a function of the density and velocity of the air.

Notice from Fig. 5-4 that dynamic pressure increases with the square of the airspeed; that is, going twice as fast will increase dynamic pressure by a factor of four. Also, see that dynamic pressure decreases proportionally with air density. Therefore, as an airplane ascends into thinner air, the dynamic pressure acting on the airplane will decrease. An airplane can accelerate until it reaches a point

$$\text{Dynamic pressure} = \frac{1}{2} \text{(density)(velocity)}^2$$

5-4 *Dynamic pressure formula.*

where dynamic pressure equals the thrust available. Using this as a constant we can fiddle with the other side of the equation and learn some interesting facts. Notice that if air density decreases we have to increase velocity to keep the equation balanced. The airspeed indicator is basically a sensor for dynamic pressure, so dynamic pressure equals indicated airspeed. This is the left side of the equation. As air density decreases, velocity (true airspeed) naturally increases to keep a constant indicated airspeed (dynamic pressure). So what does this mean in English? As air density decreases with higher altitudes, true airspeed will increase even though we don't get the satisfaction of seeing it on the airspeed indicator.

In order for the pilot to know exactly how fast the airplane is flying, the airspeed indication must be corrected for the density of the air. The pilot must check temperature and pressure altitude and *calculate* true airspeed.

True airspeed

An observant pilot purchased a cockpit poster for the Concorde and noticed that the airspeed indicator reads only to 500 knots. He knew that the Concorde routinely crosses the Atlantic Ocean at more than 1100 knots, or Mach 2. The flight crew sees the Mach needle steady at 2.0 and the indicated airspeed pointing squarely at only 460 knots at the same time. The inertial navigation system calculates 1320 mph over the ground, for an en route time of less than four hours from New York to Paris. The speed is definitely real, so how can this be?

True airspeed is easy to calculate using an E-6B computer. Simply align 50,000 feet with a typical air temperature for that altitude, say, –56 degrees centigrade, in the true airspeed window of the computer. Next, find 460 knots on the inner scale, and read a true airspeed of 1180 knots on the outer scale (Fig. 5-5).

A similar problem was encountered by a friend of mine who had just purchased a turbo Mooney. He was disappointed that the plane appeared no faster than a normally aspirated Mooney. He observed that: "It indicates 155 mph, just like the other plane, but burns 3 gallons an hour more." I explained that the turbo advantage is to be

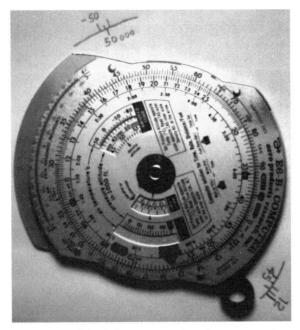

5-5 *I wonder if the Concorde pilots remember how to do this?*
1. Set temperature of −56 degrees opposite 50,000 feet in the window at the upper left, giving a density altitude of 50,000 feet (standard conditions).
2. Read true airspeed of 1180+ knots (just shy of 12) on fixed outer scale opposite indicated airspeed of 460 knots (46) on the circular dial.

able to indicate 155 mph at 24,000 feet, which translates into 232 mph *true* airspeed. A typical temperature for that altitude is −34 degrees, in case you're interested in doing the calculation yourself.

Density altitude, power, and fuel consumption

Normally aspirated (nonturbo) engines develop maximum-rated power at sea level. This maximum available power diminishes steadily as the airplane ascends. Even though full-rated power is not available at normal cruising altitudes, *cruise*-power probably is. It might take several thousand feet of altitude to prevent an engine from developing 75%, 65%, or even 45% of sea level power, which are typical cruise power settings. Cruising significantly above the altitude where the engine might develop adequate cruise power is inefficient. The benefits of true airspeed gains with the high altitudes are negated by loss of thrust from the powerplant.

A turbine engine is also normally aspirated, and suffers the same general loss of power as the airplane climbs. The power loss problem is easily solved with the turbine, however, because of the tremendous power available from such a small, relatively light-weight package. Designers pack so much power into the machine in the first place that operation at altitude reduced-power settings will still make the pilot's eyes water. Often, the engines are *flat rated*, which is an operating technique wherein the engines are run at some percentage below maximum, so that said percentage is available through a range of altitudes. A flat rating is a little like operating an engine at cruise-power settings all the time, it would take a few thousand feet of climbing to cause the *available* power to diminish below that setting.

Being much more sensitive to ambient temperature, the turbine benefits somewhat from normal atmospheric temperature reductions during the climb. Generally, as long as the air keeps getting colder, it is in the interest of the turbine aircraft to fly higher. This is limited only by the excess power available from the turbine, or by the point at which the air stops getting colder. This is why airlines cruise around 25,000–40,000 feet (depending on the season), the point at which the air temperature reaches a minimum, and gets no cooler.[1]

One benefit of the thin air is reduced fuel consumption. The fuel consumption varies directly with the power developed by the engine. Engines require leaning as the airplane climbs. If leaning of the fuel flow is neglected, it is possible to do serious damage to the engine. The principle is simple. Internal combustion requires fuel and air in the proper ratio. Too much fuel and the fire goes out, too much air and it blows away. As the airplane climbs, the density of air diminishes. This is the same as a reduction in the amount of air. The combustible mixture will naturally become fuel rich. If allowed to continue this way, the engine might suffer severe carbon deposits, premature ignition, detonation, or it might simply quit. Leaning the fuel that is metered into the engine balances the ratio as the airplane climbs. Leaning the fuel translates into less fuel burn. In most turbine engines, this occurs automatically with a fuel control mechanism.

A turbocharger allows the engine to develop cruise power through much higher altitudes, permitting the airplane to take advantage of

---

1 The official average, or geopotential of the tropopause, is 36,089 feet.

significant gains in true airspeed. Even turbos, however, reach a point where air density is simply too little to allow the production of full-rated power. The altitude at which this occurs is called *critical altitude*. Critical altitude generally equates to optimum cruise altitude for most turbo applications. Because the turbocharger increases the air density in the engine, a corresponding increase in fuel consumption is also required. This is why turbocharged engines generally burn a few gallons per hour more than their normally aspirated counterparts.

Optimal cruise altitude for high speed

Optimal cruise altitude is easy to determine if the plane has good charts. Look at Fig. 5-6. Running a finger down the speed column of the chart, you can see that 5000 feet is the optimum altitude for maximum cruise speed in this airplane. Notice that altitudes above the optimum cause a reduction in true airspeed. Too high, and the powerplant will experience such a loss of thrust that a net decrease in speed occurs.

Naturally, in the interest of time, a pilot would seek to plan flights as close to an optimal altitude as possible, but there is a catch. The pilot flying the airplane in the sample chart must be careful to cruise at a 5000-foot *density* altitude.

In standard conditions, 5000 feet would be the magic number. For every degree C above standard temperature, however, the pilot would fly pressure altitudes 100 feet lower.[2] The reverse is true in weather colder than standard. For example, standard temperature at 5000 feet is 5 degrees. If the temperature at 5000 feet is 15 degrees, or 10 degrees above standard, the pilot would optimize cruise flight at a pressure altitude of 4000 feet. And if the temperature is –5 degrees at 5000 feet, or 10 degrees below standard, 6000 feet would be the ideal indicated cruise altitude.

In general, piston aircraft will cruise at lower pressure altitudes in hot weather, and turbines (searching for cold air) will cruise at higher pressure altitudes.

2 Pressure altitude is indicated with the altimeter set at 29.92.

2500 RPM CRUISE PERFORMANCE

	MP	BHP	TAS	GAL HR	ENDR. HRS	RANGE
2500 ft	25	76	158	15.9	4.0	625
	24	72	155	15.0	4.2	645
	23	68	151	14.2	4.4	670
	22	64	148	13.4	4.7	695
5000 ft	25	78	163	16.3	3.9	630
	24	74	160	15.5	4.1	650
	23	70	157	14.7	4.3	670
	22	66	153	13.9	4.5	695
7500 ft	22	69	159	14.4	4.4	695
	21	65	154	13.6	4.6	715
	20	60	150	12.7	4.9	740
	19	56	145	11.9	5.3	765
10,000 ft	20	63	156	13.2	4.8	740
	19	59	151	12.4	5.1	765
	18	55	144	11.6	5.4	785
	17	50	137	10.8	5.8	800
15,000 ft	15	46	128	10.0	6.3	810
	14	41	115	9.1	6.9	795
	13	37	102	8.3	7.6	775

5-6 *Compiled cruise performance for a Cessna 206.*

Optimal speed for efficiency

Efficiency can be thought of in two ways, namely, the most miles per gallon, or the most time aloft per gallon. These are best range and best endurance, respectively. Looking at endurance first, the pilot's objective is simply to minimize fuel burn. This is accomplished by a careful selection of airspeed, altitude, power setting, and some rather aggressive leaning (for piston engines).

The airspeed selected is none other than the best L/D speed, or best glide. According to the aircraft drag curve, this is the point at which the airplane produces a minimum of drag and corresponds to a requirement for minimum power (Fig. 5-7). Lowest power required also equates to lowest fuel burn. You might be surprised to find out exactly how far the throttle might be reduced for level flight, when the airplane is trimmed for best glide.

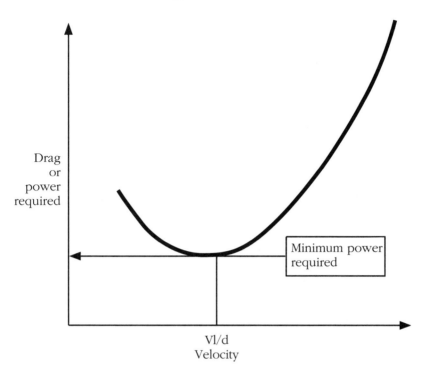

5-7 *Best endurance is found at the speed for minimum power required.*

Altitude does not appreciably affect the endurance of a piston aircraft. In fact, a long, high-power climb to altitude might be detrimental to overall endurance. For jets, on the other hand, fuel consumption is directly related to altitude. Maximum endurance in the jet would be achieved at the highest altitude and coldest temperature at which the airplane can maintain best L/D speed.

For maximum range, the pilot seeks to minimize fuel consumption and maximize speed at the same time. This usually results in a flight condition that is somewhere between best L/D and high cruise, a happy medium, so to speak. The ideal speed can be determined by reference to the drag curve again. Notice that power required and fuel consumption can be used interchangeably (Fig. 5-8).

A tangent line drawn from the origin touches the drag curve at a point corresponding to the best range speed for a given airplane. Notice that the speed is appreciably faster than VL/D, but definitely slower than max-cruise speed.

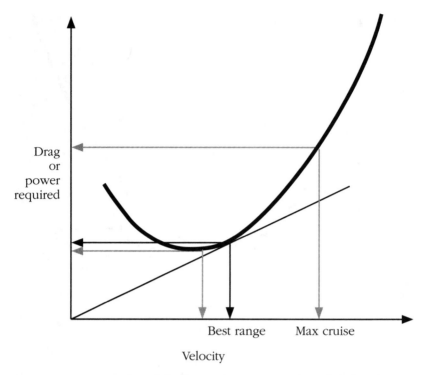

Drag
or
power
required

Best range   Max cruise

Velocity

5-8 *Power required and fuel consumption are directly related. Max-range performance occurs at the speed where a line drawn from zero airspeed tangent to (just touching) the drag curve. Although a little faster than best endurance speed, it is still quite a bit below maximum cruise.*

Ideal cruising altitude for maximum range will be the highest at which the engine can develop sufficient power to maintain optimum range speed, taking advantage of true-airspeed gains. For a jet, this altitude will also serve to reduce fuel consumption. The best-range altitude will vary, depending upon the aircraft weight.

Airplanes flown at light weights will require less power to maintain a given speed. Engine power available depends on altitude, thus, lower power settings might still be possible at yet higher altitudes. Also, the ideal range speed itself depends on angle of attack, meaning that lighter weights will cause the proper speed to be slower. The slower speed requires even less power to maintain, thus higher altitudes are practical for lighter airplanes. Under ideal circumstances, the airplane should be allowed to climb as fuel is burned away, thus benefitting from increases in true airspeed. The pilot seeks to simultaneously maintain proper cruise angle of attack and the highest altitude for the required power setting.

Navigation

There are three types of navigation, namely, pilotage, ded reckoning, and radio navigation. Of these, pilotage is by far the most accurate. It simply means that you see where you want to go, and you go there. You follow your eyes. You use pilotage when walking out the front door and getting in the car, when you land the plane and, when you thread a needle.

Ded reckoning is short for *deduced reckoning*. It is the technique that Columbus used to discover America, and Lindbergh used to cross the Atlantic the other way. It is very simple in concept, but obviously subject to error. Ironically, ded reckoning makes use of the most accurate instrument in the cockpit, the clock. The compass, the simplest and most reliable instrument, is the other half of the equation. The pilot using ded reckoning plots a course and estimates the time required to get there. When that time is up, the pilot looks down and expects to have arrived. Needless to say, this method is subject to some error caused by many unknown variables, like unforecast wind and weather. In Columbus' case, he underestimated the size of the earth, and predicted his arrival a bit too optimistically.

Radio navigation uses electronic instrumentation as eyes to verify position and progress on a planned course. It is subject to the limitations of the equipment used. Modern GPS receivers have accuracy that has been unknown in the past, but are still no substitute for your own eyes.

Wind and weather

So you've consulted performance charts, spun the whiz-wheel, checked temperature and decided on an altitude that you'd like to fly. Great. Now you need to check the temperatures at your destination, plot the data from weather reporting stations en route, consult radar weather maps, Doppler images, digitized satellite photos, teletype machines, and weather-balloon soundings to find the most favorable winds and weather. After compiling the data, you should average this and draw it out in a useful, pictorial format, and fortunately, the National Weather Service has already done all this for you.

Obviously, a 50-knot headwind at your optimal cruise altitude would do much to kill the benefits of climbing up there. Generally, winds blow stronger as altitude increases. There was a direct 50-knot head-wind for almost the entire trip when Jack flew over the pole. He minimized this by flying as low as he could when conditions permitted. Friction of the earth will often slow wind velocities near the surface to a fraction of their speeds at altitude. In fact, hot-air balloon pilots will tell you that wind blowing *any* direction can be found in the first 1000 feet agl. This is how they steer in competitions, by adjusting altitude until they find a breeze that blows the right way.

The winds aloft forecast becomes an important part of altitude selection, with one caveat: it is only a forecast. The weather people have launched balloons and rolled the dice and arrived at their best *guess*. What you might actually encounter could be very different from the forecast. The pilot, to some extent, might do as the balloon drivers, that is, adjust altitude to find the most favorable winds. Also, the time spent climbing *way up there* to make use of a tailwind might better be used in straight and level cruise to the destination.

The fastest trip will occur when the pilot has maximized both true airspeed *and* tailwinds. In addition to optimizing wind by selecting an advantageous altitude, some adjustments in course with respect to pressure patterns could also produce groundspeed dividends.

Cruise profile

Since most airplanes climb at speeds that are much slower than cruise, it is in the best interest of the pilot to establish cruise flight as quickly as possible. For short trips, this might mean cruising at an altitude far below optimum in order to get things moving or establishing some sort of cruise-climb profile. This is especially true for airplanes that do not climb rapidly. On the other hand, airplanes with high fuel consumption at low altitude must launch for thin air as rapidly as possible, or they might run out of fuel.

A friend of mine flies Learjets on contract for a local bank. Every night he makes the 45-minute, 500-mile run from Salt Lake City to Denver. He has done it so many times he has the flight down to a science. It requires 300 gallons of fuel. He makes a tight right-hand climbing turn over the departure airport, recrosses the field as he passes through 15,000 feet, and he's on the way. Cruising altitude is generally 37,000 feet. One day, they asked him to fly to St. George,

Utah, only 280 miles away. Since the flight would be short and very scenic, they chose to remain below 15,000 feet and enjoy the ride. When they landed, they were surprised to learn that they had nearly run out of fuel. The amount of air running through those turbines required an enormous amount of fuel to sustain combustion, and the fuel controller dutifully complied. This is why turbojets, like Lears, are blessed with such a high rate of climb. They need it to get to fuel-efficient altitudes quickly.

For reciprocating airplanes on a short trip, however, it makes no sense to climb to high altitudes when the destination is only 15 minutes away. The trip will be faster and less fuel burned overall if the pilot simply levels off at a convenient, rather low altitude, and points the plane at the destination. The need to climb to optimal altitude must be balanced against the length of the trip.

The flight path of the airplane, as seen from the side, or profile, view over the course of the trip, is known as the *cruise profile*. Planning the profile well can significantly affect the outcome of the trip. For example: the Concorde first achieves Mach 2 at around 45,000 feet and begins a slow climb to around 60,000 feet as fuel is burned away. The airplane is trimmed to an optimum angle of attack and maintains this throughout the cruise portion of the flight. The plane becomes lighter as fuel is burned away so the profile calls for a gradual increase in altitude instead of an increase in speed. The correct angle of attack is critical to the efficiency of the flight, so the flight profile is designed to maintain it as long as possible. Any other flight profile burns more fuel.

A large portion of the total weight of the Concorde and many other airliners is carried in fuel. Flight profiles that call for this sort of climb over the course of the trip are common in the industry because aircraft weight might change by more than *100,000 pounds* by the time the airplane lands. For the typical light plane, on the other hand, the weight of fuel carried and consumed is comparatively insignificant, negating the need to climb over the course of a normal trip. Exceptions to this rule would be long, fuel-laden ferry flights, and of course, the flight of the globe girdling Voyager.

I participated in an interesting impromptu race some time ago. My brother and I were flying a Maule, and our friend Dick was flying a turbo Mooney. Of course, in terms of cruise speed the Mooney blows the doors off the Maule, but in this one instance our cruise profile was better than his, and we could beat him to the destination. Here's how it worked: We departed Salt Lake in formation, Dick flying slowly enough that the Maule could maneuver around his plane and take photographs. After several miles of this, we ran short of film and decided to break off the formation and cruise separately to Hanksville, at that time about 60 miles away. Dick began a 120-knot climb in order to make use of the turbo's advantage and get some speed. He diverted from his course to avoid some high-level cumulus clouds and get around the south end of a mountain range. We continued talking to him on the radio and he gave us regular position reports.

When we broke from the Mooney, the Maule was at optimum altitude already. We floored the power and beat a straight-line path for the destination. We avoided clouds by going under them, and went straight over the mountain range, climbing up one side and diving down the other. Dick was somewhere to the south, and we already had Hanksville in sight. We began a gradual descent in order to bring the groundspeed up. Dick informed us over the radio that his GPS was showing 195 knots. He had climbed more than 5000 feet above our altitude. He was surprised to find that we were 3 miles ahead of him, on final for the short, dirt strip that crossed the paved runway at the airport. We flew a pattern to allow him to land first— straight in. We didn't want to make a Mooney driver feel bad.

Our flight profile for the short trip gave us an advantage over an airplane almost 60 knots faster. We flew a straighter course, more efficiently avoided weather and mountains, and kept the airplane out of winds, closer to its optimal altitude. All in all, our groundspeed in a straight-line towards the destination was in this way a little faster than a Mooney's. That is the benefit of a proper cruise profile.

Groundspeed

Increased groundspeed is the ultimate product of a well-played cruise. I'm talking about actual groundspeed that is directed at the destination, that effectively shortens the time en route. The proficient pilot considers all factors affecting the airplane during a cross-country and maximizes the beneficial ones, while minimizing the others. The pilot must think in terms of groundspeed. After all, it is groundspeed that actually gets you there.

Technique

One of the nicer features of cruise flight is its relative consistency. When the airplane is up and level, there is little for the pilot to do except consider the options. Those options are the subject of this chapter. Should I fly higher? Slower? Faster? What are the benefits and compromises behind each decision? All the theory is worthless unless it can be applied to the pilot's advantage. Here are some methods that work.

Selection of course

When I set out on my first long solo cross country, I planned meticulously for the trip. Salt Lake City to Pocatello, Idaho, to Wells, Nevada, and back to Salt Lake. The total trip: 422 miles. I carefully scanned the charts for aerial hazards, plotted my course straight from VOR to VOR and decided to cruise high above the nearest obstacle within 5 miles of my course. 11,500 feet, on average, seemed safe enough. I figured fuel consumption and planned to take a little more than four hours for the trip. Mom packed my lunch with sweet rolls and apples; I loaded the plane with a little survival gear, and took off on a crystal clear morning.

I flew about 40 miles before actually attaining cruise altitude. When I leveled the plane, the throttle was to the wall and the plane barely indicated 75 knots. Trimmed for cruise, the flight was smooth as glass. Exited and happy to be flying, having dreamed about this sort of thing for years, I whooped and hollered until I could hardly speak. After 5.8 hours on the Hobbs, and stopping for fuel, I landed again back home, having flown the exact course as planned. They told me that airplanes didn't perform like advertised, but I had hoped for at least 100 mph, not 72 mph.

I have flown nearly the same course since and averaged more than 100 mph. The 11,500-foot altitude was much too high for the airplane to deliver its best performance. Something like 7500 feet would have been ideal. Looking at the chart, I was worried about the many mountains along the route, but there is truly no need to fly extremely high above the mountains in VFR weather. In truth, the entire route could be flown at 7500 feet, never getting closer than 1000 feet to any mountain along the route. That was mistake number one.

Planning to fly from station to station on victor airways was mistake number two. It is not infrequent for users of these aerial highways to travel far out of the way in an effort to track a radial. Again, in VFR conditions, there is no need. Pilotage is by far the more efficient method to get there. Also, since air traffic might be expected to frequent the airways, there is a greater chance of collision with another aircraft while flying VOR routes. Worse, IFR traffic use the airways, and you could find yourself avoiding an airplane on instruments, the pilot inside it not paying enough attention to see and avoid.

Routes should be carefully selected to provide the most direct flight path to the destination. Obviously, mountains, restricted areas, terminal areas, and weather play parts in route selection, but going way off the straight course to follow a radial makes no sense. Plan to use pilotage along the course. Use a map and select checkpoints. As far as checkpoints are concerned, space them so that each new checkpoint can be seen from the last one, the actual spacing will vary with the weather and visibility of the checkpoint itself. Plan to use ded reckoning and radio navigation as a back-up, or verifier, to your pilotage.

Once the course is selected, check wind forecasts, temperature, and performance charts to determine the pressure altitude for the flight. Be sure to defer to FAR-mandated cruising altitudes when they are appropriate. If there is a mountain or some other obstacle protruding above your desired altitude, use it as a check point and plan to make a quick climb over it, or go around. Do not adjust the cruise altitude of the entire trip to compensate for a solitary obstacle.

Compute times en route and between checkpoints and actually fly them. Adjust your estimated times of arrival as the flight progresses. It might sound like a lot of bother, but it becomes a critical factor on trips that approach the maximum range of your airplane, and can be the basis for several critical decisions you make in flight.

With all the fancy avionics available today, you might be tempted to simply switch on the moving map and sit back like a couch potato in the cockpit. Please understand that this equipment cannot make important decisions for you. While definitely making your job as pilot easier, you are still the pilot in command and must actively follow the flight to stay in the informational loop, and that includes using a chart and watch.

The watch is really your best indication of fuel remaining in the tanks. Aircraft fuel gauges are notoriously prone to error. It is critical to safety that you know the time of departure and the time to the next fix or checkpoint.

IFR navigation and flight rules provide some extra challenges. Since most high-performance aircraft attain their best speeds in the flight levels, instrument rules greatly influence the nature of the flight. If it is possible to fly directly to the destination and you are able to navigate, do it. Where departure procedures can be accomplished visually and on course, do it. When an approach can be made visually and more directly, of course, do it. A typical IFR trip involves some delay with instrument procedures at the departure and arrival ends of the trip. If the weather permits, climb and descend in visual conditions to save time. Obviously, when the weather truly requires IFR procedures, there is no choice but to follow the procedures, but it will generally take longer than flying VFR.

Selection of cruise altitude

It really takes only a few minutes to plan a flight and select an ideal cruise altitude. First, consider all the concrete restrictions: IFR minimum en route altitudes, terrain, terminal airspace, and so on. Next, check temperatures and compute the pressure altitude you need for optimal cruise performance. Finally, check winds-aloft forecasts and modify your altitude selection accordingly. Three steps. It takes less than 5 minutes and will probably save you 15 minutes over the course of a 3-hour flight.

Flying your plan

Now that the course has been plotted, altitude selected, and time en route computed, you've departed, climbed to altitude and trimmed the plane for cruise. Passing your first fix, you note the time. (I like to write directly on the chart, instead of messing with extra papers, notes and flight log forms.) Compare your planned time with the actual time en route. Do you see a significant difference? A difference of more than a couple of minutes between checkpoints indicates unforecast winds, or unexpected performance. Ideally, you want no surprises. If your plane is not as fast as the book says, that's fine, as long as it is as fast as *you* expect. Things should go as planned or better. There should be no surprises.

A significant discrepancy between the flight plan and the flight is cause for rethinking the outcome of the flight. If you took off with enough fuel to get there, and checkpoints are coming up 50 percent too late, are you really going to get there after all? If you're relying heavily on some GPS receiver and not plotting progress as it's completed, there is a chance that some vital bit of information is lost, like the time you took off. Another benefit of tracking a flight on paper is the logging of higher speeds. If you notice a high groundspeed during the climb, write it down and note the altitude for further reference. If your predicted winds at cruise altitude go up in smoke, then experiment with other altitudes until you find something that works. Then keep a record so you have something on which to base future decisions. At least sometime early in the operations of your airplane, take off with full tanks, and, on landing top them off again. If you've kept accurate record of altitude, time en route and power settings, you'll have an excellent idea of the actual fuel consumption. You'll know what to expect. No surprises.

The *step*

So you've climbed to altitude, set cruise power and are waiting for the airplane to accelerate to cruise flight. Drag builds as the airplane gains speed. As the airplane nears cruise speed, drag has built up to the point that it almost, but not quite, equals the thrust available. Acceleration is very slow. If the plane is improperly trimmed, maneuvered strongly or suddenly, or even hit by turbulence at this time, cruise speed might never be attained during the flight. It feels as if the plane is not quite up to speed, sort of wallowing around just shy of cruise speed.

Improperly flown, airplanes might not accelerate to cruise speed quickly, but rather plow through the air like a heavily laden motorboat plows about in the water. When a boat gains sufficient speed, it begins to rise out of the water like a water-skier, planing on just a portion of the hull. When the boat reaches this condition, it is referred to as the *step,* or *plane.* Airplanes achieve a similar condition in cruise, where the balance between cruise drag and cruise thrust is delicate. The final few knots of cruise airspeed might be long in coming.

One method of establishing cruise flight quickly is to climb somewhat above the desired cruise altitude and accelerate to cruise speed while descending, with the hope of completing the acceleration as the proper altitude is established. Another, perhaps simpler method, is to leave the engine set for full climb power in level flight until full cruise speed is attained, then reduce to cruise power. Pilots using either of these procedures often report better times en route.

Trim for speed

Trim drag, as a result of improper adjustment of trim, can rob a few precious knots from the cruise condition. Keep in mind that trim adjusts control surface position, and thus, the angle of attack of the respective flight surface. It is possible to cause trim mechanisms to work against each other, which might produce unwanted drag.

Begin by trimming the elevator mechanism. Be patient here, because the airplane will not be fully trimmed until final cruise speed is attained and cruise power is set. For the time being, the pilot will have to hold pressure on the aileron and rudder controls until the elevator trim is set. Concentrate on holding the cruise pitch attitude exactly, and adjust the trim mechanism until the pressures at the pitch control diminish. Next, set the rudder ball (inclinometer) dead-center in its races and trim the rudder pressure away. Last, trim the ailerons, if aileron trim is required.

The reasons behind this order of trim have to do with the power of the trim systems involved. The most effective is pitch, followed by the rudder, lastly the aileron. It's that simple. Keep in mind that pitch trim is incomplete until the airplane is finished attaining speed. If done out of order, it is possible to get the aileron trim tab working against the rudder, with everything resulting in higher drag.

The Hudson Bay start

Some time had elapsed since I had last traveled on a commercial airliner, and I had never flown first class. Yet, shortly after wheels-up in a TWA 727, things quieted down, curtains closed, and they served me a nice meal en route to Baltimore-Washington International Airport. From there, I rented a car and drove to Petersburg, Virginia, where I first met the little Pitts Special that I planned to fly back to Salt Lake City. The tach indicated 48.5 hours, a nearly new airplane, and most of its time had been spent en route from the factory in Afton, Wyoming, to Virginia. After a careful prepurchase inspection, I plunked down my client's money and received the bill of sale.

In contrast to the plush comfort, high speed, and fancy dinners of commercial first class, the Pitts Special is noisy, uncomfortable, ill-equipped, decidedly short-ranged and arguably, my favorite of all airplanes. While most airplanes do better than the Pitts in the comfort category, the Pitts shines, perhaps better than any plane ever made, in its handling. In my experience nothing flies quite so well. Since the airplane is designed with attention completely focused on aerobatic flying, its cross-country abilities have largely been ignored.

On this day I placed four quarts of mineral oil (for the new engine) and a couple of charts in the turtle-deck storage area, accessible only after landing. The front seat became a dedicated baggage area with my duffel-bag strapped down and ratcheted in place on top of the parachute by the seven seatbelts of the aerobatic harness. I triple checked its placement to assure that nothing would interfere with the flight controls. Like the oil previously stowed, the front seat was also inaccessible during flight. I selected a WAC chart, a headset, sunglasses, and a small E-6B to carry with me in the rear cockpit, strategically wedged between the trusses and structural members of the fuselage.

With a straight edge, I plotted the course from Petersburg to Lynchburg, a short hop away. If I got lost right out of the blocks, I wanted to know about it soon, and I needed a good idea of the fuel burn. With only a magnetic compass for navigation, flying the Pitts can be adventurous. Worse yet, the plane's steel-tubing structure in the fuselage causes compass errors measured in large double-figures. Accordingly, the first leg had to be short, the airport easy to find, and the en route heading easy to establish. Besides, I had not flown this particular airplane before and if it had problems, I wanted to know about them early.

The same concept was often used by the Hudson Bay Company, more than a century ago, the first night's camp set up within a short walk back to the home fort, right outside the gates. If any unforeseen problems arose with their preparations, the remedy was still close by in the morning.

By plotting my course directly on the chart, I eliminated the problem of a loose flight log in the cockpit. I marked headings, checkpoints, fuel consumption and estimated times directly on the chart, alongside the course line. The planned flight path to Lynchburg was only slightly off course from the straight-line course direct to home, which I had plotted previously using a string with all the charts connected on my living-room floor. In the next few days, I would try to select stopping points as near as possible along that line.

Navigation tools were simple and very reliable. The plane was equipped with a wet compass, I was wearing a watch and the chart was handy. The one really obnoxious part of a cross-country flight in this plane is its lack of forward visibility. This is not to say that I couldn't see at all, just that the cowling and lower wing seemed to block the view of almost everything useful. No problem doing S-turns, of course, but that made use of the mag compass a little more difficult.

Pretakeoff checks complete, I noted the time and launched for Lynchburg, located at the eastern slope of the Appalachian range. Sea-level performance for a Pitts is terrific. The acceleration nearly peeled back my eyelids, and, pulling up, I reached a low cruise altitude by the end of the runway. I had enough of that high fuel burn, however, and I reduced the throttle by nearly half and leaned for cruise. Airspeed settled on 150 mph, fuel burn to 13 gph. I turned to the heading that hopefully would end at Lynchburg, noted the time again, and flew on.

After a short while I picked up landmarks almost 20 degrees to the left. Lynchburg? I turned, noted the new heading, checked my watch, and contacted the tower for landing. By the time I prepared for landing, my back was almost numb from lumpy pressure points in the parachute, the shoulder harness chafed my neck sorely, and my other chart had slipped out of reach under the seat. I contorted in the cockpit like a gorilla trying to scratch an impossible place. It became almost unbearable to sit still in the seat, and this after only an hour. Landed, I refueled the plane, calculated *actual* fuel burn for use in estimating the upcoming legs, chose a new heading based upon the one required to get to Lynchburg, plotted a new course and so on, and sorted through my duffel bag for towels and cushions to improve the cockpit seating arrangement.

Over the course of the next twelve legs and three days, I sorted out the course heading to the point that landmarks were invisible until they rolled by under the belly windows at exactly the predicted moment. The cockpit, after much primping and padding, became bearable for almost two hours at a time. I could easily predict and monitor fuel capacity over the course of the flight and although it was only a dismal 28 gallons, I arrived home after about 16.5 hours of flight. There is much more to tell, but I've already made my points in favor of a short hop, at first, when beginning a long trip.

General considerations for the flight profile

If you have a choice of runways, consider taking off on the runway which most favors your direction of flight. If you're worried about fuel consumed during a lengthy taxi, every extra minute spent at climb power going the wrong direction burns at least six times the fuel required for a minute of taxiing.

When a wind is present during the climb phase of flight, increase speed (cruise climb) and power settings for a headwind. When climbing with a tailwind, forego the faster cruise climb speed in favor of Vy and a high rate of climb, taking greatest advantage of the wind.

During cruise, balance altitude selection with aircraft performance and wind benefits. Use higher cruise speeds and power settings in headwinds, lower settings for tailwinds. Attempt to keep the airplane in an optimum cruise condition as long as possible. Turbulence will generally slow the airplane, causing the wings to fly at less than optimum angles of attack. It is best avoided. Use weather phenomena to your advantage.

Plan to remain at the optimum cruise altitude for as long as possible before beginning descent. Be sure not to compromise engine operating parameters (avoid shock-cooling) during the descent. Descend at optimum speed and power settings, as quickly as possible. Make sure your approach is stabilized above 500 feet agl.

Leaning

Perhaps the best source of engine information for your airplane is available from the engine manufacturer. Often the engine builder will recommend a leaning procedure that is different from that suggested by the aircraft factory. It is up to you to decide which procedure to use.

Occasionally, an engine manufacturer will determine that certain operational changes to a particular engine will produce better economy. An example of this would be the recent determination that the normally aspirated Lycoming O-540 can be successfully run *lean* of peak temperatures without damage. This procedure does not greatly affect power available, it preserves plugs, and it burns less fuel. Most engine manufacturers will issue operational bulletins with specific information of this nature.

Skills to practice

Here are a couple of wonderful drills designed to enhance your skills for cruise flight. Enjoy.

Trimming

Elevator trim does not control altitude, but rather airspeed. Airspeed is an indirect indication of angle of attack, which is what the elevator trim tab *really* controls. Many pilots erroneously attempt to trim an airplane for a given altitude, when they should watch for a stabilization of airspeed at cruise.

One of the older Beech Bonanzas, circa 1954, is a great demonstrator of this concept because it is a relatively clean airplane that accelerates to full speed rather slowly. The typical pilot will climb to the desired altitude, lower the nose to level and trim to reduce control pressure. The airplane has just begun to gain speed. If the pilot were climbing at 100 mph, and lowering the nose with initial trim allowed the airplane to go to 130 mph, the airplane still has 35 mph yet to gain. As the pilot becomes occupied with other things, the airplane continues its acceleration. Since the plane is trimmed for 130 mph, there is excess power and the plane will begin a climb. Shortly after, the pilot is exasperated at the airplane's "unwillingness" to remain level. The airplane will continue this game of *trim and climb touché* with the pilot until it has finally arrived at, and been trimmed for, its real cruise speed of 165 mph. At this point it will appear to hold altitude willingly, having no excess power available for climb.

When leveling an airplane at altitude, the pilot should keep in mind the airspeed at which the airplane wants to cruise. The pilot should then stay with the task of trimming the airplane until this speed is attained. Once this is achieved, the pilot workload is much diminished and the task of flying straight and level becomes simple.

Check the power settings and suggested airspeeds for 75-, 65-, and 55-percent cruise. Practice leveling at the appropriate altitudes at climb power, waiting until the recommended speeds are attained, and setting the power for cruise. Then trim. If all goes well, the airplane should be steady at airspeed and altitude. If you find that airspeed is steady (as it should be), but the altitude isn't, then the airplane's flying weight is such that another altitude (probably higher) should be used. Practice this procedure at each power setting until you are comfortable achieving the performance figures as outlined in the aircraft flight manual.

Compass, clock, and airspeed

This is a fun drill for practicing ded reckoning navigation. You remember the scene in *The Hunt For Red October* where a Russian submarine captain attempts to evade his pursuers by navigating through an underwater canyon? Notice that the only tools they used were a compass, a clock, a speed indicator, and an accurate chart. The navigator boasted that with these tools, he could fly a plane with no windows through the Alps.

To try this without the mountains, you'll need a safety pilot and a hood. Before takeoff, plot a round-robin course over three or four points, not in a straight line, about 60 miles long. (You can make it as difficult—longer or shorter—as you like.) Plan your headings to the nearest degree and the turns to the nearest second. Be sure to check winds and compensate your heading and groundspeed accordingly.

After takeoff, your safety pilot will watch for traffic and other conflicts while you don the hood. You should begin timing at the start of the takeoff roll and establish your initial heading as soon as practicable afterwards. Without looking out the aircraft further, your task is to navigate to your intended points and back to your departure airport. Use only a chart, a compass, the airspeed, and a clock. You might be surprised at the accuracy you attain.

Try it again, but have your safety pilot give you a visual fix at each of the en route points. Compensate your course accordingly as you fly the route. This time, I think the accuracy that is possible will be astounding. It should be equivalent to that of good radio navigation.

Getting your own figures

Since engineers and test pilots have attempted to predict the future performance of your airplane using charts, graphs, and raw data, you have a rough idea of time en route and fuel required for a given trip. Now, keep in mind that a billion variables might change that rough estimate as the flight takes place, altering, however slightly, its outcome. With this in mind, the best, and most practical, performance information available to the pilot is found by looking at past, not future, performance by means of a trend analysis. This is a technique used by airlines the world over. It has been refined by millions of hours of flight over courses spanning billions of miles. Sound astronomical? It's true, and it's uncannily accurate.

Records

Spending less than three minutes per flight, as the flight occurs, it is possible for a pilot to develop performance data far more accurate than what could be generated with charts and a calculator for an hour beforehand. It is simply a matter of keeping records and paying attention to detail. At the conclusion of a flight, most pilots record Hobbs or tach time, write something about the trip in a logbook and call it a day. In the interest of performance, however, the flight record should include accurate takeoff weight, time en route, cruise altitude, temperature, power setting, indicated airspeed, fuel consumption, route, and fuel consumed over the trip. It takes just a couple of minutes of your time, at the most, to record this information.

As time goes by, you'll have an interesting catalogue of performance over actual flights, to and from various airports. Fly the same trip enough times, and you'll have a highly accurate idea of what is required to complete it, including the variables of ATC, typical weather to be expected along the way, and seasonal changes over the year. This information is merely a starting point. You now have the opportunity to alter flight profiles, power settings and altitude until the entire trip is truly optimized. Can you see the advantage here? This is what airlines have been doing for years. They have the times and fuel required between city pairs down to a science. Altitudes are selected and planned well in advance, months even. When this information is managed well, the system works like a machine, with maximum performance and no surprises.

Get a book that you may keep handy in the cockpit and take notes. Designate each page for one destination. A loose-leaf binder is helpful because the trip pages may be kept in alphabetical order for easy reference. Have a space above each vertical column for recording

SLC to PIH

		8/83	2/84								
1. Date		8/83	2/84								
2. Type		C152	C152								
3. Takeoff weight		1580	1670								
4. Cruise altitude		11,500	6500								
5. Temperature		-1C	3C								
6. Power setting		Full	Full								
7. Indicated airspeed		78kts	98kts								
8. Fuel consumption		5.6	6.2								
9. Route		dir	dir								
10. Time enroute		1.7	1.3								
11. Fuel consumed		9.9	8.0								

5-9 *A sample trend analysis log for a Cessna 152 going from Salt Lake City, Utah, to Pocatello, Idaho. By looking back like this, future performance can be optimized and predicted with tremendous accuracy.*

the date of each flight. Make a column down one side of the page with the following information (Fig. 5-9):

1 Type

2 Takeoff weight

3 Cruise altitude

4 Temperature

5 Power setting (Torque, N1, Manifold, RPM, etc.)

6 Indicated airspeed

7 Fuel consumption

8 Route (if significantly altered)

9 Time en route

10 Fuel consumed

Notes: During a flight, pull out your book and note the various parameters called for in a single column, as though logging accounting data. When you make the flight again, record that data in another column alongside the first, with the date at the top. Soon you'll have a manual with performance comparisons much more accurate than what is possible with the AFM. Then, when you plan a flight to a familiar area, you'll get there with precision, knowing exactly the performance to be expected. Also, these records may be used to estimate the needs of an unfamiliar trip, based upon the flight performance gleaned from something similar that you might have logged in your book elsewhere.

Further reading

Airman's Odyssey, Antoine de Saint-Exupery, HBJ Books, 1984

Instrument Flying, Air Force Manual #51-37A, US Government Printing Office, Department of the Air Force, 1961

Instrument Flying Handbook, FAA EA-AC 61-27B, Department of Transportation, For sale by the Aviation Maintenance Foundation, 1971

Aerodynamic for Naval Aviators, H. H. Hurt, Jr., University of Southern California, NAVWEPS 00-80T-80, 1965

Flying in Adverse Conditions, R. Randall Padfield, McGraw-Hill, 1994

Cross-Country Flying, Padfield, McGraw-Hill, 1991

Van Sickle's Modern Airmanship, Van Sickle/edited by John F. Welch, McGraw-Hill, 1994

Cross-Country Flying, Jerry A. Eichenberger, McGraw-Hill, 1994

6

Weather

Ben and I had flown the plane for almost an hour before we climbed high enough to cross the ridge. Airspeed held precisely at 67 mph while vertical speed fluctuated between 0 and 100 fpm. The altimeter slowly crept past 8000 feet. "Three-hundred to go," I said. The back seat of a Citabria is certainly not the worst place to spend a hot summer afternoon. Visibility was great, and I enjoyed the view. We flew back and forth along the west slope of the Wasatch Range to climb out of the Salt Lake terminal area and find a place to maneuver. Back and forth we went, like endless switchbacks on a mountain road. I adjusted the harness of my parachute. An old army B-5, it had mysterious lumps that were invisible and unfelt until after takeoff when I was buckled tightly in and at its mercy; then the lumps would try to bore holes in my backside. Ben shifted around awkwardly in his seat as well, his parachute beginning to wear him down.

Temperature at the surface read close to 100 degrees F. I set the cockpit vents to blow the hot outside air straight at my face. Since it was late in the summer, the grass below was burned yellow like the sun, dried and brittle in stagnant air. We could see Morgan Valley over the pines at the top of the ridge. Almost there. "Eighty-three hundred," Ben said. He lowered the nose and gingerly nursed the airplane up to cruise speed. Air temperature was noticeably cooler. Airspeed picked up to 90 mph. We flew eastward, out of the controlled airspace. Finally, after the long climb, I got excited about the flight.

Ben, the chief flight instructor of the school where we worked, had expressed an interest in aerobatics. I was the only one teaching them at the time in the old Citabria. Ben, a veteran pilot of 30 years or more, is far more experienced than I am, yet he had never done much in the way of upside-down flying. I was honored to be in the plane with him. "Lower the nose to 120 mph," I said. Reaching that speed, we raised the nose 25 degrees and rolled left as the speed bled away. The plane went through inverted and back to upright, coming level at 120 mph, but with a 300-foot loss of altitude. Even from behind, I could tell Ben was smiling. He flew two more rolls, one right and one left. Altitude dropped to 7600 feet. We descended into Morgan Valley, happily rolling, spending in a few minutes the altitude we had gained during the previous hour.

Ben flew nice loops, and I showed him how to do snap rolls. By then, his stomach was upset and we broke away from the maneuvering for a few landings at Morgan County Airport. It had been years since Ben had flown a taildragger, and he wanted to get current. His landings were nice.

Traffic patterns for the Citabria stretched into small cross-countries. The plane would not climb fast enough. I'd like to blame it on the hot weather, but the plane wouldn't climb any better in the winter. It was old, tired, and underpowered. With only 118 hp, it took an eternity to climb to altitude. A typical aerobatic lesson was 90 percent climb and 10 percent maneuvering on the way down. Traffic patterns were huge, slow trips to pattern altitude. Ben made three pretty landings and we began the long climb back over the ridge to Salt Lake.

"Let me show you something," Ben said. He flew along the valley, scrutinizing the fields to the side of a freeway. Finding what he was looking for he flew the plane over a dry, grassy field and circled tightly. It was turbulent. After a few moments, Ben modified the turn slightly, repositioning the little airplane, and I was amazed to see the VSI show a 400-fpm climb. "I used to fly gliders," Ben explained. "There is a thermal over this field, and if we can find its core, we might get over the ridge a little sooner. The trick is to drift downwind with the thermal." I looked in amazement for some kind of clue as to where the thermal was. Ben went on explaining how to feel out the turbulence with the wings, banking into the lift. The VSI crept steadily past 1500 fpm; we were still in a 45-degree bank. A few minutes later, we topped 8500 feet and headed for home.

When we left the thermal, the airplane was its old self again, struggling for any altitude, slow to move. I couldn't help but wonder what got into it back there; it was like riding an express elevator, as though the airplane suddenly took vitamins and pulled us, musclebound and power-charged, into the sky. Just as quickly, it was over, the plane once again a meek, underpowered butterfly.

Background information

Ben found free lift and better performance by paying attention to the weather. Pilots who know what to look for can improve the performance of their airplanes; they climb better, go faster, and burn less fuel than otherwise. This is just one example of the performance gains possible with a knowledgeable and skilled pilot at the controls.

Ideally, this chapter should be written by a glider pilot. Who better to explain weather related performance than the pilot of a machine that derives *all* of its motivation from the weather? Nevertheless, powered pilots have been known to make good use of weather now and again, and I am no exception.

The following is an attempt to reduce complicated weather theory into a practical nutshell that might be remembered for good use by the average pilot. Some of the more technical explanations have been foregone in the interest of simplicity.[1]

Origin of weather

The root of weather is sunshine. The sun heats parts of the earth to different temperatures. Regions near the equator receive more direct sunlight than the poles and therefore reach higher temperatures. The temperature differential causes the air to move and circulate, at the surface, in a fairly consistent pattern, from the poles toward the equator, as in Fig. 6-1.

This would be easy to visualize, except that it is complicated by the rotation of the earth. This rotation tends to stir any recognizable circulation pattern into a mass of eddies and jetstreams that look more like my hair in the morning than anything the weather people might draw on a map. Suffice it to say, the wind blows out of the poles. There is a general high-pressure region at the poles and corresponding low pressures at the equator. Breaking the circulation pattern down into two parts, we see the following generality about high and low pressures (Fig. 6-2):

High pressures move air down and outward; low pressures draw air in and upward. The generally rising air of a large low-pressure system is theoretically capable of improving flight performance. In

---

1 At the end of this chapter are several recommended texts which may be read for further detail.

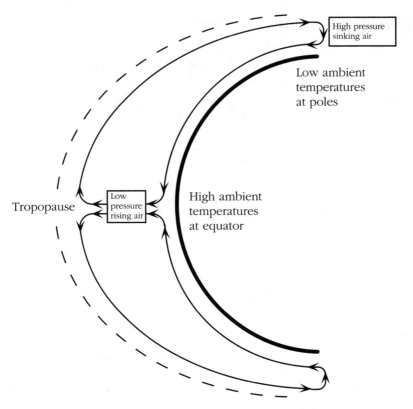

6-1 *Global circulation.*

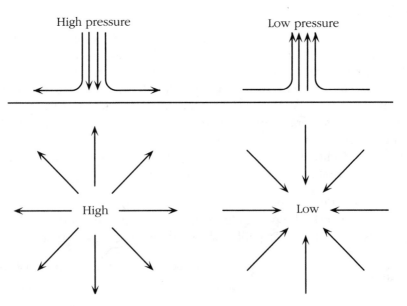

6-2 *High pressure sinks; low pressure rises.*

truth, the benefit is probably there, but is so slight that it would be difficult to notice.

When the earth's rotation is brought into the pressure theory, an interesting phenomenon occurs. Someone discovered that the atmosphere isn't really bolted to the earth's surface at all, but moves independently of the planet. If a weather balloon floating freely in the atmosphere is followed closely while it travels southward over a spinning planet, its course will appear to curve. Try rolling a marble from the center of a spinning pottery wheel to its edge. The marble traces a spiral course along the wheel as it moves toward the outside of the disk. *Coriolis* force is born. This means simply that a man named Coriolis discovered that all atmospheric motion in the northern hemisphere experiences an almost irresistible urge to deflect its path to the right, as seen in relation to the map, because of the spinning earth beneath.

Take Coriolis at face value and the air patterns around high and low pressures generally look like Fig. 6-3, as seen from above.

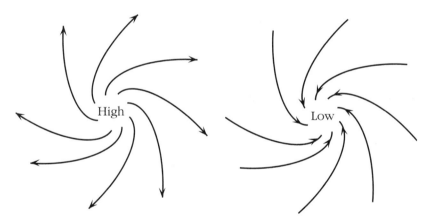

6-3 *High and low pressures with Coriolis twist.*

Notice that the air flowing into a low pressure is still favoring a bend to the right, passing around to the right of the low-pressure center.

Putting it all together, if you're planning a flight from Denver to Salt Lake City, and the weather shows low atmospheric pressure over Wyoming and a high pressure system over Wendover, Utah, which way will the wind blow (Fig. 6-4)?

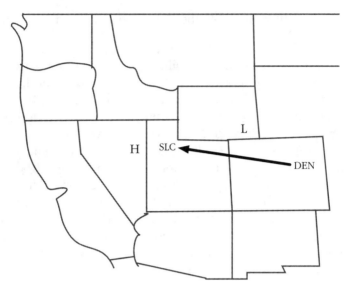

6-4 *Across windy country.*

The answer is toward Wyoming. (Because, as they say, if it ever stops blowing there, all the cattle will fall down.) Visually, it looks like Fig. 6-5:

Earth to tropopause

Meteorologists use the characteristics of temperature change in relation to altitude (lapse rates) to distinguish one atmospheric layer from another. For example, standard temperature at sea level is an average determined to be 15 degrees centigrade. In the first atmospheric layer, called the *troposphere*, the temperature decreases an average of 2 degrees centigrade for every 1000-foot increase in altitude. Depending upon the season and geographic latitude, air temperature reaches a minimum of about –56 degrees centigrade at altitudes ranging between 25,000 and 45,000 feet, at which point the air temperature remains constant for several miles above that.

The constancy of temperature at the middle altitudes gives rise to the name *tropopause*, because the air temperature pauses, or remains constant, for several thousand feet. Jet-cruising performance is most efficient at the beginning of the tropopause, as was discussed in Chapter 5. Also, a constant temperature effectively puts a lid on weather systems, sapping the energy from any thunder clouds that dare venture above that point. It is also in the tropopause that the jet stream flows.

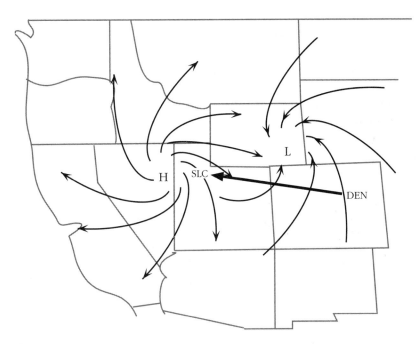

6-5 *The wind revealed.*

Above the tropopause, air temperature actually begins to increase slightly, a characteristic of the atmospheric layer known as the *stratosphere.* Aircraft types that routinely fly into this region have performance characteristics beyond the scope of this book.

When considering pressure systems in terms of atmospheric layers, weather scientists make careful pressure maps of the surface of the tropopause as though it represented a great sea. The border between it and the troposphere can be visualized as a distinct surface within the atmosphere, like a break between oil and water. The pressure map of the tropopause is literally a topographical map of the waves on its surface. A peak (ridge) translates into a high-pressure region at the earth's surface. A valley, or trough, equates to a low-pressure area. Waves in the tropopause move about like waves in the ocean, except they are much bigger in size. The waves in the atmosphere could be simulated on a smaller scale at the beach. Take a scale under water with the breakers crashing overhead, and the diver would notice pressure fluctuations showing on the scale as the waves pass. The crest of a wave overhead weighs more at the surface than the valleys in between the swells.

The Weather Service plots the barometric pressure readings at ground level and literally plays connect the dots. Lines connecting areas of equal pressure, called *isobars*, create a topographical image of the floor of the tropopause. The waves are visualized in the same way that mountains and elevation changes are topographically depicted on a map. Where the lines are closely spaced, the pressure gradient is steep, and the pressure differential is high. Much like a ball rolling down a steep mountain slope, the wind blows hardest in these areas (Fig. 6-6).

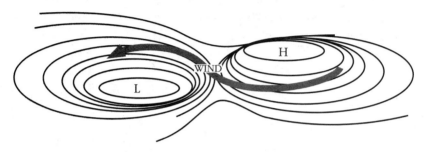

6-6 *Isobars, pressure topography, and wind. Wind blows to low pressure, roughly parallel to the isobars.*

Reading the above chart, it is easy to see where the wind blows strongest: the point at which the gradient is steepest. Also, remembering the circular flow patterns around pressure systems, it is easy to determine wind direction, as depicted by the arrow.

Wind

Wind is governed primarily by pressure patterns at altitude. An altitude of 2500 feet agl and above is considered the region where wind blows with little influence from the terrain below. Reaching ground level, however, friction and obstacles stir the air into a blinding conflagration of unpredictable flows.

The Weather Service predicts upper-level winds based on the drift they observe in weather balloons. The service releases these balloons twice daily at approximately the same time world-wide. Radar tracks the balloons as they ascend, and the flight paths translate into an estimate of wind velocity and direction at various altitudes. Combine these observations with pressure plots and other data, and you have the forecast. When all is said and done, the weather briefer looks at a depiction of wind for your cruising altitude, licks a finger and gives you a good guess.

Low-level wind might be as unpredictable as a politician. A pilot familiar with the territory might know general wind characteristics—that wind always blows up a certain mountain slope, down a particular valley, or have different habits depending on the time of day. However, wind might blow *any* direction at low altitudes. Buildings, trees, mountains, and localized weather patterns easily disturb the best of the Weather Service's predictions. The only truly reliable bit of information about surface wind is a *report*, not a *forecast*.

Now, you might be wondering what all of this theory has to do with airplane performance. Weather is probably the single biggest factor for increasing—or totally destroying—the performance of your airplane. It doesn't matter how big the airplane is, either. My folks were riding in a B-747 on their way home from vacationing in Hawaii, for example, when the captain happily announced that the airplane's groundspeed was a supersonic 812 knots! Flying high over the Pacific, the jumbo-jet encountered a terrific tailwind to the delight of everyone onboard. The winds were probably forecast to be strong, and they always blow out of the west during that time of year, but I doubt anyone in the cockpit of that 747 expected to go quite so fast, based upon a forecast alone.

Read on, we will cover a little more weather theory and then discuss how to apply it, to make an airplane perform well, indeed.

Water

Water vapor in the air can drastically alter its weather characteristics. Chemists say that water has a high specific heat. That is to say that it takes an enormous amount of energy to cause water temperature to rise even a few degrees. Ever go to a swimming party where the host forgot to heat up the pool? They say, "Don't worry, I'll just turn up the heat now." The pool might take a few days to warm up to a tolerable level. The same goes for the water heater in your house, it takes time and a lot of energy to heat water. Conversely, water will store this heat energy for a very long time, as compared to other elements, like air or earth. Turn the heat off on a warm pool and it will take just as long to cool down. As a gas evaporated into the atmosphere, water retains this characteristic, and plays a lead role weather patterns.

You remember that the average temperature lapse rate with altitude is 2 degrees C per 1000 feet. This average refers to air with an *average* amount of water vapor. The water vapor acts as a heat sink, or insulator, for the air in which it is found. Increase the water content in a volume of air and the lapse rate will decrease, dry the air and the lapse rate will be so fast you'll get frostbite by wearing platform shoes. This is evidenced by the climate in Hawaii as opposed to the climate in the Sahara. Temperatures in Hawaii are a consistent 70 to 80 degrees F. Sunup to sundown, the temperatures are consistent. Go to the desert and daytime sun heats the air to 120 degrees, but by predawn it's cooled nearly to freezing. Dry desert air will heat and cool with gusto.

Put dry air with its fast lapse rates next to relatively wet air (with slow lapse rates) and you get a condition of instability, a recipe for a thermal.

Making of a monster—cooking up a thunderstorm

Thunderstorms are basically thermals with an attitude. A thermal is a column of rising air. One glider pilot explained thermals as a rising bubble of hot air, like bubbles in a pan of boiling water. When the sun heats a landscape, differences in topography, vegetation, and surface textures promote differential heating. The air over the black tarmac of an airport would have hotter localized temperatures than the air over a nearby cornfield, for example. Soon, the air over the airport becomes hot enough to rise and it breaks free of the ground like a bubble and rises to pop and tumble airplanes flying overhead. They call this *convective turbulence*, turbulence generated by heat, which is an annoyance to powered pilots. Flying through convective turbulence is remarkably similar to the ride endured by a sprig of parsley in a pan of boiling water. Glider pilots love it, airline passengers hate it. Often, cumulus clouds mark the location of thermals and provide a sort of aerial landmark for rising air.

When conditions are ripe for thermals, little more is needed to build a thunderstorm—just add water and bake in the sun for a few hours. Thunderstorms develop whenever the following occur together:

1 Moisture

2 Instability

3 Some form of lift

Looking at each of these ingredients in order, we'll first explore the background of a thunderstorm, then attempt to create a theoretical massive death cloud in the comfort of your own home.

Moisture is the insulating ingredient. Humid air retains heat as it ascends, cooling much slower than relatively dry air nearby. This is unstable. Instability is simply a condition of different atmospheric lapse rates within close geographic proximity. Unstable air is not homogeneous, or well mixed. There are pockets of wet air and areas of dry air. Surprisingly, they don't blend well. A wet air mass will hold itself together tenaciously and not dissolve much into the surrounding sky. This is instability.

Moisture and instability combined are an explosive mixture looking for a match. A lifting action is the trigger, or spark, that sets the ball rolling. For our example, we will use a mountain as a physical wedge for lifting, but an actual lift source might be as simple as heat from a factory, a weather front, a little thermal, or an atomic bomb.

Look at Fig. 6-7. This is a classic setting for thunderstorm development: a body of saltwater, next to a desert, next to a mountain. In the morning, the rising sun begins to heat the whole area. Since everything begins at a consistent temperature, nothing happens. Soon, the air above the water is saturated with moisture while the surrounding desert air remains as dry as, well, a desert.

The air over the water has become insulated in its humidity. Its own lapse rate has become relatively slow when compared to the air over the desert. For convenience, we'll assign the rate of 1 degree C per

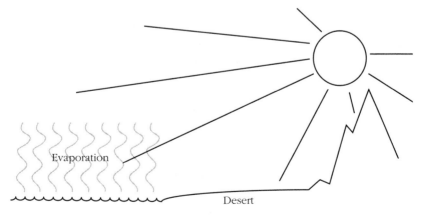

6-7 *Setting for a thunderstorm.*

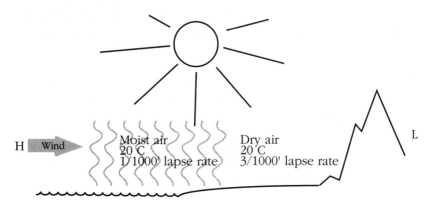

6-8 *The plot thickens with the addition of instability and a little wind.*

1000 feet to the wet air, and 3 degrees C per 1000 feet to the dry air. Two of the three ingredients for a storm are already in the pot, just by having the sun rise and heat things up. All we need now is a little lift.

Suppose a high pressure system moves in from the left, making wind blow across the water, over the desert, and up the side of the mountain. The air mass above the water moves over the desert with the wind, hits the mountain and rises. It remains in a mass. The wet air does not mix or dilute much with the dry air. We're about to witness a revolution of instability.

Assuming that the sun has heated everything to a uniform 20 degrees centigrade to begin with, what happens to temperatures when the moist air mass is elevated 1000 feet?

If everything started at 20 degrees, a 1000-foot elevation would reduce the wet air to 19 degrees, the dry air to 17 degrees (Fig. 6-9). All of the sudden, we have a temperature differential. Hot air rises. The trigger has been pulled, and the wet air mass continues to rise. Five thousand feet later, its temperature has cooled to 14 degrees, whereas the surrounding air has cooled to a relatively frigid 2 degrees. The differential is growing, and with it, the power of the updraft.

When the moist, rising air cools to its dewpoint, water will condense to liquid form and a cloud appears. This seems to happen rather suddenly, giving the cumulus cloud its characteristic flat bottom. The air mass continues to rise forcefully, condensing as it goes. Soon, water has condensed sufficiently to form drops that eventually fall as

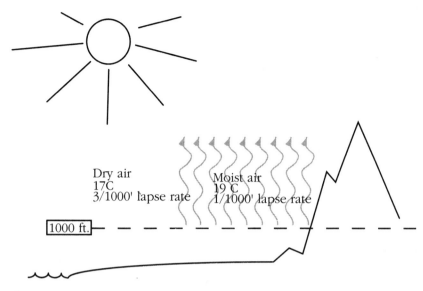

6-9 *Pulling the trigger.*

rain. When the raindrops are big enough, they will fall to earth in spite of the powerful updraft that has suspended them thus far. A pilot can easily tell the intensity of an overhead thunderstorm from the size of the raindrops. Big drops indicate very powerful updrafts booming somewhere above (Fig. 6-10).

The powerful updraft in a thunderstorm is a small, low-pressure system in itself. Air going up cannot leave a void behind, so wind rushes into a storm from all directions below becoming a low-pressure column of fast-rising air. Coriolis gives everything a counter-clockwise twist and the whole storm system becomes a whirling dervish with an appetite. If the updraft is powerful enough, the low pressure column of rising air might spin itself into a tornado and go looking for mobile home parks in the area. On a more massive scale, groups of storms might spin into a unit and shelter one another from the ravages of nights without sun, forming tropical storms and hurricanes, to be given names long remembered in the wakes of the devastation they cause.

All the motion and stirrings of the air in a thunderstorm generate massive electrical charge. The air literally rubs against itself and produces a zap like rubber shoes scuffing on a carpet floor. Get too close, and POW! Thunderstorms are certainly best avoided.

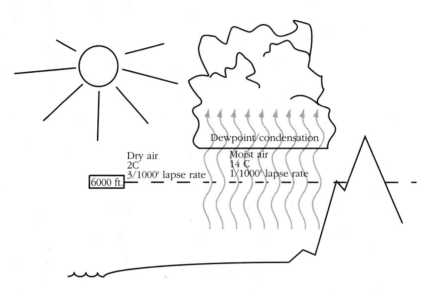

Dewpoint/condensation

Dry air
2C
3/1000' lapse rate

Moist air
14 C
1/1000' lapse rate

6000 ft.

6-10 *A little later . . .*

Deprive storms of their critical ingredients, and they die. Remember the temperature differential that causes the updraft? It might continue until the surrounding air cools no further. The tropopause effectively puts a lid on vertical weather because a booming thunderstorm will continue to cool as it penetrates this region, while the surrounding air has already bottomed out in temperature. Before long, the storm cloud's air mass has an equal temperature with the rest of the atmosphere, and vertical development comes to a halt.

When rain falls from a thunderstorm, so falls the insulation that retained its heat. The storm will cool more rapidly, losing much of its energy. The condensation process within the cloud produces some heat, but that is lost to poor insulation as the rain falls. Generally, rain marks the beginning of the end for a storm cloud. Sometimes, water might be quickly replenished by evaporation when the storm is over a source—like the ocean—but our storm in the desert goes dry in a hurry.

As the storm rains away its moisture and energy, the updrafts diminish and succumb to the falling rain. Downdrafts then predominate and the entire system crashes to earth again like a collapsing building. Sometimes the downdrafts might remain for a time after the cloud is gone. When this falling air strikes the earth, it might generate windshear and endanger airplanes at airports nearby (Fig. 6-11).

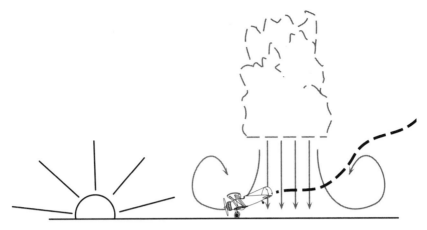

6-11 *The last gaspings of a monster—windshear!*

Stable weather

Air is stable when it's homogeneous: no areas more or less humid than others and has even, consistent lapse rates. If stable air encounters lift, whether from frontal activity, low pressures, or whatever, the cloud forms tend to be flat, layered affairs. Little, if any convective turbulence might be expected. This is the kind of weather that could drizzle about, moping gray and overcast, for days on end. To pilots, stable weather systems mean long stretches of poor visibility, rain, and if it's cold enough, ice.

When the wind blows across mountain ridges in these conditions, wave patterns might occur. The air blasts up the mountain slope, arcs over the ridge and, being stable, tries to return to its previous elevation, usually overdoing it, and spends the next several miles waving up and down like white water in the wake of a big rock. If there is enough moisture in the air, clouds will form at the crest of each wave, making the characteristic, lens shaped, lenticular clouds. Pilots are often cautioned about flying near these clouds because of the tremendous turbulence often associated with the high wind that caused them. What is not often said, however, is that a plane flown parallel to the range can be made to literally surf on the waves, picking up an extra 20 or 30 knots in cruise, or maintain normal speed with huge reductions in power. The idea behind this kind of aerial surfing is to stay in air that is going *up* and avoid the descending air on the other side of the crest (Fig. 6-12).

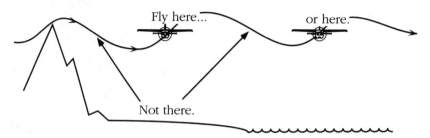

6-12 *Mountain waves in stable air.*

Fantastic mountain waves can be generated when moist, stable air from the coast makes its way over the Sierra-Nevada Range and into the desert. Combining that wet air with the dry desert air on the other side of the range, things get unstable after the first crest. The wave pattern arcs over the range, strikes the desert air and moves upward with a vengeance (Fig. 6-13). It usually does not come back down. A world altitude record for gliders was set in air like that, something over 49,000 feet. Another interesting aspect of mountain waves is that they are generally *smooth*. I know what they say in ground school, but the air in the middle of the wave can offer a lovely ride.

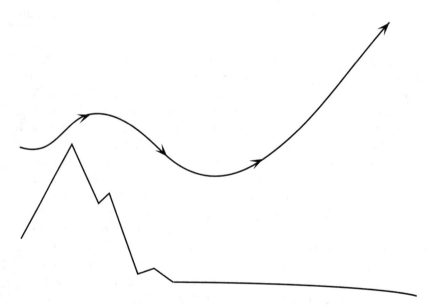

6-13 *Mountain wave in unstable air.*

Fronts

A weather front is a line dividing large air masses of different temperatures. The outside surface of a cumulus cloud could be considered a type of front; it is one temperature in the cloud, quite another in the surrounding sky. On a much larger scale, air masses the size of a continent might retain temperature characteristics much different from adjacent surrounding air. The boundary between these large air masses is a *front*.

High- and low-pressure forces come into play here and cause the air masses to move. When they move, the cooler air mass will wedge under the warmer one and remain in that stance as the front moves across the landscape.

Notice from Fig. 6-14 that the front derives its name from the direction the air mass moves. You could think of it as named after the air

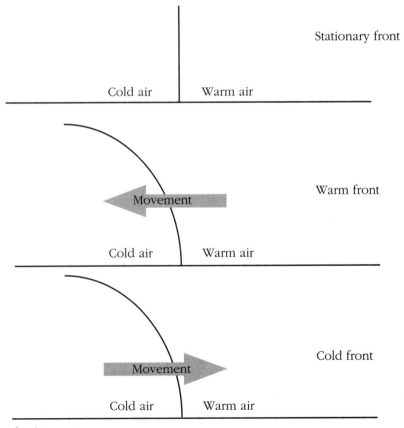

6-14 *Fronts.*

mass which is doing the pushing. See how a cold front moves along wedge-like, lifting the air that it encounters. This could be thought of as a sort of moving mountain—a roving trigger for unstable air. If the air ahead of the cold front is unstable, thunderstorms will result along the frontal line. Stable air will produce less violent weather, but clouds are still likely to form.

A warm front, on the other hand, has less of an option for thunderstorms. The warm air rides up above the air masses it encounters. If the warm air mass, itself, is unstable, then thunderstorms might occur. If not, then that's it—whatever it is, that's what you get. A cold front, by its nature as a form of lift, has much more opportunity for producing violent weather.

Aerial landmarks

Weather might be an effective tool for the pilot to maximize airplane performance. The concept boils down to a simple object: stay in air that is moving up, or in the general direction you wish to travel. We have already discussed the benefits and challenges of horizontal wind in the previous chapter. Wind blowing vertically, either up or down, is referred to by glider pilots as *lift* and *sink*, respectively. It might be difficult to remain solely in lift for extended periods of time. However, a skilled pilot can maneuver an airplane so that the majority of the time airborne is spent in lift.

This is the simple creed of glider pilots: Find the lift and stay in it. The result of their best efforts is extended flight without the benefit of an engine, truly a remarkable feat. For the pilot of powered planes, lift represents free performance gains. For example, departing Elko, Nevada, on a windy, winter day, a student and I encountered a mountain wave near the high peaks of the Ruby Mountains, east of town. We slowed the Beech Bonanza to best angle of climb speed, found the center of the wave going up, and hung on for the ride. The vertical speed indicator literally went around the dial twice, for an average climb rate of more than 5000 feet per minute. We had cruise altitude in the proverbial blink of an eye. Flying downstream in the wave presented other difficulties, but we simply let the airplane flow along with the wind, sinking and rising like a piece of driftwood in a fast river. Groundspeeds were 40 knots faster than normal cruise, slicing 30 minutes from the flight to Salt Lake City— free performance gains from vertical wind.

Cumulus clouds and ground formations make excellent indicators of the presence of lift. Cumulus clouds (non-thunderstorms), for example, are formed by lift, and mark the center of a low-pressure elevator. Think of them as a landmark. Remaining in the lift below a cumulus cloud might require tight maneuvering, however, as most thermals are quite narrow. Gliders frequently circle in them with bank angles near 45 degrees and speeds just above stall to keep their turn radii tight. For the fast-moving cross-country traveler, cumulus type thermals are hardly more than sharp bumps in the road. A savvy pilot will occasionally observe cumulus clouds hanging about in rows, or lines in the sky. If the airplane is guided down these cloud streets on the upwind side, tremendous gains in lift can be realized as in a mountain wave, allowing the pilot to reduce power to save fuel and still increase speed.

Mountain ranges will produce lift up their windward slopes. If the pilot is aware of wind direction and willing to fly rather close to the mountainside, the same benefits can be realized. The endurance record for gliders was set primarily by remaining in mountain-ridge lift for more than 60 hours.

Areas at the surface that tend to get hotter than their surroundings are good thermal generators. Dry, yellow fields are warmer than green, irrigated land, for example. Huge mall parking lots and factories put out great amounts of heat. In many cases, continuous thermals might rise from such terrain throughout the warmer part of the day. The pilot eager for altitude on a hot, high-density-altitude day might divert the flight path slightly over a parking lot and develop a more comfortable climb using a thermal.

On the down side, where lift is present, sink might also be found. Cool areas at the surface cause air to descend. There is a back side to a mountain wave. Just as a pilot learns where the lift is, careful attention must be paid to avoiding sink; it's part of the game. I've heard many arguments from pilots who are convinced that no downward wind, no matter how strong, might actually take an airplane into the ground. They say that the wind cannot blow through the earth, and must, therefore, change direction before hitting the ground. Thus, an airplane caught in powerful sink might simply wait until the air bottoms out against the earth, at which time the *sink* nature of the air will change. It's a nice theory, but easily shot down by the bugs that hit a car's windshield. Obviously, the air is deflected by a slanted windshield, but insects still manage to splatter themselves against the glass. Pilots caught in powerful sink might soon hit the dirt if steps aren't taken to extricate themselves from the situation.

Turbulence

Turbulence as felt in the airplane is caused by quick changes in angle of attack. Suppose you're flying along in smooth air. Invisible to you up ahead is a region of air blowing straight up. The plane is at cruise speed when it penetrates the vertical gust. Since the direction of the air striking the wing has changed, so has the angle of attack, which is momentarily increased by the vertical gust. The result is a rather sudden increase in lift, felt by the plane's occupants as a bump. Recent research has been conducted into this phenomenon and an airplane constructed with a wing that is allowed to pivot freely in angle of attack. The wing is designed so that it naturally seeks an optimum angle of attack independent of the airplane fuselage. The results are a smoother ride in turbulence and rather idiot-proof stall characteristics.

For the normal airplane, turbulence is merely annoying unless the momentary increases of lift exceed design loads and cause structural damage. An airplane maneuvering hard in turbulence runs a risk of damage because the turbulence causes stress to the airframe in addition to that already produced by maneuvering forces. A fighter plane pulling 9 Gs hits a 2-G gust and momentarily pops 11 Gs on the meter, for example. For this reason, airplanes experiencing turbulence must be maneuvered gently.

Another way of minimizing the spikes in lift due to turbulence is to slow down. The airplane wing produces lift based on speed and angle of attack. Turbulence causes angle of attack changes that are quite unpredictable. Slowing reduces the lift potential of the wing so that even extreme, momentary angle of attack changes do nothing more than stall the plane. Don't let the stall scare you, because even though the airplane stalls quickly in turbulence, it will unstall just as quickly when the plane moves from one bump to the next. For the pilot, the procedure in heavy turbulence is simply to slow down, keep the plane right side up, and hang on for the ride. It has exactly the same effect as slowing a car on a bumpy road; the bumps are still there, but they lose their bite.

Technique

One of the simplest techniques for averaging more time in lift than in sink is to slow in areas of lift. Slowing allows the airplane to be affected by the updraft for a longer period of time, maximizing its effects as the lift is traversed. Conversely, the pilot should increase speed when sink is encountered in order to pass through it quickly. This might often require the pilot to lower the nose and accelerate when faced with a strong downdraft. It sounds a little goofy, but increasing speed in this manner might cause less overall loss of altitude than trying to fight the downdraft by slowing to climb speed. Slowing prolongs the time the airplane is exposed to the sink and allows the sinking air to steal more altitude.

Thermalling

To use a thermal for gaining altitude requires a prolonged time spent in the thermal. Often, thermals might be so narrow of cross section that the airplane must circle tightly to stay within them. Since the thermal is invisible to the eye, the following technique can be used to find its center and stay there. This is exactly what Ben accomplished when he made the Citabria climb over the mountains.

The plane is flown at the best L/D or glide speed (conveniently close to Vy). There are two reasons for this. One, going slower than this hampers climbing performance, and two, speeds significantly faster cause the plane to pass through even big thermals before the pilot can react. When the plane penetrates an area of lift, the pilot paying careful attention will feel the lift surge before it registers on the VSI. Experience will be helpful here in making the decision to remain and circle in the thermal or to press on for a bigger one. When considering the lift worthwhile, the pilot banks the plane tightly in the direction most likely toward the thermal's core, where lift is the strongest. Simultaneously, the pilot slows the plane to Vx, which improves the tightness of the turn and maximizes climb in a confined area.

The actual location of the thermal's core is found by a hit and miss procedure. Initially, a thermal might cause one wing to rise sharply as the lift is encountered. Logically, the pilot will bank in the direction of the upended wing, hoping that lift is stronger to that side of the plane. It works great in gliders, with their huge wingspans; however, the typical airplane's response to this will be much more subdued. While the plane is tightly circling, the pilot pays careful attention to vertical speed. The pilot modifies the spiral a few yards one way or another, trying to maximize the climb. During this procedure it is equally useful for the pilot to become sensitive to the feeling of sink, as the airplane might periodically fly out of the thermal in its hunt for the core. If the pilot is successful, the airplane will be drawn to the core by gentle, natural forces within the thermal, much like a piece of scrap paper in a whirlwind. When this happens, the pilot has an express elevator ride to altitude.

A word of caution. With the airplane circling tightly at speeds very near stall, mishandling of the controls could invite an immediate spin. That would do little to improve the rate of climb. Be sure to keep the airplane well coordinated and at angles of attack less than stall at all times.

Regarding angle of bank within the thermal: Some pilots avoid steep banks while thermaling, preferring the efficiency of more moderate bank angles. Many glider pilots, however, observe that the thermal itself is the best source of lift and believe that whatever bank angle is necessary to stay in its core is most appropriate for the highest rate of climb. From a powered-pilot's perspective, the thermal is merely supplementary to the engine, and whatever bank angle is convenient for a high climb rate will be the most practical.

When through with the thermal, the pilot rolls the plane out on heading and flies away. If the pilot wants to keep looking for more thermals the speed should be set again at Vy until the plane encounters worthwhile lift again.

Catching the wave

I flew a Cessna 310 from Idaho Falls to Salt Lake City a few years ago. The course line parallels several mountain ranges all the way. The wind blew at the time, but not hard enough to produce anything more than light chop. I trimmed the plane for cruise, indicating about 180 mph, and sat back to watch the world go by. It seemed peculiar that the clouds formed into long rows, parallel to our flight path. They appeared to be lenticular shaped in cross-section, but each about 20 miles long, looking like the way cut alfalfa lays down in long rows before it's bailed. Mountain wave? I knew the wind was blowing from the west, so I adjusted the plane's course to fly just west and below one of the lines of clouds.

The plane responded with a nice climb, about 600-feet per minute. I adjusted the trim until the plane held altitude, and the airspeed settled on 195 mph. There it stayed for the rest of the flight. We were surfing on a cloud! It was fortunate that the clouds were pointing at the destination because the plane and I enjoyed an extra 15 knots groundspeed the entire trip for doing practically nothing. We could have easily lost that much speed and more by flying along the down side of the wave, but as it was, the trip was delightful.

Look for signs of mountain wave activity. If the plane is in need of a boost, maneuver into the upside of the wave. Wherever possible, avoid the downside, it might wipe out the climb performance of the best airplanes. If the course requires the plane to fly perpendicular to the wave, it is best to allow the plane to rise and fall with the air, within reason. Trying to fight it and hold altitude can be nightmarish and destroy cruise performance at the same time. Just relax and act like a piece of driftwood (Fig. 6-15).

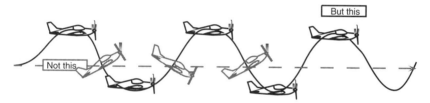

6-15 *Act like driftwood in a mountain wave.*

The turbulence that might be encountered in mountain waves is very real. Certain areas below the wave, and especially right behind the mountain crests themselves, can produce turbulence so violent that a plane flying into it could literally rain out in little pieces. Please study the conditions carefully before flying in these regions.

Ridge lift

If wind is blowing at all, nearby hills and mountain sides can provide a steady lift next to their slopes. Wind simply blows up one side of a mountain and down the other. The pilot who is aware of wind direction can maneuver the airplane in the lift on the windward side of the mountain and stay there for hours, if desired, tracking back and forth along the slope. The hapless pilot on the other side of the slope would not be so lucky, having to fight turbulence and sink in the lee of the mountain (Fig. 6-16).

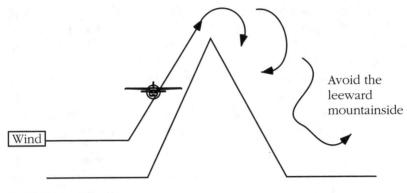

6-16 *Ridge lift.*

While turning in the vicinity of terrain, as when maneuvering in ridge lift, it is critical that the pilot carefully judge separation from the mountainside. In a course reversal, turning in directions away from the slope is often the only safe choice.

Tailwinds from thunderstorms

For a pilot tearing along in the northern hemisphere, solitary thunderstorms might provide a little push if the plane passes to the right of the clouds. Since a thunder cloud is essentially a concentrated low-pressure system, air will circulate into it with a counter-clockwise twist at low altitude. That means a pilot passing on the right of the cloud will encounter a slight tailwind, and one passing to the left will most likely face a headwind, with the strongest effects found at altitudes below the level of the cloud base (Fig. 6-17).

The procedure works great for the pilot scud-running among widely scattered thunderstorms. Be cautioned again, however; thunderstorms generate vicious aerial hazards and venturing too close to them could invite disaster. On the other hand, mild cumulus clouds also mark low pressure regions and offer impressive scenery to the pilot looking for a tailwind.

Pressure-pattern flying

On a scale much larger than thunderstorms, large pressure systems might be played to advantage in the search for favorable winds.

In Fig. 6-18, a pilot attempts to fly from Denver, Colorado, to Los Angeles, California. Over the course of the flight, weather patterns first

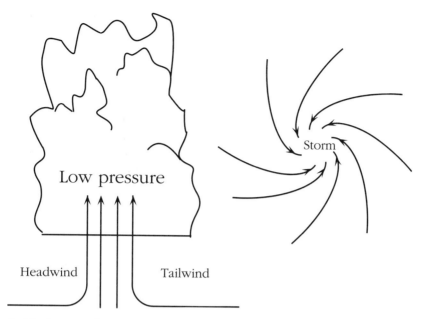

6-17 *Air circulation around a thunderstorm.*

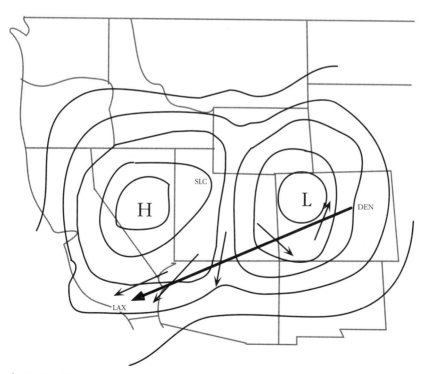

6-18 *Stubbornly navigating through pressure patterns.*

produce left crosswinds, then right crosswinds, and finally tailwinds, requiring the pilot to compensate left, right, and straight, respectively. Each time the heading is adjusted off course to maintain a straight ground track, some percentage of the plane's speed is given up to fight the wind. A couple of knots here, a few there, and the trip takes longer than necessary. There is a way for the pilot to establish a heading at the beginning that will allow the plane to drift around with the wind, and yet ultimately end up over the destination. In this way, groundspeed toward the destination is maximized because the plane has been essentially pointing at the target from the beginning. It might look like Fig. 6-19.

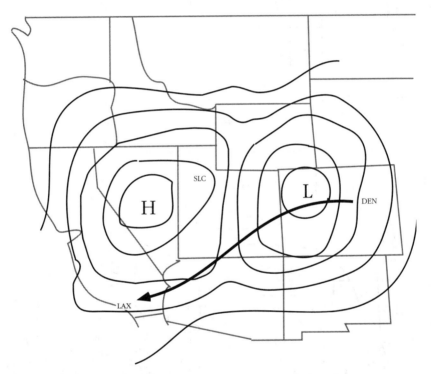

6-19 *Taking a path of least resistance on a single heading.*

The key to the procedure is a formula developed by Dr. John Bellamy that allows pilots to calculate net wind drift over the course of a flight with the use of barometric pressures from the departure and destination airports. The formula looks like Fig. 6-20:

$$\text{Drift in nautical miles} = \frac{(\text{pressure at destination} - \text{pressure at departure})\text{ K factor}}{\text{True airspeed}}$$

K factor	Latitude (degrees north)
540	22-25
480	25-28
440	28-31
400	31-34
360	34-38
330	38-43
300	43-50
270	50-55

6-20 *Recipe for pressure-pattern navigation.*

Assuming the pressure over Denver is 22.92 and pressure for the same altitude over Los Angeles is 23.10, average latitude for the trip as obtained from charts is about 35 degrees for a K factor of 360, and the airplane's true airspeed is 160 knots, the formula would look like Fig. 6-21:

$$\frac{(2292 - 2310)(360)}{160} = -40.5 \text{ Nautical miles}$$

6-21 *Pressure-pattern navigation applied.*

Notice that the decimals in the barometric pressures are dropped, and that the answer is in nautical miles of drift. A negative answer indicates drift to the left of the destination, a positive answer predicts a net drift to the right. Taking the –40.5-mile drift generated by the formula, our pilot knows that a heading aimed from Denver straight at L.A. would cause the plane to end up 40.5 miles to the left of course. The solution is to aim 40.5 miles to the right of L.A. from the beginning, and hold the heading until the plane arrives, allowing the wind to blow the airplane precisely over Los Angeles.

In this way, the pilot can minimize wind corrections and maximize actual groundspeed toward the destination. It allows the plane to follow the path of least resistance, so to speak.

Skills to practice

The skills to learn from the weather can literally occupy a lifetime. Experienced glider pilots develop an eerie sixth sense about weather and lift. For the powered pilot, efficiently using weather-generated lift to advantage also takes a lot of practice. In order to facilitate that practice and have a ball at the same time, try turning your powered plane into a glider.

I'm not suggesting that you throw away the engine and attempt to dangle from a tow-plane; just throttle back to a power setting that allows your plane to approximate the glide of a good sailplane. Set your airspeed at best glide, and adjust the power until the plane shows around 200 feet per minute descent. You are now a "glider." Go find some lift and see how long you can stay in the air. You'll learn more about weather that way than you ever will by reading a book like this one. Keep in mind that your airplane is somewhat disadvantaged in thermals by a sailplane, due to your airplane's relatively high glide speeds; but it might benefit from strong lift nonetheless.

You'll find that sunny, unstable weather produces the best thermals, ridge lift is preferred in windy weather, and when you can get them, mountain waves are incredible.

At such reduced-power settings, your airplane will burn a bare minimum of fuel, which should allow you to fly for extended periods of time at comparatively low cost. When you are skilled at finding adequate lift with power set for 200 feet per minute, try it with the throttle set even lower. Do not be tempted to actually shut off the engine to complete the glider simulation—that is sheer foolishness. Simply enjoy the safety a running engine provides, and if you find yourself too low, just advance the power and look for lift elsewhere (Fig. 6-22).

The skills you'll develop in this manner could be invaluable in an emergency situation. A famous dead-stick landing of a Boeing 767 was possible because the plane's captain had some glider experience. He used various forms of lift to stretch the powerless plane's glide more than 200 miles from cruise altitude, finally landing in a place called Gimly. Thus was born the "Gimly Glider."

6-22 *Develop a sixth sense for weather—think like a glider pilot.*

Further reading

Aviation Weather, FAA AC 00-6A, 1975
The Joy of Soaring, Conway, Soaring Society of America
Proficient Pilot, Barry Schiff, Aircraft Owners and Pilots Association, 1980
Song of the Sky, Guy Murchie, Ziff-Davis Publishing Co., 1954
Wind, Sand and Stars, Antoine De Saint-Exupery, HBJ Books, 1967

7

Maneuvering

It has been said that the road to good judgment is paved with experience and experience is created by bad judgment.

The rented Cessna 172 was a little dirty, but certainly adequate for a local flight. I wanted to be as impressive as possible with my newly found skills and made a little show about every slight technicality I could find during the preflight, my hands unnecessarily flitting about the instrument panel in what I believed was an impressive display of aeronautical prowess.

There I was, 18 years old with almost 80 hours in my logbook, a private pilot, like Walter Mitty at his best. I could have been flying the space shuttle. It didn't get any better than that. I finally looked over at my friend Ron, whom I quite expected to be in a rapturous state of awe with my flying abilities. He appeared unimpressed with me, paying attention to the view out the window. I looked away, silently wishing for some aerobatic skills. I thought he'd be impressed if I could show him that view upside down.

Ron commented that an airplane ride was not the sky-in-your-face wrestling match with death that I had played it out to be. He said it was more like riding around in a car that had a great view. I said sure, but your car can't go this fast, referring him to the airspeed indicator's blistering 105 kts. I secretly wished we were in an F-16.

We were flying south along the Wasatch Mountain Range, and the view, in spite of me, was indeed fantastic. As we passed one of the canyons, the ground seemed to climb into the clouds. The overcast hung about in the midst of the rocks like a brilliant veil of draperies and the canyon road wound dark and cavernous among the cliffs. I asked Ron if he would like to go up the canyon and inspect the snow conditions at Snowbird ski resort. He nodded. Surely *this* ought to be impressive, I thought. Somewhere in the back of my head I began to hear the admonitions of my Dad. He had said something about the inherent dangers of flying around in these mountains, but I couldn't think of anything in particular, and I felt that I could always turn around. Besides, we were almost 6500 feet high (Fig. 7-1). What could go wrong?

7-1 *What could go wrong?*

As we entered the canyon, it was soon apparent that we could not progress much farther without penetrating the scattered veil of clouds. I began to turn from the middle of the canyon, but the rocky crags rushed over to meet the airplane with such alarming speed that I turned back to my original heading. We were too close, I thought. I flew more to one side of the canyon, carefully checked airspeed and raked into a steeper turn. The rocks on the other side rushed the plane with equal aggression and again forced me to back down and resume my original course. The clouds were really close by then. I couldn't turn around. At 6500 feet the canyon was too narrow. It was then that I considered what lay ahead.

Snowbird was one of a couple of ski resorts near the end of Little Cottonwood Canyon, which is short in length and very steep. The mountains to either side are well above 10,000 feet. The canyon terminates in a beautiful glacier-formed basin, which contains the resorts, the floor of the basin being 9000 feet and ringed on all sides with rocky cliffs. It is an awe-inspiring sight from the ground and truly spectacular from the air. But I couldn't see it, as about then we penetrated the clouds.

Fear caused little beads of sweat to ooze from my face and I began to breathe rapidly. I was blindfolded, a prisoner facing the firing squad. The situation might have been different had I been able to see. I could have seen the ground reach skyward faster than the airplane could climb, perhaps with me making repeated attempts to turn out of a canyon already too narrow for escape. I might have dodged the ever-present cliffs to crash-land in the trees near the mountain road. But being blind like this, like driving lead-foot through a canyon with your eyes closed, all I could do was prepare for impact.

My 1.4 hours of instrument experience was inadequate, mountains or not. To remain in the clouds very long would mean disorientation, vertigo, and a screaming dive into the heart of the earth. I held the wings level, maintained heading and established a climb speed of 59 kts—the best angle climb—for what it's worth. We emerged from the clouds briefly, crossing a break in the overcast with water droplets on the windshield and a cold flood of sweat on my forehead. I noticed that we were headed a little askew of the road below and turned slightly to match it. We entered clouds again. Luminescent from the outside, the clouds felt like a cold, smothering shroud from within. It was like putting my head under water. I could hardly think and wanted to hold my breath . . . maintain wings level . . . What was that heading again? Ron still had his face pasted to the window and was making some observations about the view. I'm sure he said quite a bit, but I heard only two of his comments: "Wow, it's really neat inside these clouds," and "Oh look, I can just see the cliffs out this side of the plane." My head jerked that way in time to see the cliffs passing eerily off the right wing tip. I banked slightly left and they faded away in a cloudy gloom. Some pine trees appeared out my window, raking by like bony fingers trying to snag us. I banked a little to the right. The light dimmed as we slipped farther into the overcast, plunging deeper into an airborne sea. My feet began to shake uncontrollably on the rudders. I tried to stop them by pressing hard on both pedals, but it didn't help.

"We're dead," I thought. The altimeter was just passing 8000 feet, breaks in the clouds were less frequent and I had no idea exactly where we were. The cliffs to either side were invisible; the boxed end of the canyon waited somewhere ahead. I was beginning to lose control. The stall horn sounded—we were trying to climb too steeply. I lowered the nose. Any minute now—I wondered how it would be. Would I have time to react, or would our bubble suddenly burst with an explosion of rock and charred aluminum? Would we actually make it to the end of the canyon, or scrape and tumble along the sides? I considered telling Ron, but maybe the morticians would prefer him peaceful. My lips began to quiver, and inside I began to pray.

Ron saw skiers down there. Then I saw the wires of the Snowbird aerial tramway go by. They were *close*. This is it for sure, I thought. I was in agony waiting to be hit, flinching at thoughts of crushing cold and granite rock. I banked hard left. I'll take the side of the canyon. Turn now. Die now? I didn't care. No more waiting. It's over. I could feel the unseen canyon walls rushing the airplane. I made no attempt to maintain altitude. Just make it quick. I wanted to close my eyes.

It took a few years for me to understand what happened next. The airplane simply turned around, with little help from me, and descended out of the cloud layer. The one saving element was a slower airplane. I had unwittingly slowed to 59 knots in a dismal effort to climb. A slow airplane will turn much tighter than a fast one. For me, inexperienced and frightened, lost in the canyon, blindly turning against invisible granite rock, it was a miracle.

Ron was still talking about the view. It was beautiful. I could have cried. The airplane was diving away from the clouds in a steep left bank. We were most of the way through the turn. The mouth of the canyon stood ahead like the pearly gates, sunlight splashing behind it from breaks in the overcast. We poured out of the canyon and flushed across the valley to Municipal Airport II. I didn't want to fly anymore. I wanted to stand on the ground. I wanted to stop shaking.

The landing was a fluke. It was a good one, the rare greaser that seems to surprise you when you're not really trying. Taxiing in, I began to feel better. I must be good, to look death in the face and land like that. Good thing I didn't tell Ron. I was going to act like this was all in a day's work. We stopped. I opened the door and stepped outside. My knees buckled, and I fell like a soggy towel onto the left main gear. I would have sucked my thumb had I thought about it. Ron said, "Are you okay?"

Background information

Had I known the secret of really tight turns it would have been easy to get out of the foregoing situation before it was serious. The secret is to slow down.

Speed and turn radius

To explain the inflight relationship between speed and turn radius first requires a careful look at a car. In an automobile, the physical position of the front wheels in relation to the rear defines the path that the car will follow. Short of a skid, the prescribed track will not change whether it is driven slowly or very fast. The occupants, on the other hand, will experience a greater lateral acceleration (sideways G) with the higher speeds. So the driver of a car manipulates the steering wheel to define the turn radius, and that radius is constant regardless of speed. It is the load factor, or sideways G, that is variable with speed.

Unlike a car, an airplane can maintain the load factor in level flight constant while the turn radius changes with speed. For example, referring to Table 7-1 we see that a level turn at 60 degrees bank requires lift totaling twice the weight of the airplane, or two Gs. If the airplane were traveling at Mach 3+, like an SR-71, or 90 knots with a Cessna 152, the pilots would still be burdened with two Gs. No more. No less. But the turn radii are radically different. The difference lies in the fact that the Cessna might be doing several lazy pirouettes around a big moose down there while the Spy plane is blasting through Utah, Idaho, and half of Canada before it turns even once.

Table 7-1
Bank angle and load factor.

Angle of bank	Load factor
0	1.00
15	1.04
30	1.15
45	1.41
60	2.00

Note: Valid only for turns in level flight

The pilot can manipulate the controls to produce a bank and the direction of lift is changed, creating the horizontal lift component that produces the turn. Imagine an arrow that is always perpendicular to the wings showing both the direction and intensity of the wing's lift (Fig. 7-2). It is the lift vector. Since a bank causes the lift vector to angle off to one side, its influence could be broken down into a part pulling to resist gravity (vertical arrow), and another part causing a turn (horizontal arrow). The horizontal part, or horizontal component of the lift vector, is the key to turning. The magnitude or intensity of the total lift vector illustrates how much lift, or load factor, the wings are producing.

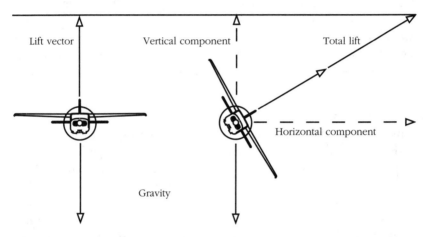

7-2 *Lift vector and bank.*

Angle of bank determines the load factor in level flight. Imagine the airplane in the figure rolling through several bank angles, with the lift vector always needing to produce enough lift in a vertical component to oppose gravity. You can visualize that steeper banks require progressively greater load factors to keep the airplane in level flight. By level flight I mean that the airplane is neither climbing nor descending through the turn. Again, the load factor remains constant at all speeds for a given angle of bank. The airplane has the uncanny ability to naturally modify the tightness of the turn to match the speed it flies. If a fighter plane were to match the tight turn of a Cessna 152, it would need bank angles approaching 90 degrees and ridiculous G loadings just to stay over the field. The pilots of the 152 might scoff, but if they were traveling that fast, they'd have squashed faces and wear funny suits, too.

When I slowed the Cessna in that frightful situation among the cliffs, I wanted only to climb. Best climb speed for that model 172 is 59 knots, far slower than the 105 knots possible at cruise. I had attempted first to turn in visual conditions from full cruise speed. The turns were quite steep, probably near 60 degrees of bank. However, at cruise speed in a 172 this turn was not sufficiently tight to fit in the canyon. Later, at 59 knots, roughly half of the original speed, the airplane turned easily inside the canyon. That turn was also at least 60 degrees of bank.

The story illustrates the relationship between the tightness of a turn and the airplane's speed. If the pilot wants to turn quickly, the plane has to slow down. You might ask why bother with a slow turn anyway? I've heard pilots say that they will never, ever wind up in a situation like mine in the canyon, and heavy maneuvering near stall speed is just inviting trouble. Sure, I say. And to avoid any serious maneuvering at slow speeds you might just want to avoid rotating for takeoff, or flaring to land, or turning base to final. You might even avoid flying at all in wind, because the wind has related effects during ground-reference maneuvers. This is a valuable lesson and skill. If pilots were better skilled in the techniques described here, there wouldn't be so many stall/spin accidents in the landing pattern, let alone bad landings on the runway.

Lift

We are taught from the first day of ground school that lift is an essential force among the primary four that pull on an airplane. We are then led into a complicated and often confusing series of explanations involving a dead Swiss scientist (Bernoulli) and low-pressure airflow. These explanations are true, of course, but difficult for a pilot to visualize and apply. When it is boiled down and scrubbed, lift is still just a force.

The airflow around a wing can be extremely complicated, and for our purposes it is not worth explaining, except for two simple facts that you might remember from your high-school physics class: In order for the airplane to go up, it has to push a lot of air down (for each action, there is an equal and opposite reaction), and a force results from an accelerated mass ($F = ma$). If the airplane accelerates an air mass down, the force results in the opposite direction, which makes the airplane go up. Simple.

Looking at Newton's declaration in more specific terms would give us this: Lift (force) is equal to airspeed (mass) times angle of attack (acceleration).

The pilot can control lift by varying airspeed and angle of attack. Increased airspeed allows the wing to affect a much greater volume of air, effectively increasing the available mass that can be acted upon. Increasing angle of attack gives a firmer downward push to the passing air. If we assume that the amount of lift required is approximately equal to the weight of the airplane, we observe an inverse relationship between speed and angle of attack. If the airplane is flying slowly, that is affecting a small amount of air, the angle of attack must be relatively high in order to support the weight. As the plane gains speed, the airplane will develop more lift and the pilot must reduce the angle of attack to maintain level flight (Fig. 7-3).

7-3 *Maule flying at high angle of attack and 28 mph indicated. The flight path is parallel to the ground.*

The stall

No discussion of lift would be complete without a look at the stall. Many pilots believe that a stall is caused by flying too slowly. This is inaccurate. *A stall occurs when the wing is flown at too great an angle of attack. Period.*

A snap roll is proof that angle of attack, not airspeed, causes a stall. This maneuver is executed by first pulling hard on the stick to initiate a stall and then literally spinning the airplane with the rudder. It is usually done at a speed well above stall speed to make the roll happen faster. The airplane does not need to slow down to stall.

The concept of *stall speed* exists because of the inverse relationship between airspeed and angle of attack; that is, the plane is flying slowly so the angle of attack must necessarily be high. The stall speed, then, is the speed that requires a maximum angle of attack in order to produce enough lift to fly.

Angle of bank and stall speed

What about the increase in stall speed at high bank angles? I knew one pilot, a doctor, who was so concerned about stall speed in a bank that he posted the manual's figures dead center on his airplane's instrument panel. It looked something like Table 7-2.

Table 7-2 Stall speed.

Angle of bank (degrees)	Speed (mph)
Level	72
30	77
45	85
60	101

I suppose he was convinced that if he were flying along at 80 mph and happened to roll to a 60-degree bank, the airplane would stall. Fortunately, that is not so. The facts behind the stall speed question are wonderfully simple. I'll show you.

Most pilots should be familiar with the technical reasons why an airplane turns, that the horizontal component of lift causes the airplane to change direction. I try to explain this to my aerobatic students with the following visual imagery. See yourself in the cockpit with a big golden pointer poking out the top of your head. This is the direction of the wing's lift, or lift vector. If the wing is lifting hard, the vector is long, or has a high magnitude. If it is short, the wing is hardly working. Throughout a normal flight, the magnitude and direction of the lift vector are often rapidly changing. When the wings are level with respect to the horizon, 100 percent of the lift directly opposes gravity. If the airplane is rolled to a 45-degree right bank, half the lift is resisting gravity and the other half is pulling the airplane to the right, causing a turn. If the plane is rolled to a 90-degree bank, all the lift will cause the plane to turn and none will make it fly. The airplane will descend unless it has some other source of lift.

Figure 7-2 is a visual depiction of an airplane in a steep bank as compared to an airplane with wings level. Notice that the banked airplane must produce much greater total lift—through increased angle of attack—just to maintain level flight. This is why airplanes in this situation experience a higher stall speed. If the wing is producing lift equal to several times the weight of the airplane it will stall at a higher speed. The wing behaves as if the lift it is required to produce *is* the weight of the airplane, and we all know that a heavy airplane stalls at higher speeds than a lightly loaded one.

My friend's airplane, a Beech C 23, has a gross weight of 2450 pounds. When it is flown at 72 miles per hour and maximum angle of attack, it can produce 2450 pounds of lift. If all of that lift were directed vertically, the airplane could maintain level flight at 72 mph. By level flight I mean that the plane is neither climbing nor descending. If the pilot were to bank the airplane to 30 degrees, the direction of lift, or lift vector, would no longer be vertical. In doing so, some of the airplane's total lift is used to pull the airplane to a new course. Great, but at 72 mph there is not sufficient lift to sustain level flight as long as some percentage of the total lift is used to turn the plane. In a typical turn, the pilot simply pulls a little harder on the yoke to compensate for lift diminished by bank angle. In this turn, however, the plane at 72 mph is already at maximum angle of attack and the plane will stall if the pilot pulls any harder. The problem is the amount of lift available. If the pilot can't increase angle of attack, then the only remaining option is to fly faster. According to the manual, 77 mph is sufficient to produce a vertical lift component equal to 2450 pounds in direct opposition to gravity while the airplane is banked 30 degrees; and 101 mph is minimal for 60 degrees. "Okay," my friend would say, "you haven't told me anything other than what I already know." I'll go further.

Who said that the pilot has to maintain level flight in the turn? As long as the pilot does not exceed the critical angle of attack, the airplane *will not* stall. Angle of bank by itself has nothing to do with angle of attack. Even the sacred stall speed itself does not guarantee stalled flight.

All of the figures given for stall speed and angle of bank imply one very critical item: The pilot is maintaining level flight in the turn. Angle of bank taken by itself is not going to stall the airplane. If the pilot turns steeply from a slow speed, level flight might be impossible but the turn can still occur and control be maintained. The pilot merely has to give up some altitude to remain in controlled flight. Figure 7-4 depicts an airplane in a hard turn at minimum speed.

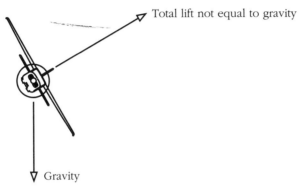

Total lift not equal to gravity

Gravity

7-4 *A hard turn at minimum speed.*

The principle was first demonstrated to me by a now-retired flight examiner. He asked me to fly the Piper Arrow at minimum speed, which I did, the airspeed needle hovering just above a stall. Then he requested that I demonstrate a turn while maintaining that speed. I complied by placing the airplane into a coordinated 10-degree left bank. He asked me to go to a 60-degree left bank and maintain the speed. I looked at him with something akin to an expression of shock. He nodded, and I hesitantly complied. The airplane had insufficient power and lift to maintain level flight at the slow speed in the turn, which required me to lower the nose and descend. By descending the required lift was reduced and the stall was prevented. The examiner wanted to see that I would do just that, and keep the airplane in controlled flight. I observed two things from the experience: first, that a steep turn can be accomplished at minimum speed if the airplane is allowed to descend, and second, that we were pointing the other direction almost instantly.

The fateful turn out of the canyon was like this. The airplane was near minimum speed and I turned at a very steep angle. I made no effort to maintain altitude and thus prevented the stall. The result, of course, was that I am able to write this 12 years later. The turn could have been even tighter if I had extended the wing flaps in an effort to slow down even more before beginning the turn.

Stall speed and load factor

Load factor is a measurement of the lift, or load, on an airplane wing expressed in units of gravity. One G means that the wing is lifting *one times the weight of the airplane*. It also means that the airplane structure is having to endure the same forces produced by the wing; that is, supporting one G, or the weight of the airplane. If the plane were at five Gs, the wings would be producing lift equal to five times the aircraft's weight, and the structure would be supporting the same.

The lift required of an airplane wing is rarely constant, in fact, the only real consistency is that the lift is constantly changing. For example, as an airplane roars down the runway, accelerating to flight speed, the lift potential of the wing grows rapidly. When the pilot's control movement lifts the nose wheel from the runway and points it skyward, the lift rapidly increases with the increased angle of attack, and the airplane lifts from the ground. As the pilot turns on course, the wings are banked and lift is again increased to sustain the climb in the turn, then reduced as the wings are leveled. When the airplane accelerates to cruise speed, the variations in angle of attack become more subtle, due to the high lift potential at speed. Throughout the trip, turbulence might cause minor changes in angle of attack, which momentarily boost the lift, and occasionally kill it, which the pilot feels as bumps. If the pilot makes an adjustment in altitude, lift is modified to make the change. Any time the airplane's direction is changed, whether up or down, left or right, it is accomplished by a controlled variation of lift.

The lift potential of an airplane wing is directly related to its speed. The wing has a limited range of angle of attack with which to work. If the critical angle of attack is exceeded, lift is lost and a stall occurs. Stall speed is the minimum forward speed at which the wing can produce lift equaling one G at maximum angle of attack. If the airplane is flown faster than stall speed, lift greater than one G is possible. If the pilot desires to perform maneuvers requiring lift in excess of one G, speeds greater than stall are necessary. The stall speeds in level turns reflect this speed requirement and are directly related to the load factor necessary for the turn. If a two-G level turn (60 degrees bank) is desired, then the pilot must fly the plane at least fast enough to produce two Gs worth of lift. Obviously, if the airplane is flying at speeds with lift potential greater than two Gs, the pilot simply moderates the angle of attack accordingly; he doesn't pull as hard. The relationship of angle of attack and lift, and lift and G, is where the term *pulling Gs* comes from. To increase angle of attack, the pilot *pulls* on the elevator control.

A great illustration of Gs, turn radius, and load factor can be found in the barnstormer's pet maneuver, looping the loop. The pilot, in this case, desires to perform a 360-degree turn in the vertical plane, fly a circle stood on end. This involves a continuous change in the airplane's direction of flight, and lift in excess of one G is required. Typically, the maneuver requires a minimum of three Gs, often more. So here comes the intrepid barnstormer pilot in his Waco biplane. Stall for the Waco is 55 mph. Our pilot, however, tears by at 140 mph with his silk flying scarf flapping in the breeze. At 140 mph, plenty of lift is available for a loop. The pilot pulls on the stick until he feels his face and body sag with the weight of 3.5 Gs. The airplane's nose comes up rapidly, going through the horizon and nearing vertical. As the airplane's flight path changes through the vertical, gravity and aerodynamic drag combine to cause a *rapid* loss of airspeed. Lost airspeed means lost lift, and a tighter turn radius. Believe it or not, this is easily managed by the pilot. As speed bleeds—gushes—away, the pilot must relax the elevator pressure. The airplane, now quite slow, can no longer produce 3.5 Gs of lift. Possible G loading has diminished with the speed. The pilot moderates the pressure on the elevator controls both to prevent the stall and also to widen the loop's arc. If the pilot did not back off the elevator, the loop would run the risk of becoming a sort of flop. No longer round, the radius would substantially tighten over the top due to the airplane's slow speed, making a sort of cursive letter "l." The airplane at the top of the loop has almost neutral elevator position and *zero* G. At this point, stall speed is irrelevant. The wing is producing no lift and the critical angle of attack has not been exceeded. At speeds so slow they don't quite register on the airspeed indicator, lift potential is almost nil. Angle of attack is neutral. The airplane sort of orbits over the top in weightlessness, the nose describing a lovely arc, falling back towards the ground. Half done, the airplane starts down. As speed increases, the loop risks becoming wider, but potential lift also increases. The pilot applies more elevator. Increased G and high speed at the bottom of the loop keeps the radius of the arc about the same as it was over the top.

Load factor and drag

Since the very beginning of ground school, we are informed that airplanes are affected by a combination of parasite and induced drag. Parasite drag is associated with the forward motion of the airplane. The faster the airplane moves, the greater the air's resistance to it. Induced drag, on the other hand, is *lift* induced. The greater the lift, the greater the lift-induced drag.

It would seem logical, then, that an airplane at high load factors is experiencing an increased amount of induced drag. The drag increase under load can be so great that it becomes an effective speed control mechanism. Conversely, an airplane under power will accelerate fastest with the wing completely *un*loaded—zero G. This is commonly practiced by fighter pilots when the need arises for a rapid escape; they push the throttle forward and shove the stick to weightlessness to maximize acceleration.

An air force instructor-pilot recommends that students flying the T-38 perform the loop maneuver by establishing a speed of 500 mph at 10,000 feet msl. The aircraft is pulled to six Gs and flown over the top at 20,000 feet. As the plane arcs downward, the throttle remains forward and the pilot controls the speed with load factor, increasing the load to retard acceleration. Similarly, the commercial-pilot flight test requires a demonstration of a steep spiral. In this case, speed control during the 60-degree bank spiral is best maintained by variation of load factor.

Maneuvering speed

As long as we're on the subject of maneuvering, we should discuss the limiting factors. Maneuvering speed is the result of a structural limitation on the airframe. Currently, a normal category airplane is certificated capable of withstanding 3.7 Gs of stress, or lift. Exceed that, and the pilot runs the risk of bending or breaking something. The capacity for exceeding the load limits of an airplane are related directly to the airplane's speed. Remember, potential lift, or load, increases with speed. An airplane flying at stall speed cannot be overstressed. The wing will stall at or very near one G.

There is some speed, faster than stall, at which the lift available equals 3.7 Gs. This is maneuvering speed. If the pilot were flying at maneuvering speed, theoretically, the elevator control could be pulled to the stop and the airplane would go to 3.7 Gs before stalling, or unloading, the lift. If the airplane were even a smidgen faster, the load limit might be exceeded before the wing stalls. In theory, a plane flown at or below maneuvering speed would be incapable of doing itself damage from aerodynamic forces. The plane should always stall and unload the lift before structural damage is done. That's theory, of course. Snap rolls and the like at maneuvering speed are best not tried "at home."

One of the peculiar features of maneuvering speed is the way it changes with different weights. If an airplane were lighter, maneuvering speed would be *slower*. That seems a little weird, but is true. Suppose we fly an airplane that weighs 1000 pounds and is rated at five Gs. The wing at maneuvering speed might produce 5000 pounds of lift. If the same airplane were lighter by half, weighing 500 pounds, maneuvering speed would be much too fast—5000 pounds of lift would suddenly become ten Gs.[1] Okay, you say, the wing will still support 5000 pounds of lift without breaking, and that fact does not change, regardless of the weight of the airplane. True, the wings might not fall off but all is not well. You see, the whole plane, not just the wings, is stressed to five Gs. Certain components in the plane have *not* changed weight. These might include the flooring under the pilot seat, instrument panel mounts, the instruments themselves, etc. This means that at ten Gs, a floor rated for five Gs might cave in and send the pilot out through the bottom of the plane. Therefore, in order to preserve G limits for the weakest part of the airplane structure, maneuvering speed must be reduced for lighter aircraft weights.

On the other hand, the load limit itself might be raised somewhat for an airplane at lighter weights if the wings and ancillary structures are compatible to the load. This is common with military airplanes. Where an F-16 might be loaded with bombs and ammunition, the load limit might be reduced to reflect the weight of the airplane, or perhaps to accommodate the load sensitivity of the more delicate cargo. After the airplane has dropped its stores, the allowable load limit might be increased again, reflecting lighter weights and the

1 The lighter weight has a slower stall speed and a lower total lift requirement to reach maximum G. This results in a much slower Va, or maneuvering speed.

need for combat maneuvering, etc. For the pilot of the typical general aviation airplane, the load limit increase at light weight can be disappointingly small, perhaps a step from normal category limits up to those of the utility category, an increase from 3.7 to 4.4 Gs. These limits are commonly indicated in the aircraft manual, if it has one.

The concept of negative load also needs some attention. Certification rules dictate that the normal category airplane withstand –1.5 G. Negative G is lift force in the opposite direction of positive load. A 1.5-G limit might seem decidedly weak, but most airplane wings are lousy fliers when they are upside down. I used to instruct in a Citabria that would do beautiful inside loops. Upright, it would stall at less than 50 mph. Upside down, it could barely sustain itself at 102 mph. Full speed inverted was 105 mph, anyway—fat chance of making enough lift to break the 2-G negative limit without exceeding other parameters, like *never exceed speed* (Vne) in the process.

I knew another pilot who taught taildragger skills in the same Citabria. He was not qualified in aerobatics, but one day made this startling announcement: "I did an outside loop in the Citabria." Having flown that airplane quite a bit upside down, I had to ask how he did it. He seemed very excited and enthusiastic as he told the story:

> *I was out with a friend over the lake. I did three aileron rolls and came out of them headed straight down. The airspeed indicator was going through about 180 mph and I thought, 'Hey, why not push it on through,' so I did. The engine quit as soon as I started pushing on the stick, but the plane sort of coasted around and kind of stalled coming up the other side. It was great!*

I thought he was kidding and watched his face carefully. He was serious. I considered what he was telling me. To be going straight down after doing aileron rolls means that he messed them up. To be doing 180 mph in the dive meant that he forgot to throttle back, probably exceeding the RPM limitation. The Citabria's red line is 150 mph. At 180 there might be enough negative lift available to do the loop, but it would take about three negative Gs and the airplane was stressed for only two. The airplane had no inverted system, so of course the engine would quit when he went negative. I asked him if he was aware that the plane was *way* outside of its limits on that one. "Sure," he said, "but that's what the parachutes are for."

I walked over to where the airplane was parked. A simple inspection revealed a host of problems. The front windshield was loose in its mountings, the engine was leaking more oil than usual, the left wing could be jiggled at the root, where it attached to the fuselage. The left aileron attachment brackets showed signs of stress and were loose, with two wing ribs broken, one inboard and one outboard of the aileron itself. That pilot was lucky to be alive. I had one last thought. If he was pushing negative Gs in a high-wing, strut-braced airplane, and the wing had broken, it would have folded around the fuselage, blocking the cabin door. Parachutes would have been useless.

To this day, if I get on some airliner and see him in one of the cockpit seats, I'm getting back off.

The spin

Along with all of this slow-flight maneuvering and stalls, comes the danger of spins. This is the evil lurking behind the stall. For inexperienced pilots, it would seem like some kind of tornado vortex that can violently grab a plane, spin the pilot dizzy, and spike him at the ground like a football in the end zone. It is why some of these pilots visibly shake at the prospect of stalls and slow flight.

The spin falls into the category of poststall maneuvering. The airplane must first be stalled in order to spin. The spin usually develops from some yaw or roll input during the stall. The input generally stems from propeller or torque factors, or perhaps incorrect positioning of the flight controls. Often, poor rigging of the airplane wings or tail will also cause the aircraft to depart the stall in a spin.

Once the airplane is established in the spin, a strong rotational inertia can develop. The airplane behaves like a big flywheel. This rotational energy can be difficult to overcome with flight controls that often have only rudimentary effectiveness in stalled flight. It is imperative, therefore, that the pilot recognize the spin in its very early stages and initiate appropriate recovery procedures before the rotation fully develops. Failure to do so might lead to a spin situation that is unrecoverable.

The FAA believes that simple avoidance of the stall is sufficient to prevent the spin. Where private-pilot check rides once required that the pilot demonstrate spins and spin recoveries, current practices dictate only stalls and stall avoidance. The FAA's argument is that airplanes are more spin resistant than they used to be, and spin training itself involves certain risks. So, the requirement to demonstrate spins has been relegated solely to the domain of candidates for flight-instructor certificates. I believe that by making this decision, the agency overlooks a serious and potentially threatening aspect of flight for all pilots.

Lack of spin experience can prevent the pilot from recognizing a developed spin, let alone recovering from it. I have routinely placed flight-instructor candidates into various types of spin gyrations. Many of these excellent pilots fail to realize that they are spinning, and because of this their recovery actions are often erroneous. I know it seems odd, that with the airplane pointed down and rotating that the pilot does not recognize the spin, but it works like this. The airplane appears to be pointed straight down. The pilot's natural reaction is to pull back, having never before experienced a stall with the nose so far down. Secondly, the airplane is rotating, sometimes rather violently. Again, the pilot reacts with opposite aileron and in doing so, holds the airplane squarely in the spin until it hits the ground. Several crashes have occurred this way, the pilot pulling fiercely on the controls all the way to death.[2] The only solution to the problem of spin recognition is to gain experience with spins of all types under carefully controlled conditions. The conditions should include an aerobatic airplane that is capable of all types of spins and strong enough to allow for training mistakes. The instructor should be well versed in spin dynamics for that airplane. The goal is to allow the pilot to quickly *recognize* a spin and immediately begin recovery.

In general, the following actions will bring about a prompt spin recovery in nearly all aircraft types; this recovery method also works for nonspin situations in which the pilot might be disoriented:

1 Throttle back to idle, or lowest in-flight setting. This slows the spin development, making the maneuver gyrations less energetic.

2 Neutralize all flight controls. The last control input the pilot made is usually the wrong one. Bringing the controls to neutral allows the inherent stability of the airplane to take effect.

2 See the story introduction for Chapter 1, for an example.

3 Identify the spin direction and apply opposite rudder. By this time, the airplane is usually unstalled and flying again.

This approach to spin recovery is called the Beggs recovery technique. It has been carefully developed by experienced pilots and works well, but still requires experience and training to be useful. Please don't try this without a competent instructor. Many first timers can't even remember rule number one when the world goes topsy-turvy. Remember: Power-off, Hands-off, and Opposite Rudder.

The aileron stall

Here is yet another caution of near-stall maneuvering. This one can bring about a spin departure to the complete surprise of the pilot. It is caused when the ailerons are abruptly or aggressively used during slow flight. Rolling to the right, for example, is accomplished by moving the right aileron up, lessening angle of attack in that area, while the left aileron deflects downward, increasing angle of attack at that side. Basically, the left wing sits at a higher angle of attack than the right one. If this is done to extremes when both wings are already near maximum angle of attack, the down aileron might exceed critical angle of attack, and stall. The result is a rapid—and I mean *rapid*—roll over to the stalled side, followed by a spin.

This phenomenon is easily avoided by smoothness of control input. A pilot making ham-handed control inputs is just inviting trouble. If the pilot is delicate on the controls, applying gentle pressures to accomplish the necessary maneuvering, the angle of attack differences between the wings will be slight and this type of stall effectively avoided.

The concept of energy

Energy is an important factor in maneuvering. It is defined as the airplane's capacity to work, a measure of its capability to move. Energy also has a direct bearing on an airplane's ability to maneuver. Energy is defined as the combination of altitude and airspeed. In general, flight is safest under conditions of relatively high energy, and dangerous when energy gets low.

If we go back to the intrepid barnstormer pilot in the Waco biplane discussed in the stall speed and load factor section, we see a dramatic illustration of energy. As the plane was pulled up into the loop, it was high on energy due to its relatively high speed. At the top of the loop, speed (kinetic) energy had been traded for altitude, or potential energy. Down the backside of the loop, the altitude was again converted into speed. The total energy of the airplane, altitude plus speed, remained almost unchanged throughout the maneuver.

If we look at energy from another standpoint it might have a more practical interpretation. Suppose we are sitting in a Cessna 152 that is dangling from a hot-air balloon. If the balloon were, say, 100 feet high, there is no way we would allow the airplane to fall. From only 100 feet, the plane couldn't develop sufficient speed to fly and we would hit the ground. If the drop were from 10,000 feet it would be another story. From that high, the airplane would fall a while, develop flying speed, and fly away. The situational difference between the two starts is potential energy. The higher drop afforded sufficient energy to fly, the lower one did not. Now suppose the airplane were to fall from the lower altitude while moving forward at 100 mph. Things would be altogether different. At 100 mph and 100-feet high, a Cessna 152 has plenty of energy to climb away from the balloon. Energy, then, is the capacity of the airplane to fly, and is a combination of altitude and airspeed.

The pilot must play energy to advantage for successful maneuvering. The barnstormer performed a loop by trading airspeed for altitude and then back again. Aerobatics in the Citabria is a similar story. We climb to altitude for several minutes before maneuvering. Once high enough, we dive for airspeed and loop and roll and so on, each time trading some altitude for airspeed in the process. After a few maneuvers, the airplane would be down on energy, and low. We commence a climb back to altitude before doing it all over again. The Pitts is another story. With its huge engine comes a capacity to gain energy quickly. The Pitts can loop from level flight, without requiring a dive to gain airspeed. In fact, in a Pitts, a skilled pilot could perform the same aerobatic maneuvers as the Citabria and *gain* altitude, increasing overall energy. The capacity to gain energy is generally related to the power of a given airplane and can be an important safety factor. This is probably one of the reasons why one of the world's safest airliners is also among the most powerful—the supersonic Concorde.

When maneuvering, the pilot should play the energy state of the airplane so that there is never a need to rapidly gain energy. Referring to my experience in the canyon at the beginning of this chapter, the C-172 was caught at the mouth of the canyon with a dire need to climb. The need exceeded the airplane's ability and I was nearly history. Ron, on the other hand, later said that he thought the airplane could just go vertical and fly out of the canyon—like an F-16. How would it be? Unfortunately, the C-172 does not have the 50,000 hp of the fighter plane. A better energy situation in the canyon would be to explore it from the top down, flying down the canyon toward the mouth, a condition of trying to dissipate energy rather than build it.

At times when the airplane is required to maneuver in close proximity to the ground, such as in crop dusting, the energy state is a large factor in the pilot's mind. It is critical that energy be maintained, not allowed to dissipate, or the airplane could easily crash. The duster pilot's techniques for managing energy and turning will be discussed in the following section.

Consider an emergency, like an engine failure. If the plane is at high altitude when the engine quits, the pilot has energy stored in the altitude with which to glide around and find a suitable landing place. If the plane is at low total energy, that is, low to the ground and at slow airspeed, the condition becomes somewhat perilous. Getting caught low and slow is an oft-spoken recipe for disaster. See an airplane on final. Power back, flaps down, a couple of hundred feet high with the runway ahead. Now introduce windshear and the plane hits dirt. If the airplane were high on energy, the windshear could be effectively countered.

But on the other hand, the need to dissipate energy is a common one. A plane that is high on energy becomes very dangerous while trying to land. Energy as a capacity to fly is also the capacity to do damage when the plane is flown into something hard, like a runway. Ideally, the pilot should allow the airplane to touch ground with a bare minimum of energy remaining. In doing so, the airplane is less capable of doing damage to itself or other structures and easier to stop. Dissipating energy becomes a *critical* factor when maneuvering for a short-field or emergency landing.

Groundspeed and maneuvering

Groundspeed might at first seem unrelated to maneuvering, but it is actually quite important. Most maneuvering is done in reference to objects on the ground: using the runway and traffic pattern, turning out of canyons, following a road, chasing bear, etc. Speed, as discussed previously, has a profound effect on the airplane's ability to turn. When the pilot is maneuvering in reference to the ground, it is *ground*speed, rather than airspeed, that is the deciding factor to determine turn radius over the ground. With this in mind, anything that affects groundspeed is also a factor. Therefore, wind, heading, ground track, and groundspeed become key factors in maneuvering.

Okay, we're flying an F-16 near supersonic speed in the middle of the jet stream. We've got a King Kong headwind and the airplane's groundspeed is zero. Besides the obvious factor of running out of fuel before we get anywhere, we've got a very interesting situation here. The jet is effectively hovering. If we throttle back in this headwind we could go backwards over the ground; change heading slightly, and our path over the ground could pivot on a dime. Ridiculous, you say? Let me get more realistic.

A friend and I flew the Maule one day in a stiff breeze. By stiff, I mean about 30 mph. The Maule can fly comfortably at 40 mph. Out of Salt Lake City International airport, the airplane rotated on the numbers and made a near vertical climb to pattern altitude. Not that the airplane was pointed straight up, or that anything was different in climb attitude from the cockpit, but since the airplane was climbing 1500 feet per minute and moving forward at barely 25 mph, the climb angle was outrageous. The tower made some comment to that effect and asked me to fly crosswind leg when able. Fine, we had only to move the nose about 15 degrees from runway heading to make a perfect 90-degree turn over the ground (Fig. 7-5). I made the attempt to fly downwind backwards, slowing the airplane as much as possible, but at best could only hold position, hovering, so to speak. I turned a one-eighty and proceeded to get flushed—blown away—on the downwind leg due to the tailwind and resulting high groundspeed. When we turned base, the airplane again had to be pointed nearly parallel to the runway to maintain a proper ground track. The turn from downwind to base required a heading change of 165 degrees and a correspondingly large bank to stay in the pattern. The fun part came when we were on final and a Mitsubishi (MU-2) was over-running us from behind. The tower asked us to break off the approach and move to one side. We complied, hovering off to one side waiting our turn to land while the MU-2 went sailing past. On landing, the airplane rolled about 30 feet. My point is this: With groundspeed running the gamut between nearly zero and

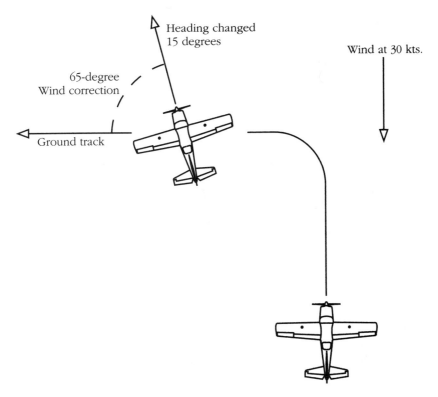

7-5 *Heading and ground track in a high wind.*

high speed, the *airspeed* was normal, regular speed normally flown in the traffic pattern. It was the groundspeed that made these unusual antics possible.

Groundspeed is entirely based on *heading*. I know what you are thinking now, something like "I thought it was the wind all of this time." The wind is only part of it. When the F-16 is going straight up, impersonating the Space Shuttle, its groundspeed is zero. Whether an airplane has a headwind or a tailwind depends entirely on which way the airplane is pointed, the wind direction being relatively constant. The plane's track over the ground is also variable with the wind. Any heading not directly into or away from the wind means that the airplane is traveling over the ground in a somewhat different direction than where the nose is pointed. This heading/groundspeed/ground track relationship is key to ground reference maneuvering, and the reason behind the FAA's required maneuvers in certification flight tests.

Technique

So there we are, back in the canyon again with a real need to turn around. What method is best? How is it done?

The high performance turn

Perhaps the ultimate in high performance turning can be found in the stall turn, or *hammerhead*. Correctly performed, this maneuver allows the airplane to pivot 180 degrees around the yaw axis within its own fuselage length. We will explore this maneuver first and embellish its concepts into a more practical high-performance turn procedure for the typical general aviation pilot.

The hammerhead turn is begun from a speed near cruise, often faster, depending upon the thrust of the airplane involved. The pilot pulls the airplane to vertical, verifying attitude by reference to the wingtips' position on the horizon. As speed rapidly decays, the pilot carefully anticipates the moment when the airplane will come to a halt in the vertical. Just before the airplane stops, the pilot applies brisk rudder and allows the airplane to pivot on the vertical (yaw) axis, swapping positions of nose and tail, like a diver doing a jack-knife from the springboard. As the airplane rotates about its vertical axis, the plane's upward momentum should be completely nil, it should appear as though the airplane is suspended, for an instant, while the turn occurs. As the plane points back to earth, momentum builds and the airplane follows its own path back the way it came. Properly done, the hammerhead turn—or stall turn, as Europeans call it—has *no* turn radius. The plane pivots around its vertical axis like an insect pinned to a piece of cardboard.

The major difficulty in performing the hammerhead turn is timing the rudder input. It requires much practice and an airplane strong enough to tolerate mistakes, like falling backwards in a whipstall or tailslide. Otherwise, there is little in this maneuver that could not be duplicated with most airplanes. The pilot pulls vertical to dissipate speed. As speed bleeds away, possible turn radius is tightened. If the maneuver is properly timed and the airplane turns when it comes to a complete stop in the air, there is no way to turn tighter. High performance, indeed.

Two other high-performance turns, as far as horizontal turn radius is concerned, are the *Immelman* and its counterpart, the *split-S*. Max

Immelman, a pilot in World War I, got credit for inventing the turn in which the airplane pulls though the vertical as though doing a loop. At the top of the loop, before the airplane would start back down, the plane is rolled upright and flies away. The turn radius in this maneuver is entirely in the vertical. Properly done, the horizontal displacement of the airplane's ground track during the turn should again be nil. The split-S is the Immelman in reverse. The pilot slows the airplane at altitude, rolls inverted and pulls through the vertical down and back to level pointing the other direction (Fig. 7-6). Although the Immelman and split-S maneuvers require little in the way of horizontal travel—they could be done in the alleyway between two skyscrapers—they require enormous changes in altitude.

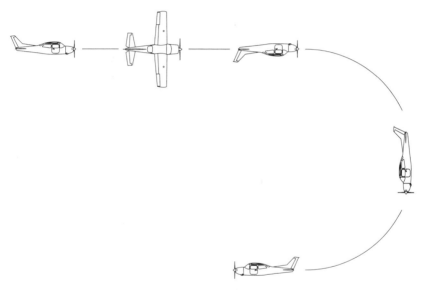

7-6 *The split-S.*

For all of the preceding maneuvers, there is the ugly possibility that they are flown incorrectly. For the hammerhead and Immelman, this could easily mean loss of control and a spin. The split-S might cause the plane to exceed design speed or load parameters and come apart in the air. For them to be safely attempted, a proper airplane should be used and the pilot should possess aerobatic skills that are beyond the scope of this book.

And these maneuvers are not yet finished at recovery. After performing a stall turn, Immelman, or split-S in a Piper Cherokee, for example, the lucky surviving pilot should march right over to the mighty FAA and relinquish all applicable licenses and ratings. That's what the FAA hopes, anyway; I'm often amazed at the naiveté of government agencies. A more likely scenario is that the pilot bolts for the nearest hiding place, while the FAA begins a methodical manhunt to find the pilot and revoke privileges: license suspension. It's an ugly situation.

The FAA declares that to exceed 60 degrees of bank, or 30 degrees of pitch (up or down) is to perform aerobatic maneuvering. If the pilot wishes to do this, then it must be within the limitations of the airplane, all occupants must be wearing parachutes, visibility must be better than 3 miles, they must be located off the airways, at least 1500 feet above ground level, out from over a populated area . . . and on and on. That is another story. Our purpose is to turn with minimal radius and stay within the limitations of the airplane, as well as the law.

This brings us to the ubiquitous crop duster. This is not to say that crop dusting is particularly safe, but it has an excellent demonstration of a high-performance turn done legally, albeit a few feet from the ground. It is a low-budget hammerhead turn, right above the trees and power lines. It is critical that the airplane dissipate no energy during the maneuver, each time trading airspeed for altitude and altitude back to airspeed again with no losses. If the airplane were to sacrifice energy while in the turn, for example, there might be insufficient energy remaining to pull out of the turn and the machine would hit the ground. To watch a good crop duster is akin to watching a skate-boarder inside a half pipe, back and forth across the fields and up with a turn at both ends.

Crop dusters fly the length of their row, turn off the spigots and pull up, both to dissipate airspeed and maintain energy (exchanging that airspeed for altitude). They roll to a 60-degree bank when the speed nears the stall and pull just hard enough to turn and yet maintain control, usually with the stall warning beeping away. The airplane descends through the turn and completes it by coming level with a turn radius not much greater than the airplane's wingspan. It is very pretty to watch—a legal, nonaerobatic hammerhead.

So, there are two options for the tightest turn. One is to slow to near standstill like the crop duster and do hammerhead turns. The other is to turn in the vertical plane, like the Immelman and split-S. These two options can be used at the same time to the advantage of the general aviation pilot.

First, the pilot slows to minimum speed. If the airplane is easily controllable with flaps down, then flaps should be used. With the airplane at minimum speed it should be rolled to 60-degrees bank and pulled to maximum angle of attack. For most airplanes, this will require a sacrifice of altitude until the turn is completed. The loss of altitude further tightens the turn radius by inclining the plane of turn downward, as in a split-S. Under normal circumstances the altitude loss should be minimal. The pilot must be careful to keep the airplane in controlled flight, avoiding a stall and possible spin departure. The airplane's turn rate will, in this way, be maximized without going aerobatic.

A variation of this maneuver is more conservative of energy. In this case, the pilot first pitches the airplane up sharply—less than 30 degrees (for legality's sake)—to reduce airspeed, and applies flaps within the parameters of their operating envelope but only to the extent that lift is maximized and drag penalties are small, again to minimize forward speed in the turn. When speed is at a minimum, the 60 degrees of bank is introduced and the pilot pulls to maximum angle of attack. Again, a loss of altitude is required to maintain controlled flight, but that is negligible because of the altitude gain in the pitch-up. This method is basically a modified version of the crop-duster turn, but hopefully performed at a higher altitude (Fig. 7-7).

Maximizing the turn performance of an airplane is an important factor in safe flying, and one that, unfortunately, is not taught often enough in the general aviation mainstream. I hope that these insights into the concepts of high performance turns will be of some assistance to you. The skills to practice section describes several drills that should be effective in developing your technique for maximizing an airplane's turn performance.

Ground-reference maneuvering

Ground reference is the most common type of maneuvering. Turning out of a canyon is obviously done with reference to the ground in an effort to avoid smashing into canyon walls; but ground reference

7-7 *Slow speed and steep bank make a tight turn.*

has a much wider scope. Making a cross-country flight involves directing the airplane's heading to some distant point on the ground. Flying the traffic pattern, staying in the aerobatic box, circling your house, hitting the runway, and taxiing to the hangar are all ground reference maneuvers; even the definition of pilotage as it applies to air navigation is a specialized type of ground-reference maneuvering.

The primary consideration in ground-reference flying is the wind. Several factors change with the influence of the wind. They include groundspeed, ground track, climb and descent angles and, indirectly, turn radius. We will follow each of these effects as they relate to a standard traffic pattern, probably the most common ground-reference maneuver of all, with emphasis on the techniques that a good pilot would employ to maximize landing performance.

Please reference Fig. 7-8. This is a representation of a standard traffic pattern as described in the Aeronautical Information Manual. There is much to be said about the legalities of flying the traffic pattern. These topics are beyond the scope of this book. One point that bears clarification, however, is the physical dimension of the pattern. If, at any time, the airplane is unable to make a successful landing on the runway in the event of an engine failure, the pattern is too big. It will be assumed, except when noted, that the wind is blowing down the landing runway, as depicted.

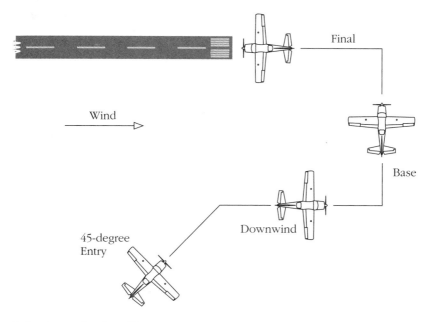

7-8 *A standard traffic pattern.*

The first characteristic that the wind imparts to the airplane in the pattern is a variable groundspeed. As the airplane enters the pattern on the downwind leg, the airplane's speed over the ground increases beyond the true airspeed by the amount of the wind. If the plane had a true airspeed of 100 mph, for example, a 20-mph wind at downwind leg would increase groundspeed to 120 mph. It is important to note that the indicated airspeed, as viewed by the pilot, is unchanged. Increased groundspeed on downwind will shorten the time the pilot might spend there. If the pilot is accustomed to completing a lengthy prelanding checklist on the downwind leg, a substantial tailwind might carry the airplane into the next county before the checklist is finished. The wise pilot will begin the checklist early, perhaps before entering the downwind leg, so that it will be complete before the airplane flies out of gliding range to the runway.

Increased groundspeed at the base turn appreciably widens the turn radius, the same effect that increased airspeed has on turns in flight. If the pilot begins the downwind-to-base turn without compensating for the increased groundspeed, the turn might be widened to the point that the airplane overshoots the final leg before completing the base turn. High groundspeed means a big turn radius, and the pilot must compensate with a correspondingly high angle of bank. This is where the steep bank and stall speed come into play. Understand that the airspeed as viewed by the pilot is unchanged with the wind, say 100 mph. If the airplane stalls at 101 mph in level flight and the turn requires a large bank angle, like 60 degrees, with that angle of bank the pilot faces a potential disaster. The only solution is to give up on the notion of maintaining level flight. This is where a lot of stall/spin accidents happen. The pilot tries mightily to make the plane turn as in a normal pattern. The plane hints at a stall during the turn and the pilot reacts with a reduction of elevator pressure. Then the pilot notices the rapid descent because of proximity to the ground. The pilot, now somewhat alarmed, pulls harder on the elevator control and stalls the airplane. Obviously, this is a situation to be avoided. The skilled pilot might anticipate the large cost of altitude in this turn and fly higher on downwind or delay beginning the descent until established on base leg, knowing that the downwind-to-base turn will cause quite a drop anyway. Another option is to fly high enough on downwind to enable a steep base turn.

One of the easiest ways to visualize the downwind-to-base turn is to view the aircraft wind-correction angles from above (Fig. 7-9). Notice that the airplane is required to change heading substantially more than the normal 90 degrees. This is a reason why the turn is necessarily steep. The reverse effect occurs during the base-to-final turn. Because of a reduction of groundspeed during this turn, it may be accomplished at substantially reduced bank angles. Notice that the airplane makes somewhat less than the 90-degree heading change at this point.

If the runway has a substantial crosswind such that the airplane had a tailwind while on base leg, the base-to-final turn could be very dangerous. It is basically like the downwind-to-base turn discussed earlier, but closer to the ground. This is how the majority of the stall/spin accidents in the pattern occur (Fig. 7-10). In this case, the required steep turn is exacerbated by the pilot's desire to complete the turn in alignment with the runway, often cross-controlling the airplane with a heavy dose of pro-turn rudder. When the airplane stalls in this condition, a spin is very likely. A wise pilot in this case might fly a wider downwind leg to lengthen the base leg portion of the pattern and allow for a wider turn, or fly a higher base leg in anticipation of an altitude loss during the turn, or, in extreme winds, fly a pattern to the opposite side of the runway. In any case, the plane

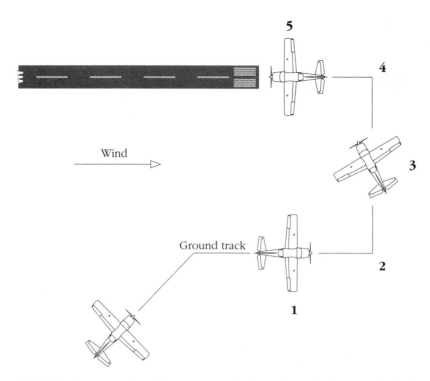

7-9 *Wind-corrected traffic pattern. Airplane has a high groundspeed on downwind (1) that decreases turn performance and requires a steep bank. To make this necessary wind correction on base, the plane must turn more than 90 degrees (2). On base leg (3), heading does not match the ground track. The final turn (4) is less than 90 degrees, relatively slow, and may be achieved with shallow bank angles. The final-approach path (5) has a much steeper descent because of the headwind.*

must not be allowed to stall. If it appears that the airplane will over-shoot the runway, the pilot should go ahead and do so, perhaps going around the pattern again for another try.

Turning the final leg and into the wind presents an interesting view to the pilot. The descent angle is different. Angles of climb or descent are based on rate of altitude change and groundspeed. If the airplane normally approaches with a forward speed of 65 knots and a descent rate of 500 feet per minute, for example, the descent gradient is 462 feet per nautical mile, an approach angle of 4.3 degrees. If the airplane's groundspeed is slowed by the wind to 45 knots with the same descent rate, the gradient becomes 667 feet per nautical

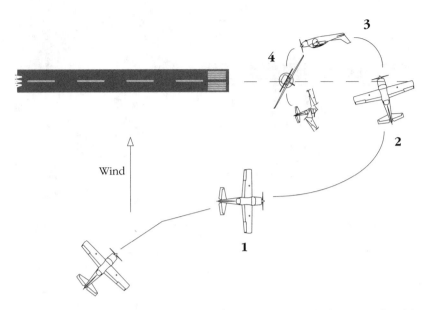

7-10 *A disaster in the traffic pattern: Airplane drifts laterally (1) because of faulty wind correction, setting up a very short base leg. High groundspeed in base turn takes the plane across the extended centerline (2) of the runway. The pilot anxiously makes a steep correcting turn, leaning hard on the rudder (3) and pushing the "ball" way out of center. Airplane stalls (4) and the flight ends violently.*

mile, a much steeper approach angle of 6.3 degrees. The wind basically slows the airplane's forward progress while the descent rate remains constant. The approach angle can take on a parachute-like quality, becoming abnormally steep. A steep approach angle made far from the runway would require the pilot to add power just to reach the runway threshold. Without the added power, the plane would come down short. If the pilot does not anticipate this, an engine failure from an otherwise safe and normal approach position could place the airplane in the dirt short of the runway.

To compensate for a higher than normal approach angle, the skilled pilot would turn from downwind to base leg sooner than in a no-wind situation. This has the effect of shortening the final approach leg and placing the airplane in a position requiring a steeper approach (Fig. 7-11). From this position, the airplane could still reach the field in the event of an engine failure.

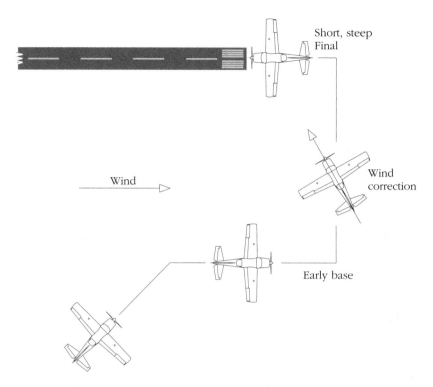

7-11 *Traffic pattern in the wind again, but set up for a short, steep, final approach. The pilot anticipates the wind's effects on final approach glidepath and positions the airplane for the steep descent, avoiding the need for high power settings during the approach.*

The steep approach can cause the added distraction of blocking the view of the touchdown point. To illustrate, visualize moving forward toward a point in front of the airplane. The point is directly visible out the forward windscreen. Now suppose the airplane is *hovering* into a headwind that matches its forward speed. If the plane were to descend slowly to the ground in this manner, the point of landing would be directly below the airplane. The pilot's view of the landing point would be blocked by the floor of the cockpit. The view out the cockpit during a wind-affected steep approach is similar, although not so extreme. The view to the landing point is usually blocked by the nose of the airplane as the plane descends. Inexperienced pilots will generally lower the nose in this case and approach at a higher speed, but the high speed does little to shorten the landing rollout and is simply poor technique. A proper approach requires practice, and when used to advantage, the wind can dramatically shorten the landing roll.[3]

The landing flare

The landing flare is accomplished in the same way as a turn. The plane must momentarily produce lift greater than one G to cause the change in flight path direction from downward to level above the runway—a *flare* at the bottom of the approach path. Since increasing speed is not an option here, the lift must be created by increasing angle of attack. It is for this reason that typical approach speeds are some margin above stall. If the plane were to approach *at* stall speed, the landing flare would be nearly impossible to achieve by normal methods, the wings' angle of attack being already maxed. The actual speed of the approach and flare varies widely with the particular airplane and situation.

Skills to practice

Now it's time to fine-tune those maneuvering skills by practicing a few drills. Please remember that enlisting the aid of a good instructor will be helpful to keep the flight safe and within the plane's limitations until you are proficient enough to try them alone. Some drills will not require the assistance of a flight instructor. However, if you're ever unsure, get one.

Airspeed transitions

Taking an airplane from cruise speed to minimum speed can make things busy in the cockpit of most airplanes. It is a time fraught with altitude deviations and mental saturation. Consider the typical process. The airplane is trimmed and comfortable in cruise flight. The pilot begins the deceleration process by reducing power. The lessened thrust over the tail surfaces also diminishes the effectiveness of trim and the airplane begins a pitch excursion. The pilot applies elevator pressure to compensate and initially trims the plane. Soon the slowing airplane is running up the induced side of the drag curve and the required angle of attack increases quickly. The pilot increases power substantially to counter the increased drag, but now has to fight with a very effective trim system whose authority was in-

---

3 Discussed in Chapter 9.

creased with the power change. The pilot has to aggressively *retrim* to keep things in order.

Pitch response to power change is characteristic of airplanes with a thrust line above or below the center of gravity. Trim effectiveness can also be variable with thrust as it passes over the tail surfaces. In some planes, it is pretty benign, but the Maule and several others require a lot of muscle just to keep the nose from going ballistic with the combination of high power and nose-up trim. I heard of the crash of a Convair 580 that took off with the elevator trim mistakenly dialed in for full nose-up. The resulting force was so powerful at takeoff power that the airplane went vertical at liftoff, looping back around and smashing into the runway in spite of the flightcrew's efforts to hold the nose down.

The airplane is trimmed before the deceleration occurs, and retrimmed once the slow-flight situation is established. It is out of trim during the entire transition phase. If the pilot constantly maintains a trimmed condition throughout the maneuver, the workload is quite high, the time required to complete the transition is increased, and the chances for a mistake, such as an altitude bust, are also increased.

The secret of a smooth airspeed transition is to do it fairly quickly and trim only once. Reduce power as much as possible. If the engine can tolerate it, reduce power to idle. When the airplane pitches nose down with slower speed, just hold the attitude, don't trim out the pressure yet. As the airspeed comes into the flap operating range, apply flaps completely (if desired). When the airplane is near the desired speed, apply sufficient power to maintain that speed. Then establish the proper attitude for the plane's configuration and *finally*, trim. Most light airplanes will require very little, if any, trim adjustment, because the trim tab position at cruise flight and flight in the landing configuration are often very similar.

Practice speed changes, or airspeed transitions. Work on smoothness and precise control. Take the plane from cruise speed to minimum-controllable airspeed and back again, never allowing the altitude to deviate or the heading to change. Pitch attitudes should progress smoothly with airspeed changes, not bobble and porpoise with the control inputs of an over-anxious pilot. When you have a handle on speed transitions in straight flight, try it again while maintaining a constant rate turn. You will notice that the airplane requires much less angle of bank at slow speed to keep the turn rates consistent with those at cruise.

Now that you are proficient at these speed changes, you might wish to improve your skills further by attempting them with a safety pilot in simulated instrument conditions.

Accelerating/decelerating 360s

Performing 360-degree turns while accelerating/decelerating is simply an airspeed transition flown in a two-minute turn. Establish the airplane on a cardinal heading in level flight. Begin a standard-rate turn and simultaneously slow the airplane. At standard rate, you have one minute to fully slow the plane. When the airplane has turned 180 degrees, the stall warning should be sounding and the plane should be already configured for landing. At that point, you should begin accelerating the airplane back to normal cruise and cruise configuration such that cruise speed is reached just as the airplane returns to its original heading. A constant altitude and standard-rate turn should be maintained throughout the maneuver.

When you think you are pretty good at this one, bring along a safety pilot and practice it again in each direction with the hood on. To do it well, the airplane's attitude must be in constant flux throughout the maneuver, everything changing at the same time, pitch, power, bank—everything.

Chandelle

The FAA requires commercial-pilot candidates to demonstrate a chandelle turn as part of the flight test. It is unfortunate that most pilots who have not prepared for the commercial flight test really don't understand the subtleties of the chandelle. Many mistakenly think that it is some kind of aerobatic maneuver, and are surprised when they learn its true nature. The chandelle in its most basic form is simply a 180-degree climbing turn. The stipulations placed upon the commercial candidate, however, require the candidate to convert forward energy into maximum altitude gain without loss of control in the process. The maneuver becomes an exercise in energy management, timing, coordination, and control, exactly the skills under scrutiny by the FAA and certainly worth a closer look in this text.

A proper FAA chandelle begins at maneuvering speed from straight and level flight. The pilot simultaneously rolls the plane to 30 degrees bank, applies maximum power and initiates a pitch-up for climb. The pitch attitude is slowly increased to reach a maximum with 90 degrees of heading change. At that point, the controls are manipulated to maintain the pitch attitude constant while the airplane continues to decelerate in the climb. As the plane decelerates, the turn rate increases. One of the stipulations of a proper chandelle is that the pilot maintain a constant rate of turn. To accomplish this, the pilot must gradually lessen the angle of bank during the latter half of the turn, as the airplane slows. The maneuver finishes with the airplane nearing a stall, 180 degrees from its original heading. There should be a substantial gain in altitude and no overall energy loss.

During the chandelle turn, the pilot trades speed for altitude. The energy state of the fast airplane at the beginning of the maneuver matches the energy state of the high airplane at the turn's end. If the energy is poorly managed, it is evident in a poor altitude gain at the end of the maneuver or a stall at some point in the turn. The chandelle is an excellent opportunity for the pilot to develop an understanding of energy and its proper management.

The official description of the chandelle, as the FAA requires it, is available from numerous maneuvering texts. It is also described in some quantitative detail in the FAA's own *Practical Test Standards, Commercial Pilot-Airplane* book. I recommend that you obtain some of these materials and become proficient at the chandelle, if you aren't already.

The lazy eight

Yet another energy-management maneuver is the lazy eight, which is basically two toned-down, crop-duster turns, performed back to back. From above, the maneuver looks like an "S" turn. The name *lazy eight* comes from the path that the aircraft nose describes around the horizon when viewed from inside the cockpit; it looks like the number eight laying on its side.

Again from maneuvering speed and level flight, the nose is pitched up smoothly to decrease airspeed. The pilot is restricted by the FAA's definition of a *proper* lazy eight to 15 degrees of bank until the aircraft heading changes 45 degrees.[4] Pitching the nose up slows the

4 *Proper*, in this case, means whatever will satisfy the FAA and result in a successful check-ride. The definition/description is found in the *Practical Test Standards*.

airplane and accelerates the rate of turn. The pilot can easily demonstrate this aspect of the maneuver by rolling to 15 degrees and pulling the nose up until stall. Observe the turn rate with the same 15-degree bank. Initially, it will be barely noticeable. Near the stall, however, the turn will be rapid. Passing the 45-degree turn point, the nose should be at maximum pitch and the airspeed near stall. The pilot is then allowed to increase bank to 30 degrees and lower the nose to the horizon. The nose should reach the horizon again as the heading changes through 90 degrees.

Halfway through, the nose is allowed to fall below the horizon and bank is decreased to 15 degrees as the nose reaches its low point, near 135 degrees of turn (Fig. 7-12). The maneuver is complete when the pilot levels both pitch and roll at a heading 180 degrees from the entry. Airspeed and altitude should be the same at completion of the maneuver as they were at the beginning. At this point, the maneuver is repeated in the other direction.

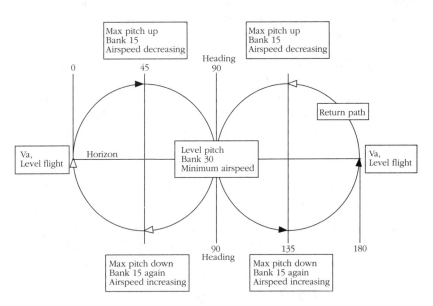

7-12 *A lazy eight as seen from the front windscreen.*

Common errors are numerous. They include stalling, poor coordination, not completing the turn, and gains or losses in altitude. It is the latter that needs addressing here. If the pilots have difficulty completing a full 180-degree turn, it is because they are not holding the airplane at slow speed long enough. Most of the turn occurs when the airplane is near stall. If the pilots shy away from the slow speeds, eager to fly fast again, the airplanes will respond with incomplete turns. The lazy eight can be flown through a full 360 degrees of turn if the pilot is willing to keep the airplane slow long enough.

The problem of altitude variations is one of energy. Most airplanes can gain energy in the lazy eight if they are left at full throttle. That means that the end of the maneuver is either faster or higher than the beginning. The solution is to fly the maneuver at a reduced power setting. If the airplane comes out of the turn too low, then energy and power must be increased. It will take some experimentation, but pilots can easily modify the power setting until their lazy eights are completed with identical parameters as what the pilots began with. It is really an energy management maneuver. Once the correct power setting is achieved, take note of it for future reference.

Stalls

I know that this seems hardly more than what is already required by the FAA, but it needs attention anyway. The goal here is to learn the feel of the airplane *exactly* at the point of the stall and to be able to maintain that condition indefinitely. The pilot should be able to fly the airplane at a speed just above a stall continuously, through turns, climbs and descents. No spins allowed.

Spins

I have to come out and say it: We *all* need spin training. The only way to become proficient and safe in the slow-flight regime is to learn to tackle its difficulties with a minimum of fuss, and that includes recovering from spins. It is not enough to experience only the spin departure. I suggest that all pilots find an instructor who is competent, rent a proper airplane and learn to master—and then enjoy—spins.

Accelerated stalls

The FAA defines a couple of procedures to induce or demonstrate an accelerated stall. The name comes from the fact that the airplane can be made to stall at a speed much higher than *stall speed*. In every case, the methods involve loading the airplane in some way—

pulling Gs. The critical factor in performing an accelerated stall is the load on the airplane.[5]

The first and most practical method used for the accelerated stall is to establish a steep turn and progressively pull on the elevator control until the stall occurs. In this way, the load factor can be made to increase gradually and the pilot can easily learn the feel of the airplane in this condition. It is the *feel* of the plane when it is about to stall that is so valuable to the pilot. Learning that feel is the purpose of this exercise.

A second method of stalling the airplane is to slow to some speed marginally above the stall—about 1.2 Vso and load the airplane sharply until the stall occurs. This method involves greater risk due to the sharpness of control input. If the airspeed is too high, the wings might be over-stressed and leave the plane.

The purpose of doing accelerated stalls is for the pilot to learn the nature and behavior of the airplane at high angles of attack while under load.

Dutch rolls

Fly the airplane at a constant altitude. Select a heading reference-point on the nose. While holding that point on the nose, roll the airplane back and forth, from a right bank to left bank, as if waving the wings. The rudder ball should be kept centered throughout the maneuver (Fig. 7-13).

Aileron and rudder pressures should be coordinated throughout the maneuver. Keep the *ball* in the center. Right aileron would dictate right rudder, left aileron-left rudder, and so on. You will be able to hold the heading-reference point because the airplane is not allowed to remain in a bank long enough to produce a turn. This maneuver is sometimes done incorrectly with the use of opposite rudder to prevent the turn. Now you know better. When you have mastered the Dutch roll, practice the maneuver at different speeds, including speeds very near the stall. You will notice that slow speeds generally require more rudder input to coordinate with the ailerons, due to increased adverse yaw at high angles of attack.

---

5 It is imperative that the airplane's structural load limits are *not* exceeded.

7-13 *Dutch rolls.*

All normal turns should begin this way, that is, with a coordinated bank in the direction of the turn. Practice half a Dutch roll, a 90-degree turn, half a roll the other way, a turn, and so on.

Boxing the horizon

A rectangle is drawn on the horizon using the aircraft nose as the pencil and the view out the windscreen as a slate. The nose is first raised, then while keeping wings level, right or left rudder is introduced to swing the nose laterally above the horizon. The wings should be held completely level throughout the maneuver. At the completion of the lateral swing (usually to the point of maximum rudder deflection) the nose is brought below the horizon and opposite rudder is applied to complete the box. Nose up, right rudder (left aileron), nose down, left rudder (right aileron), and so on (Fig. 7-14). This requires crossed controls.

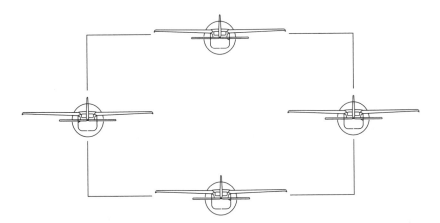

7-14 *Boxing the horizon.*

A variation on this maneuver is to keep the rudder ball centered and use bank to produce the lateral translation. The nose is first raised above the horizon, then, with coordinated control inputs, the airplane rolls into a bank. The bank angle is held constant and the nose is made to scribe a line across the horizon in the direction of the bank. When the top of the box is completed the aircraft is rolled out of the turn in coordinated fashion, and the nose is allowed to drop below the horizon. The pilot then begins a coordinated roll the other way, and so on (Fig. 7-15).

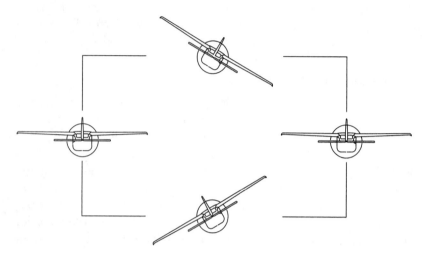

7-15 *Boxing the horizon with the rudder-ball centered.*

Try drawing other shapes on the horizon until you develop perfect control of the airplane. Draw them while holding the wings level, and again while keeping the ball centered. Some of the harder shapes include the circle and triangle. When you feel really capable, use the airplane nose to write your name on the horizon.

The benefits of better aircraft control are numberless. Dutch rolls, boxing the horizon, and writing your name with the nose in the sky are some exercises that can be safely practiced while flying alone, perhaps during a cross-country someplace, when you get a moment.

Ground-reference maneuvers

The broad category of ground-reference maneuvers is described in detail in numerous FAA texts and related publications. They are well portrayed there. Most pilots perform these maneuvers to the satisfaction of the FAA for a checkride and then never do them again. I suggest that these maneuvers be practiced often.

The best time to practice ground-reference maneuvering is during conditions of high wind. If wind is not available, it can be simulated by maneuvering in reference to an object in motion on the ground, like a car on a highway. Flying multiple turns around a speeding car is a terrific challenge for the pilot who attempts to remain a constant distance away from the car and fly a consistent altitude. In my experience, it has always caused the driver of the car to slow down. I guess the driver thinks that plane up there is the highway patrol. Delightful.

Once the pilots have mastered the turn around a car on the highway by adjusting angle of bank, they might attempt the same task by different techniques, such as variation of altitude, as with on-pylon eights. If the car is too fast for comfort, you can find several things slower, simulating less wind—these include boats, horses, balloons, you name it.

Aerobatics[6]

This is the ultimate in the art of aircraft control and maneuvering. I have heard arguments pro and con about the benefits of aerobatic training. Having taught aerobatics for a number of years, I have observed a great many students master this art. In no case has it made the student unsafe. To the contrary, the student gains a greater awareness of the airplane's limitations and greater ability to maneuver within those limits. I believe a safer pilot is the result.

Getting your own figures

Quantifying the maneuvering characteristics of a given airplane can prove a formidable task even for the professionals. Grading the maneuvering capability of a pilot in nonsubjective terms is practically impossible. Good maneuvering skills are often described with somewhat nebulous terms like *smooth*, or *deftly handled*. They are completely subjective as far as the pilot is concerned, hardly the sort of precise definition that we've come to expect from a performance standpoint.

---

6 Aerobatic training is something that may *not* be self-taught with any degree of safety. With this in mind, I suggest that you find a skilled aerobatics instructor, a capable airplane and take a few lessons.

It seems that bold pilots often try to define their skills in some way, to prove their abilities by doing the craziest stunt or most daring maneuver. This usually culminates in a type of record-setting flying that cannot be exceeded: They tie the record for low-altitude flying by hitting the ground. The most-skilled pilots combine excellent aircraft control with superb judgment and are safe. Pilots of this sort might accomplish the incredible while maintaining a high degree of safety. The exercises that precede this section are valuable in developing a pilot's ability to control the airplane's attitude, energy and situation. There is yet another attitude to master, however. It is that of the pilot. Fantastic flying ability and lousy judgment are a deadly combination. Please practice these skills at high altitude and stay within the design parameters of the airplane.

Figure 7-16 depicts the aircraft structural operating envelope. The boundaries of the envelope are defined by designers and test pilots as the upper- and lower-limiting load factors and Vne, or never exceed speed. During heavy maneuvering, the airplane might venture near these structural limitations, the edges of the envelope. This is to be expected, and the airplane is certainly designed to fly anywhere within the set range. It is the pilot's responsibility to see that the defined limits are not exceeded.

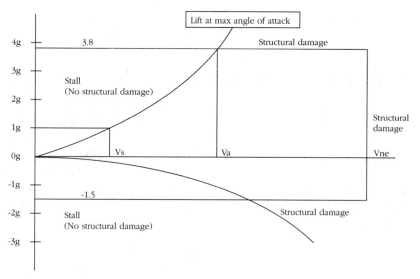

7-16 *A typical structural operating envelope or velocity/G diagram.*

The purpose of getting your own figures for this chapter is two-fold. First, the pilot must fly the airplane until the plane's handling characteristics are second nature, until the plane becomes a figurative extension of the pilot's body. This is easier to do in some airplanes than others. The good ones are said to *fly* nicely: i.e., handle very well. Poor handling characteristics from a given airplane will require more practice for the pilot to master it. So be it. Second, there is one maneuver that needs experimentation and an individual quantity to be useful, and that is the gliding turn.

Should a power failure occur just after takeoff with the runway behind, exactly how high do you need to be to be able to turn back to the runway? Pick a calm day to develop the figure. Establish a stable, power-off glide and record the sink rate. Still gliding straight ahead, at altitude, vary the airspeed slightly until the sink rate is minimized. You should be in the neighborhood of Vx, or maximum angle of climb speed. Once established with an airspeed target, select a bank angle and use a stopwatch to measure the time that it takes to turn 180 degrees. Take note of the altitude loss with the turn. Try it again, but change the bank angle slightly. You are working towards a happy medium: a bank angle and airspeed combination that minimizes altitude loss and maximizes turn rate in a power off glide.

Practice until you are comfortable with your parameters and can achieve the same figures every time. Remember the altitude loss required for the turn. In the event of an engine failure on takeoff, look at the altimeter. If there is less altitude available than required for your turn, then the runway is not an option, land somewhere ahead.

It might surprise you to find that the runway behind you is not a safe option for an emergency landing until you are rather high. Typically, altitudes of at least 500 feet are needed, but that can vary greatly, depending on the airplane, its forward speed, and the wind. A glider might be capable of a return to the runway in as little as 300 feet. The Pitts needs about 1000 feet to turn around.

If you fly a twin, then turning might be a silly option. Use the other engine to climb away. That's the idea, anyway. Most twin-engine trainers are marginal on one engine, to say the least. In the Cricri, single engine flight is barely possible for me. I'm a bit too heavy for the airplane. My partner, who weighs 50 pounds less than I do, can fly the airplane all day on one engine. I have had an engine failure occur three times during low passes down the runway. In each, I was about 100 feet high, going 120 mph. The optimal turn was a pull to gain altitude and reduce speed to 78 mph and bank to 45 degrees. The plane gains about 300 feet in the pull and then descends during the turn like a crop duster. After three engine failures from similar positions (the engines were notoriously unreliable), I can say that the method works pretty well. Each time, the airplane was able to make the turn and land on the runway. If the plane had a lower energy state than that, I would have landed straight ahead in the fields.

To summarize, practice until flying the airplane becomes second nature, like moving your own body. Stay within the structural limitations of the airplane design, and practice the 180-degree gliding turn until the exact energy condition needed for a return to the runway is consistent and predictable.

Further reading

Fighter Combat, Tactics and Maneuvering, Robert L. Shaw, Naval Institute Press, 1985

Airline Transport Pilot and Type Rating Practical Test Standards, FAA-S-8081-5

Commercial Pilot Practical Test Standards-Airplane, FAA-S-8081-2

Stick and Rudder, Wolfgang Langewiesche, McGraw-Hill, 1994

Basic Aerobatics, Geza Szurovy and Mike Goulian, McGraw-Hill, 1994

Stalls and Spins, Craig, McGraw-Hill, 1993

Aerodynamics for Naval Aviators, H. H. Hurt, Jr., University of Southern California, NAVWEPS 00-80T-80, 1965

8

The approach

Greg had a problem. For some reason the left engine had quit again, the propeller sitting there just four feet from his face, dead still. It was no surprise really—the engine had a talent for quitting and seemed to do so rather abruptly about every third flight or so. Greg shook his head. "Stupid two-stroke engines," he muttered. The engine failure was usually caused by a carburetor glitch or something with the single-ignition system.

He followed his usual single-engine procedure. He split the rudder-ball one half to the right and gingerly raised the pitch attitude until the airspeed settled exactly on 78 mph. Two-degree bank to the right, into the operating engine. In the past he had just flown back home to land. The plane flew well enough on one engine. But this time there was something wrong; for some reason, the plane wouldn't hold altitude. In fact, the little plane struggled to hold a 100 feet per minute descent, coming down with the airport out of range. Greg looked around for a place to land. Although too far from the airport, he wasn't far from his house. Maybe if he landed near a telephone he could call his wife to bring the trailer and pick him up.

A French-designed Cricri (Fig. 8-1) has tires hardly bigger than those on a go-cart. In fact, they came directly from an electric, motorized wheelchair. With landing speeds above 40 mph, there is no way they'd survive a soft-field landing. "I have to pick a road," Greg thought. At 100 feet per minute, Greg had about 10 minutes before the plane hit the ground, time to study the landing area. He picked a lonely road, and checked it carefully for automobile traffic. He would need to avoid a few powerlines, some strung across the road. After circling the stretch of road a couple of times, Greg positioned the plane for the approach. Throttling back the right engine, he established a normal descent and aimed his approach path between some wires that were spaced a little farther apart than the others.

8-1 *Greg had a problem . . .* Dan Sullivan

There would be no going around; no second chances. Every foot of altitude lost could not be regained. Slowly descending, he committed to the landing. Accuracy in the approach was everything. Speed was critical. Go too slow and the plane would come down too quickly; go too fast and it would float above the road in ground effect, stretching a short landing into an alarmingly long opportunity to get nailed by a car. Best to get down in the right place, stopped, and off the road. Greg looked long down the road. No auto traffic up ahead, at least none that he could see. If there were traffic, he was committed to land anyway. Greg wanted to honk a horn and tell everyone to get out of the way.

The right engine was blasting along. It made an uncanny noise, like a chain saw with a stuck throttle. Get 15 pounds of angry hornets together, hit them with electric shocks 6000 times per minute and harness the fury of it all, and you get the idea of the way the little engine sounds. It was adapted from a chain saw: 15 horsepower and 15 pounds, a single-cylinder dynamo, and the other one was broken.

Pitch attitude adjusted for 70 mph. At this point, the little plane approached the first of the cross-wires. It could have been six feet thick and painted fluorescent pink, so completely did the wire capture Greg's attention. Like the flick of a shadow, it passed under the plane. The next string of wire waited ahead. To misjudge and hit it in this plane would cut Greg in half. The canopy is barely ⅟₁₆ of an inch thick. The pilot is enclosed, but protected only from the wind. If the plane hit the wire, the canopy would offer no resistance at all. What a messy thought. Greg nudged the nose down and flashed under the second set of wires, with his wheels about 10 feet above the road.

Something caught his attention . . . horseback riders. Their faces turned around to see what was making all the racket. Greg saw every detail of their faces. He saw wide eyes, open mouths, and heads turning in unison as though watching the ball in a tennis match while the little plane popped, sputtered, and buzzed down the road. No cars. Greg throttled the right engine back completely and flared. There were telephone poles on both sides of the two-lane road, but with a wingspan of only 16 feet, the plane fit nicely between them, a few feet to spare on either side. He landed better than usual, the plane slowing to taxi speed on the still empty road.

He taxied toward a house. Reaching it, he pulled into the driveway, killed the engine, and climbed out of the plane. The owner of the home sat on the porch, looking just like the horseback riders, mouth open but no sound coming out. Greg smiled. It's not every day that a plane taxis into your front yard, and this one is the smallest twin-engine plane in the world. "Borrow your phone?" Greg asked.

Background information

Greg nailed an approach to a spot landing. His methods were born out of a dire need for accuracy. Hitting the obstacles or missing the landing point could have been fatal. The techniques he used are common to all airplanes and are critical to high-performance (short) landings.

Approach speed

Some time ago, I observed a student pilot consistently miss his landing point time after time. He made a textbook perfect approach, holding his desired airspeed exactly; the directional and glidepath control were flawless. He crossed the numbers at the proper height and began the flare, only to float two or three hundred feet past the mark. The touchdowns were not bad, but this particular student was bothered by his failure to land where he was aiming. Too many pilots find *spot* landings difficult. Some solve the problem by flying *navy style*. They simply smash their airplanes into the spot, not bothering to flare. This works if you have arrester cables, grappling hooks, and an airplane with the legs of an iguana, but it is not proper for most airplanes. The problem was his approach speed. It was too fast.

A typical pilot makes beautiful approaches with regard to airspeed. We are taught from the first lesson that airspeed is everything, that "thou shalt maintain thine airspeed lest the earth rise up and smite thee," to quote a famous phrase. I have observed several pilots take this to extremes, adding double the wind-gust value, 5 knots for the kids, another 20 knots for the insurance premiums, and then doubling that, just to make sure. The result is a flaming approach that would make a fighter pilot's strafing run look like grandma driving to the Sunday bazaar. The plane is usually flown into the runway at warp speed and then the brake pads are cooked off as the pilot barely makes the last exit from the runway. These pilots often consider themselves the only safe ones out there. An acquaintance of mine used this procedure to land a Cessna 152 on a 4000-foot runway. He was concerned about a high weight condition and used 120 knots on final—exactly twice as fast as it should be. He missed the entire runway and muttered that the airplane did not perform like the book said it should.

How slow?

Okay, there you are on landing approach to a short runway, you consult the book and it says to use an approach speed of 1.3 Vso (stall in landing configuration) which would be about 46 mph. You're too fast.

Suppose we fly an airplane which has a gross weight of 2600 pounds and the book and test pilots agree that a stall results if it is flown slower than 35 mph. This means that the wing produces exactly 2600 pounds of lift at maximum angle of attack and 35 mph. Slow down more than that (without stalling) and you get less than 2600 pounds of lift, so you have a 35 mph stall speed. Now suppose you fly your airplane alone with the fuel tanks nearly empty. You and your airplane weigh only 1800 pounds. With the wing at maximum angle of attack and 35 mph you will still get 2600 pounds of lift. That is 800 pounds more than you currently need. You can fly slower, maybe a lot slower—like 29 mph.[1]

1 See "Getting your own figures," at the end of this chapter.

The book speed of 46 mph is for your airplane at gross weight. You stall at 29 mph. A quick calculation 1.3 times 29 gives an appropriate approach speed of 38 mph. To use the *book* speed in this instance is to fly 8 mph too fast and could result in a disastrous float.

1.3 Vso

At what speed should we fly a short-field approach? Flying too slowly will not produce sufficient control to flare and we could crash; too fast, and we miss the runway altogether. This is where the idea behind 1.3 Vso comes into play. The shortest landings are born of the slowest possible approaches. Approaching at stall speed leaves too little reserve lift to permit a flare. The rule of thumb of 1.3 Vso is designed to provide just enough speed to permit a flare at the end of the approach, and leave the airplane at stall just as it meets the ground. Anything above that speed will have to be dissipated after the flare while the airplane is suspended in ground effect. It is desirable to avoid excess speed in the short-field landing.

The most accurate method for calculating a suitable approach speed is to stall the airplane at your desired landing weight at a safe height. The pilot should carefully observe the airspeed at which the stall occurs. Often the needle will fall well off the scale. The stall horn and other aerodynamic indicators will consistently predict the stall, however, as they directly indicate angle of attack. Taking into account the inaccuracies of the airspeed indicator as described in the aircraft manual, the pilot should then derive the approach reference speed, using 1.3 Vso as a starting point.

The figure of 1.3 times the stall is not cast in stone. For very light aircraft with extremely slow approach speeds, 1.3 Vso might be easily doubled or lost entirely by a mild wind gust. In that situation, some sacrifice of landing performance in the interest of safety might be wise in rough air. Pilots often use slightly higher speeds in gusty conditions, increasing the approach speed by half the gust value. Sometimes the airplane will require a speed slower than 1.3 Vso. I have flown bush planes that were so responsive to throttle adjustments that a landing flare could be accomplished with throttle alone and the airplane barely above a stall. It depends greatly on the situation and particular aircraft.

The important thing to understand is that too much speed on approach makes a short-field landing next to impossible and can be every bit as dangerous as flying too slowly.

Angle of attack

It is not exactly proper speed that we're after, it's proper angle of attack. Take, for example, the navy pilot again. The navy jet might lose more than half its weight during the course of the flight as it burns fuel and expends weaponry. The proper approach speed for a 40,000-pound airplane leaving the carrier is quite different from the correct approach speed for a returning plane weighing 20,000 pounds. With such a large weight variation, the approach speed varies as well. The pilot needs a constant, something that is the same, regardless of wild weight changes. This constant is angle of attack. The wing always stalls at the same angle of attack, regardless of weight or speed. The pilot of the navy jet uses an angle of attack indicator as a primary reference on the approach, letting the speed go where it might. The results are obvious; landing a high performance jet on the deck of an aircraft carrier is proof enough.

Pilots of the typical light airplane use airspeed as an angle of attack reference because the lift characteristics of straight wings vary much faster than swept wings with angle of attack changes. The typical angle of attack gauge in a straight-wing airplane is more difficult to accurately manage than airspeed. Besides, airspeed indicators are relatively cheap. The rules are the same for both the navy pilot and the general aviation pilot, however, even though the numbers and their variations are not. The pilot of a light aircraft must typically determine the stall speed for its particular loading and then go 1.3 times that value for a short-field approach reference speed. Pilots who are very familiar with their aircraft can eyeball the proper approach attitude or angle of attack by visual reference out the windows.

Glidepath control

Once we have determined the proper angle of attack or approach speed, we need to hold that constant and get firm control of the glidepath. Faulty glidepath control is the big letdown in a great many general aviation fatalities. Most pilots who are new to the short-field approach procedures in the Maule, for example, find themselves over-controlling the approach path, making throttle adjustments too big and generally going everywhere but in a smooth descent to the point of touchdown.

Airspeed should be established and maintained with careful variations of pitch attitude. This leaves the throttle and flaps as the only way to fiddle with the descent. If the throttle is advanced to climb power, the airplane will begin climbing. Simultaneously, the pilot will have automatically raised the nose to maintain the target airspeed. Most propeller driven airplanes will climb nicely at 1.3 Vso because this is surprisingly close to Vx. If the throttle is closed, the natural response is to lower the pitch attitude, again keeping constant airspeed. Of great help in the approach is to trim the airplane to the desired speed, so that little additional control manipulation is required to keep it there. In truth, power and angle of attack work together to nail an approach, but for the purposes of this discussion, pitch for speed and adjust power for glidepath. Get it backwards, and we could go for an exciting ride up the back side of the power curve.

The power curve and approach control

Several airplanes are incapable of climbing at full power in the landing configuration when their angle of attack is high. They can be flown well behind the power curve in this condition. If a pilot attempts to slow down too far on the approach, the airplane might be committed to hit the ground long before the pilot is ready for, or even aware of, it. I will illustrate:

Here's the young navy pilot approaching the aircraft carrier again. He's dizzy from all that combat flying and not making wise choices. He slows the plane to approach speed and concentrates on the short, pitching deck of the ship. To the navy pilot, perhaps more than any other, short-field landings are a matter of life and death. Judging himself a little low on approach, the pilot raises the nose to arrest his descent. The airplane slows and begins to descend faster. Adding power to regain approach speed, the pilot simultaneously raises the nose further to climb a little. The airplane continues decelerating and falling like a brick and the pilot is really excited. He has the stall-warning system blaring away, has applied full throttle and the airplane is still going to smack the water. He crashes because he flew the airplane behind the power curve. The plane slowed to a condition of such high drag that the available thrust was insufficient to maintain level flight, or even a normal approach glidepath.

Getting behind the power curve is a fairly common phenomenon with airplanes, even the high performance variety used by the military. I am informed that a T-38 flown carelessly can develop descent rates as high as 20,000 feet per minute in this manner. The solution is simple. Maintain the proper speed or angle of attack. There is little room for error. On the one hand, the pilot needs to slow down in order to stop on the runway. On the other hand, too slow and the plane might fall out of the sky like a lead sinker while still on final approach. If the navy pilot in our example would have first increased power when the airplane was low while simultaneously maintaining an angle of attack at which the airplane could climb, the landing would have progressed to a happier conclusion.

Slowing down to steepen the approach

In light of the previous discussion, it might seem a little strange to suggest that an approach can be steepened by slowing down, but that is the case. Considering the airplane's capabilities and the pilot's skills, slowing down on approach might afford almost parachute-like descents. Just as many airplanes are susceptible to the ravages of the power curve, many more are capable of climbing at Vso in the landing configuration, offering tremendous advantage to a pilot in approach. A word of caution here, however. An airplane that can climb at slow speeds and high angles of attack might only be capable of such a feat when flown at lower density altitudes. Power available at high altitudes might diminish such that the airplane is placed behind the curve when the pilot is counting on a climb.

I know what you're thinking now, probably something like the old axiom: "Want to go up, pull back. Want to go down, pull back all the way." I'm not advocating that the pilot stall the airplane on final approach or get behind the power curve at all. Still, incredibly steep approaches are possible as a result of careful speed adjustment on final. In the Maule, for instance, drag increases immensely with slower speeds. When flying a 70-mph approach and too high, the pilot might elect to slow to 60 mph while reducing power. The airplane is still well inside the power available for climb. The drag increase at that speed, however, is often sufficient to severely steepen the approach and improve landing accuracy.

It looks like this in a Maule: The pilot has selected full flaps, established a 70-mph approach speed and is aiming for the end of a very short runway. It appears as though the airplane is a little high and is going to land long. The pilot raises the nose to slow down. Initially, the plane appears to climb as the speed dissipates. The point of landing is almost invisible now, below the cowl, maybe requiring a glidepath descent angle of 45 degrees, or so. The pilot reduces throttle initially, to prevent climb as the plane slows, and manages speed carefully. As the plane settles down and stabilizes in a steeper descent, the pilot has some difficulty seeing the landing point, as it is practically between the main gear, and the plane is descending at an angle that feels like that of an elevator. The pilot looks out the side windows to check the touchdown point. The descent feels like a parachute. The nose is rather high, but the plane is not stalled and the landing point is assured. If the pilot advances power, the glidepath will flatten; full throttle, and a go-around is still possible.

If we look at the same situation again and try lowering the nose to counter the high approach position, the pilot will be forced to go around: we're back there at 70 mph again and a little high. The pilot sees this and lowers the nose to steepen the descent. The plane responds by accelerating to 80 mph. At 80 mph, (best L/D for a Maule) the plane has less drag than 70 mph and becomes a much better glider. The pilot will observe a general flattening of the approach angle and miss the landing point entirely. A go-around is inevitable.

A word of caution, particularly in airplanes using the slow, steep approach like the Maule: very slow approach speeds might preclude the possibility of a landing flare. If the Maule pilot does not increase either power or speed prior to reaching the runway, the airplane will slam into the asphalt with the ferocity of a falling house. I can vouch for the strength of the landing-gear in the Maule, because I was once surprised by just such a landing. The solution to the problem is the timely application of power to make the flare possible, which slows the descent rate and provides enough elevator authority to adjust pitch to a landing attitude. Another flare technique from the very slow approach involves a dive from about 200 feet to regain sufficient speed to flare. The dive creates a technically unstable approach by initially steepening, then flattening it as the plane flares, which equates to a touchdown quite close to the approach aim-point anyway. The latter method would be the only flare choice for this type of approach if the engine has failed.

Slip

Crossed controls are a wonder as a glidepath control. Place the plane in a slip, pull the power, and witness a free-fall that would make a sky diver envious. Do it with skittish passengers, however, and the hysteria and potential vomit in the cabin might require the pilot to hose down the upholstery.

The real danger in approaching with crossed controls lies in stalls and potential spins at low altitude. The pilot who uses a slip to approach a short runway might be tempted to slow down. In an effort to descend, the plane is placed in a slip. There we go, crossed controls, slow speed, and short final. Many airplanes have nasty stall characteristics when the controls are crossed. If the pilot were to stall in this condition, the outcome could be fatal. As a result of this, slip procedures usually involve somewhat higher speeds on approach.

Higher speeds during a slip are fine, but the idea of a short-field approach is to slow down as much as possible, and the demands of a slip are contradictory to this concept. Therefore, the shortest landings are made following slow approaches that make little, if any, use of a slip in the final segments of the approach.

Induced drag

Induced drag gets its name from the fact that it is caused by lift, or that it is lift induced. Remember that lift is the result of a downward push the wings apply to the airflow around them. This redirected airflow is the culprit behind induced drag. The lift created by the wing does not necessarily pull in direct opposition to gravity, but perpendicular to the average direction of airflow around the wing (Fig. 8-2).

With higher angles of attack the airflow is directed farther down, inclining the lift vector more and more rearward. You begin to see how a wing at high angles of attack will produce lift that pulls substantially *against* the forward motion of the airplane (Fig. 8-3).

Now place the wing at high angle of attack close to the ground. Air moving around the wing is deflected downward, but does not continue long in this direction because it is stopped by the ground. The airflow direction is abruptly changed to level. The average direction of the airflow around the wing is changed by proximity to the ground. Since lift pulls 90 degrees to the direction of this airflow, ground effect will cause the lift vector to lose much of its rearward incline, greatly reducing induced drag.

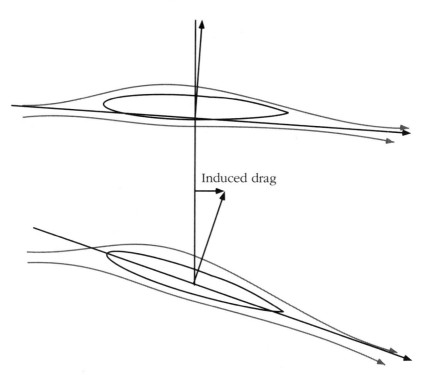

8-2 *The lift vector pulls perpendicular to the average direction of airflow patterns around the wings. High angles of attack cause the airflow to be directed more downward, inclining the lift vector aft. This increases lift-induced drag.*

Any excess speed on the approach that is carried close to the runway in the landing flare becomes very difficult to dissipate in ground effect. Even lowering the flaps at that point will cause the airplane to float farther down the runway, as the plane benefits from the lift, but does not experience much drag from the flap extension. The solution to the problem of ground effect and floating past the touchdown point is to approach at the correct speed so that no dissipation is needed.

Point of touchdown

Aim the short-field approach so that the airplane will touch down in the first few feet of runway. One of the flight-training schools for the high-performance experimental Lancair IV preaches that pilots should plan to touch down about ⅓ down the runway, saying that it is better to roll off the end of the runway at 40 mph, than crash short

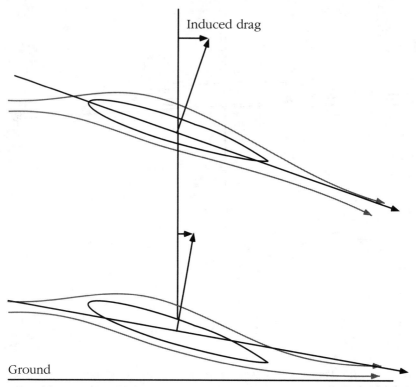

Induced drag

Ground

8-3 *The average direction of the air moving around the wings is changed by proximity to the ground, inclining the lift vector forward and reducing drag. This is ground effect.*

of it at 110 mph. The point is well taken, but the object of a short-field approach is to make maximum use of the space available, and that includes an accurate approach to the *very beginning* of the runway. Pavement left behind by landing long is a waste and ruins the finest short-field landing performance of any airplane.

Planning for a miss

A quick check of terrain beyond the runway before the airplane is committed to land is helpful in planning a missed approach or go-around. Many runways in forbidding terrain are one way in, one way out affairs, meaning that the plane and pilot are committed to land from far out on the approach, because a go-around is impossible thereafter. In addition to terrain conditions, aircraft configuration might also limit missed-approach possibilities. When the airplane is deep into the landing flare, for example, full flaps, gear, and stall speed sometimes combine to place an airplane well behind the power curve. If the pilot decides to abort the landing from that position, wheels a couple of feet above the runway, the landing might happen anyway. These things should be weighed carefully in the pilot's mind as the approach progresses. Is everything satisfactory? Will problems with the approach be solved before they are critical? A decision to abort the approach made early greatly facilitates the airplane's ability to actually go around and try again. A decision too late means that a crash, or undesired landing, might be inevitable.

Early in my experience as a flight instructor I encountered a poorly-planned go-around first-hand. Verle, the student, and I were flying touch and goes at a nearby, uncontrolled airport. A crosswind increased steadily over the course of the flight. The crosswind capabilities of the little Cessna 152 were soon matched, then exceeded by the mounting wind. By the time we prepared to leave the pattern and fly home (where runways pointed into the wind) I guessed the wind speed at about 30 knots. As we were about to leave, one of us posed the question: "What if we *had* to land here, in this wind?" I was immediately struck with the idea that perhaps, in wind that strong, the airplane could be landed *across* the runway, and losing my short and ill-fought bout with foolishness in making such a decision, decided to try it.

The runway had no parallel taxiway, but had a widened area at one end that was large enough to permit pretakeoff checks to be accomplished while out of the way of landing traffic. I told Verle what I intended to demonstrate and arranged for the pattern to take us down final into the wind, directly toward the widened apron at the runway's end. I figured that if 75 feet of runway width was insufficient for landing, then that apron—almost 150 feet wide—would do nicely. Besides, if there was a problem, I could always go around, right?

I glanced beyond the apron and observed hay fields, a few fences, and a single row of telephone lines, maybe a mile away. There were no serious obstacles to worry about, the airplane could easily clear everything out there. I concentrated on airspeed, and settled in for the approach. Working the flaps fully down, I set the trim and grooved down final while carefully reducing speed. We crossed the weeds at the side of the runway still 3 feet in the air, and airspeed set at 35 knots indicated. I figured that a wind of 30 knots would mean only 5 knots to kill at touchdown. It looked a lot faster than that, and suddenly I felt stupid. The runway was *not* wide enough to land on, and the plane would end up in the field on the other side. I decided to go around and quickly pushed the throttle to the wall. Engine noise and RPM increased, but little else happened. The little plane stayed about 3 feet high, the stall horn was still blaring away, and we floated across the runway and into the weeds on the other side.

Three feet high, and unable to climb, I had to consider the problem of the barbed-wire cattle fences up ahead. They were still 50 yards away. The plane was so far behind the power curve that climb was almost impossible unless we could gain some speed in ground effect. We stayed 3 feet high until the airspeed slowly crept up to 38 knots indicated. I began nursing the flaps up, one degree at a time, eyes glued on the airspeed indicator and the fence line just ahead. By the time we arrived at the fence, the plane was still 3 feet high, but the flaps had been reduced to 20 degrees and airspeed increased to 41 knots. Gingerly, we raised the nose of the airplane and it arced over the fence, then lost speed and descended back to a few feet above the ground with the stall warning sounding all over again. Airspeed quickly increased to about 42 knots. But the telephone wires were next, about ¼ mile away. The plane was accelerating, but slower than evolution itself. It seemed as though my heart were thumping in cadence to the engine at full throttle. The airspeed seemed painted across my eyeballs, increasing slowly, about 1 knot per 50 yards. We needed 55 knots for Vx, but I was willing to accept a little less—*anything* that would get us over those wires.

The wires were almost on top of us. I considered flying under them, but imagined passing too close and shedding part of our vertical stabilizer. Flaps were at 10 degrees, airspeed at 51 knots and we pulled up from about 10 feet. The wires moved quickly from their position above the airplane to pass across the nose and finally under. I tensed for impact, wondering if we would pass close enough for them to snag the wheels. They didn't. From 50 feet, the stall horn actually sounded reassuring. The plane had a little altitude to work with, and we quickly found our way to the climb side of the power curve, airplane cleaned up, airspeed set and a healthy climb showing on the meter.

I promised myself never to try that again.

If I had aborted the approach before committing the airplane to minimum speed, the go-around would never have become so stressful. The little plane could climb just fine from a higher speed, farther out on the approach. Of course it was stupid to attempt that particular approach in the first place. It was a bad situation. It is important for the pilot of any airplane to make the abort decision early. Delaying the decision and pushing a bad approach might close later options to landing, and perhaps running off the runway, or a crash. The choice is yours.

Technique

Of the many ways to approach a landing, perhaps the most consistent one is known as a *stabilized* approach. In this technique, the pilot attempts to square away as many variables as possible long before the airplane arrives at the runway threshold. The plane is trimmed and stable, flying (hopefully) a straight path and smooth descent to the runway. With practice, this type of approach produces by far the most predictably smooth and accurate landings.

Military aircraft use a version of the stabilized approach concept designed to make maximum use of their outstanding speed and to facilitate a rapid recovery (or landing). In a typical overhead approach, the fighter is flown at relatively high speeds down the runway and banked sharply under G load, allowing the pilot to slow down and descend at the same time. They might pull three to four Gs just turning around the pattern. The approach is still a stable one, although stable at different parameters than the typical one G straight-in, airliner approach. From either situation, any anomalies in the approach are easily recognizable to the pilot and can be corrected well before the airplane nears the ground.

Point of aim

Pilots aim at a landing point on the runway during the approach. They flare. The landing point goes by and the airplane touches down far beyond. I have witnessed student and commercial pilots do this every single time and wonder why they keep landing long. The landing flare requires a little room to complete if the pilot wishes to flare at all.[2] (Naval aviators seem to think that the need to flare in landing reveals a pilot with a squeamish personality.)

2 Which will be discussed in the following chapter.

The point of touchdown will occur somewhere beyond the aiming point used for the approach. If the pilot desires to touch down at the very beginning of a short runway, for example, the approach should be aimed at a spot before the touchdown point. The approach aim point and the actual landing point will be different. In this case the approach might be aimed for the weeds just short of the runway. Exactly how far before the touchdown point to aim the approach is subject to practice and experimentation with a particular airplane (Fig. 8-4).

8-4 *Some aiming points for an accurate landing.*

Alignment errors

Airplanes with curved windshields present an optical illusion to the pilot as to what exactly is straight ahead. Most pilots look out the center of the windshield, where it is relatively square to the airplane's direction of motion. Yet, sitting off to the left side while looking through the center of the windscreen requires the pilot to look slightly to the right.

Pilots who do this often find themselves landing on the left side of the runway, or making last-second adjustments to the approach just prior to the landing flare. This happens because they maneuver the airplane down final so that the runway appears to them in the center of the windscreen. As the runway looms closer, the skewed line of sight that the pilot is using becomes a factor requiring an approach adjustment. For most pilots, the final adjustment is almost subconscious.

To prevent last-minute adjustments to an otherwise stable approach, learn where forward is, as seen through the window from the pilot seat. This often compels the pilot to look through the curved portion of the windscreen directly in front of the left seat. The view will take some getting used to, but better approach alignment with the runway will result.

Getting your ducks in a row

A little preparation early in an approach does much for the subsequent landing. As with all other aspects of flying, the variables involved are multifaceted and ever-changing. During approach, the pilot works to bring all variables into focus on the landing simultaneously. The object is to arrive at the point of initiating the flare at the proper height, speed, position, direction, and configuration. In most cases, the flare point will be the first instant in the approach at which all of these factors are set together at once. Taking them individually, we get a good idea of what the pilot is attempting to achieve: shepherding each variable in a general direction to peak and come into focus at the proper time.

Height, for example, should be decreasing gradually and smoothly until the plane begins the flare. There should be few *steps,* or plateaus, in the final segment of the descent path. Some pilots would suggest that obstacle clearance can be enhanced by flying closely over obstacles blocking the approach at minimum speed and then diving for the runway sharply before initiating a flare. In practice, however, descent variables are changing so quickly in the final moments preceding the flare that most pilots are unable to achieve any kind of consistency in this procedure, usually losing hold of some other variable in the process, like airspeed. The most consistent and predictable method of obstacle clearance is simply a straight, stable descent aimed to pass closely over any obstacles that would block a normal approach to the runway (Fig. 8-5). The pilot adjusts the descent while long out on the approach, stabilizes its progress early, and flies a straight, steep glidepath until initiating the landing flare.

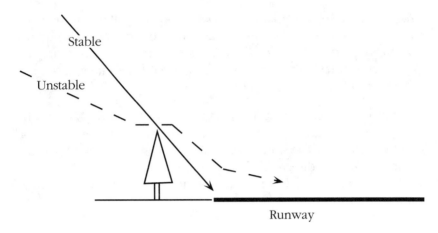

8-5 *The "no step" approach.*

The safety-conscious pilot seeks to cause a steady deceleration of airspeed throughout the final approach segment, arriving at the flare with exactly the proper speed. Airspeed need not be set at 1.3 Vso until the very last part of the approach, just prior to the flare. For a plane that stalls at 30 mph, for example, a textbook, 1.3 Vso approach speed would be 40 mph. This is quite slow. In an effort to avoid prolonged exposure to gusts and windshear during approach, the pilot of this airplane might begin the final segment of the approach somewhat fast, say 60 mph, gradually slowing down on final to begin the flare at 40 mph. Airspeed is managed in this way to progressively decrease to an ideal figure by the time the airplane reaches the flare point.

Minor corrections to a plane's flight path are required throughout the approach. For the pilot, concentration is focused on the aiming point of the approach, where the plane needs to be for the flare to begin. It is critical to the success of a short-field landing that the plane be positioned correctly for the landing to occur. It is a simple matter of pilotage, from the beginning of the approach to its conclusion the pilot sees where the plane needs to be and manipulates the controls to get there. It is very helpful for discrepancies in the progress of the approach to be caught and corrected early. The small correction made early is much easier to achieve than a large adjustment made late.

Perfect alignment with the runway is much easier to achieve when it begins far out on the approach. Runway position might demand that the pilot fly the plane around obstacles on short final with runway alignment attained only in the last moments of the approach, making the landing substantially more difficult. Where possible, the pilot should seek to establish alignment with the runway as early as possible, needing only small corrections to the flight path as the approach progresses.

Configuration changes usually require trim and attitude adjustments in the airplane. If these adjustments are required when the airplane is very close to the runway, it might be very difficult for the pilot to achieve the perfect conditions for landing. For this reason, landing configuration should be established early on the approach, giving the pilot time to adjust for the change itself and stabilize trim and attitude variables before they become critical. Many airline operation specifications require pilots to make no configuration changes below 400, 500 or even 1000 feet agl. This is the concept of a stabilized approach. It allows the pilot to nail down some variables early, leaving only airspeed for final adjustment in the end.

A perfect approach is the result of the pilot setting up all the requirements early and stabilizing as many variables as possible prior to the landing—getting all the ducks in a row.

Crosswinds

There are several methods for combating crosswinds. The simplest would be landing in a crab, like the old Ercoupe, which had no rudder pedals, or the F-104 Starfighter, which did, or setting the wind-correction angle into the landing gear like a B-52 bomber. Better yet, the Helio Courier had wheels that would castor like those of a shopping cart, permitting the plane to land and roll going almost any direction.[3] Mechanical marvels aside, crosswind-landing techniques are many and varied.

The most tried and true methods boil down to a slip or a crab, or some combination of the two, both of which have been discussed at length in several other publications. From a performance standpoint, the control authority required for landing in a crosswind might necessitate somewhat higher speeds on approach, ultimately extending the runway requirements of the airplane. Some taildraggers, for example, can be very unruly in a three-point landing attitude during a

---

3 Trouble was, it went in every direction when the pilot tried to slow down and taxi, as well.

8-6 *Wheel-landing the Maule.*

crosswind. Their pilots should simply attempt a two-point, or wheel landing, but accept much higher approach and landing speeds as a result. Tri-gear pilots often forgo the use of maximum flaps in favor of better control authority during landing. Again, the plane will stall at a higher speed, 1.3 Vso would be faster, and a longer runway would be required (Fig. 8-6).

Control authority

Some airplanes have limited control authority at very low speeds. In the Maule, for example, short-field approach speeds are slow enough to limit elevator and aileron authority to the point that a normal flare is impossible and full aileron deflection might be required to simply counter engine torque or light crosswinds. The lack of elevator authority is a factor that surprises the pilots. The plane feels comfortable enough on a slow final approach until the pilot pulls the yoke all the way to the stops to initiate the flare and nothing happens. This results in a facsimile of the carrier landing. The solution is very simple. Add power. The extra propwash over the elevator improves its authority immensely when it is needed in the flare and serves to flatten the approach angle at the same time. If propwash over the tail is not available because of jet power (no prop) or an engine failure, higher speed might be required for adequate control.

Another solution is to trim the plane full nose down. That's right. Trimming the nose down deflects the trim tab *up*, making it a type of leading tab that enhances elevator effectiveness in the flare. The pilot, of course, will have to resist the natural nose-down tendencies of the out-of-trim elevator to maintain a landing attitude.

Skills to practice

The following exercises are designed to enhance a pilot's ability to control airspeed and glidepath on an approach. These skills can be practiced in complete safety at altitude before attempting them on approach. The idea is for the pilot to master the techniques behind minute and precise adjustments in glidepath while shepherding the airspeed to a minimum at the correct moment.

Controlled flight at 1.3 Vso

Stall your plane in the landing configuration and observe the airspeed. Check the manual for indication errors and figure 1.3 times that value. Set the plane up to fly at this speed, trim it as well as possible and play with the glidepath while holding the speed exactly on target.

Set the power for level flight. Gradually reduce the throttle until the airplane indicates about 500 feet per minute descent. Add power again to climb. Each time the power is adjusted, note the change in pitch attitude required to hold the speed.

Pull the power to a normal approach setting. When the correct speed, as determined earlier, is nailed down, memorize the attitude required to hold it there. Pay careful attention to the view outside and try to figure the exact point at which the approach is aimed. It will be the only place outside that appears not to move. It will be a spot on the ground that seems to sit still and grow larger, while the rest of the world stretches by.

Practice adjusting the power setting and attitude slightly until you have firm control over airspeed and the approach glidepath simultaneously.

Flight at Vso

For the fun of it, set up a landing configuration and reduce power for a descent. Raise the attitude until the stall is imminent and maintain that condition in the descent. Try keeping the airplane just shy of a stall while playing with the power to produce a climb, level flight, or descent. If the plane will not climb like that, even with full power, you're flying one that can get behind the curve. If this is the case, increase speed one knot at a time until the plane can just hold level flight. Take note of this speed. It is the speed on approach below which the plane is committed to a landing, and a go-around from low altitude is unwise.[4]

Power-off approach

Try pulling power completely—or as much as possible—and approaching at 1.3 Vso to a particular spot on the runway. For this exercise, it would be wise to pick a place about ⅓ down the runway, just in case you misjudge and come up short with an engine that won't relight. As always, control airspeed with pitch attitude, but this time adjust the glidepath with variations in flaps, gentle slips, and approach path. If you're high, gentle S-turns might use up some of the altitude, or you could extend the traffic pattern slightly. If low, delay the final configuration change or airspeed reduction for later, keeping the airplane cleaner for a better glide. At touchdown, see how close you come to your intended point of landing.

Spot landings

This should more accurately be called the *spot-landing flare* drill, because it concentrates on the approach speed more than the actual landing. As described earlier, 1.3 Vso is only a rule of thumb, or starting point for a good approach. The actual ideal speed for your airplane might vary. To find the ideal speed, pick a calm, nongusty day, start with a 1.3 Vso and land. If, during a normal flare, the plane floats, the speed was too fast. Reduce the speed very slightly and land again. You are looking for the approach speed at which the airplane has sufficient energy to flare, and that's all, thereby minimizing the float. When you get there, don't go any slower or you might empathize suddenly with the no-flare arrival methods of the navy.

---

4 Getting below that speed with enough altitude to accelerate in a dive and then climb is not a significant problem.

For airplanes with rather delicate landing gear, the no-flare arrival could damage them (and possibly you) severely.

Once the proper speed is ascertained, pay close attention to the difference between the point used for aiming the approach and the point of touchdown. Do this several times until you can eyeball this accurately. Next time a spot landing is required, simply aim the approach that far to your side of the landing point, set the speed and flare. It's almost automatic.

Getting your own figures

Here comes a little math. In light of the procedures outlined above, proper approach technique is a matter of practice and skill. There is little that the pilot can do to actually quantify, or stick a number to the approach itself, short of using the proper speed or attitude. Feel free to measure the landings at the end if you wish, but actual landing distance will change remarkably with subtle changes in wind, temperature, altitude, braking, or even runway surface, nullifying any noticeable effect on the landing or the approach itself unless you compare several landings under identical conditions.

Approach speed is best determined in actual flight, with a gradual and almost painfully systematic reduction in speed until everything works the way it is supposed to. You should pay attention to unstable conditions, gusts, and weather for safety's sake. If the approach speeds for your particular airplane are very slow, say, less than 60 knots, even small gusts might have a frightening effect on your airspeed during final. It is wise in that case to plan your approach to reach minimum speed only when landing is assured, that is just prior to the flare.

Stall speed, and therefore approach speed at lighter weights, can be interpolated from known figures in your manual with the help of a calculator. As I said, here comes a little math:

The formula for stall speed looks like Fig. 8-7.

Everything in the formula is easily found in the manual except the constant, K, but things can be rearranged to give us that (Fig. 8-8):

$$\sqrt{\frac{2 \times \text{weight}}{\text{density} \times \text{wing area} \times \text{Clmax}}} = \text{Stall speed}$$

density × wing area × Clmax = constant, K, so:

$$\sqrt{\frac{2 \times \text{weight}}{K}} = \text{Stall speed}$$

8-7 *The stall formula.*

$$\frac{2 \times \text{weight}}{\text{stall speed}^2} = K$$

Cessna 152 weighs 1670 lbs and stalls at 46 kts, so:

$$\frac{2 \times 1670}{46 \times 46} = K = 1.58$$

8-8 *The formula rearranged for K.*

Now that K is known, we can rearrange the formula again to solve for speed and plug everything back in with reduced weights. For a Cessna 152 again (Fig. 8-9):

You might want to make a table indicating suitable approach speeds for the landing weights at which you most commonly fly. To make things easier, show the weights relative to how many seats are full in the plane, i.e., one speed for you alone, another for you and a friend, and still another for all the seats full, and so on. Simple.

Further reading

At the Edge of Space, Milton O. Thompson, Smithsonian Institution Press, 1992

F-104 Starfighter in Action, Lou Drendel, Squadron/Signal Publications, 1976

Bush Flying, O'Meara, McGraw-Hill, 1990

$$\sqrt{\frac{2 \times \text{weight}}{K}} = \text{Stall speed}$$

Cessna 152 weighs 1670 lbs gross,

1470 lbs solo

1323 lbs solo with empty tanks

K = 1.58; so stall speeds are:

46 mph, gross (from the manual)

$$\sqrt{\frac{2 \times 1470}{1.58}} = 43 \text{ mph, solo}$$

$$\sqrt{\frac{2 \times 1323}{1.58}} = 41 \text{ mph, solo, no gas}$$

8-9 *Applying the formula to a Cessna 152.*

9

Landing

It was a crisp and clear fall morning when we met at the hangar and discussed the upcoming test flight. My task was to evaluate the airplane, learn its handling and capabilities, and then teach Scott to fly it. I made the first flight alone.

I was taxiing away from the hangar in the little taildragger with Scott following closely behind in his truck when the airplane encountered a patch in the asphalt, a shallow chuck-hole not more than an inch deep, that I couldn't see from my vantage point, looking over the nose. The lip of the hole was just big enough to catch the front edge of the wheel fairing on one side, break it from its mounts and rotate it forward, around and under the tire. A quick jolt, and the little airplane wasn't going anywhere.

Scott and I assessed the damage and determined to remove both wheel pants and continue with the flight. One of us lifted the wing tip while the other removed the bolts that secured the wheel fairings. With the wheel pants removed, we were presented with the sight of a rather unusual landing gear mechanism. The airplane had drum brakes that must have come straight off the shelves of the go-cart supply store. They were actuated by cables instead of the usual hydraulics. Since neither of us was a mechanic, we were unfamiliar with the arrangement and puzzled over it for a few minutes.

"What do you suppose holds the tire on?"

"Must be these lug nuts, like a car. I can't imagine anyone would design the wheel skirt to secure the wheel. We haven't pulled any cotter pins."

"Looks good to me."

"Me too. Let's go flying."

Back in the airplane, I taxied to the end of the runway and completed the pretakeoff check. With my heart pounding I advanced the throttle and found myself airborne about when it was all the way forward. The airplane jumped off the runway like a little insect. I was delighted.

The elevator controls were hair-trigger sensitive, feather-light and unstable in the pitch axis, while the ailerons were much heavier and less responsive. I felt them out carefully during the climbout and noticed a slight shudder just as I was turning crosswind. It went away immediately and I took it as perhaps an unusual response to turbulence.

At a comfortable altitude and a few miles away in the practice area, I began to explore the controls. Steep turns demonstrated a neutral stability around the longitudinal axis; slow flight and stalls were benign and controllable. The first aileron roll was such fun that I burst out laughing. Loops and hammerheads were tiny, a few hundred feet high at most. Almost all of the aerobatic maneuvers could be accomplished in an extremely confined area. It was a new experience for me and completely delightful. There was only once, coming out of a loop, that I again felt a little shudder in the controls, like a thump on the tail. It was here, then gone. I fiddled with the stick for a minute, felt nothing unusual, and again dismissed it. "Scott is going to love this plane," I thought.

On the way back to the field I considered the landing. Three point would be best, and maybe a few practice approaches to get a feel for the descent angle. It struck me that maybe I should again check the tires to make sure there was no other damage to them that we might have missed on the ground. I peered out the lower fuselage side windows at the left wheel. *It was gone.*

It is difficult to describe how I felt at that moment, but a healthy part of the sensation was anger. I couldn't believe that I could be so stupid. I remember shouting over the din in the cockpit—nothing intelligible, just a primeval curse. My heart pounded in my throat. I looked out the other side of the cockpit in hopes that the right wheel would at least give me *something* to land on. It was just a protruding axle, like the left side. That explained the strange shudder in the controls. "Idiot!" I could just see it. At gatherings of pilots from then on: "Hey, did you hear about the guy who took his wheels off and then went flying?" Then the crowd roars. There was still a rushing in my ears and a flush to my face when I began to get a handle on the predicament.

Okay. It looks like I'm going to crash-land. Nothing but bare pegs to land on. The plane will most likely flip over on the first contact with the ground, wooden splinters from the shattered propeller will explode against the runway and the plane will slide crazily across the asphalt on its back. It will be scrap. What a waste. I felt badly for the airplane because I truly liked it. I tried to call Scott on his hand-held transceiver but there was no answer. I called the airport unicom for an advisory.

"Was that *experimental* ————?"

"Affirmative."

"Well, I hate to be the one to tell you this, sir, but we think you're missing a wheel."

"Me too. I'm missing *both* of them."

Scott came on the mike.

"Lewis, are you okay?"

"I'm fine now, but I feel terrible about what this is going to do to your airplane."

"Never mind that, I just hope you come out of it okay."

I could get hurt. The thought occurred to me for the first time. Ouch. I took a close look at the canopy bow and imagined the runway smashing through the Plexiglas and into my head. Instinctively, I squirmed down lower in the seat and tightened the lap belt. I thought about landing in the lake, but it didn't seem any better and the grass probably wasn't any softer than the asphalt either. "Hey Scott," I asked, "what about a big semi-tractor trailer going down the runway. Maybe I could land on that?" He thought it was a crazy idea.

As I passed over the field, the ramp looked black with people. There were blue and red lights and news cameras flashing all around. I lost any hope of sneaking this landing away in the shadows and avoiding a load of embarrassment. It was difficult to think clearly, so I just flew the pattern for a while and tried to figure out what to do. I practiced a few approaches and learned the feel of the airplane. It could sure slow down. With me alone in the airplane the stall speed must be close to 26 mph. On one of the passes, a mechanic on the ground noticed that the brake pads were still attached to the axles.

"Maybe, if you're lucky and the landing is perfect, they will slide a little," somebody suggested.

It was the best idea so far, and I was ready to come down. This would be the first time I had landed the plane. When I was turning base, ready to commit myself and the little airplane to ruin, there was one last comment on the radio to help my confidence:

"Try to make the landing as close to the emergency equipment as you can."

"Okay," I replied, though I later wondered if that request really came from the rescue vehicles or the news cameras that were set up nearby.

Again, it is a little difficult to describe the sensations of the moment. My concentration was so finely focused on putting the airplane on the runway that everything else sort of blurred away. My purpose was completely focused on slowing the airplane to as near a crawl as possible. I had some success in the effort and at last chopped the power completely as the tailwheel contacted the runway. The main-gear struts immediately smashed onto the asphalt while I hung on and became a highly interested passenger. I pinned the stick in the full aft position with both hands. The plane scraped and gouged the asphalt for a couple of seconds, then stopped. I shut down the systems and opened the canopy to stare into the lens of a local news camera. At exactly that moment, as with the experience in the canyon 10 years before, my brain turned to tapioca.

Background information

The purpose of the landing flare is to minimize energy and sink rate at the moment the airplane meets the ground. In the case of the crash-landing described above, a good landing flare made the difference between success and pain. The perfect high-performance landing flare dissipates *all* excess energy from the approach, leaving the airplane rolling smoothly on the runway at minimum speed. It is a pilot's maneuver, elusive in its complexity, requiring the dexterity of a ballerina, the timing of a moon shot, and the eyeball of an artist.

It is the single maneuver by which the skills of all pilots are judged. All of this for a simple turn at the bottom of an approach.

Watching a pilot's face during the final moments of landing gives me the impression of a card player in a game of chance. Concentration is certainly there, but an element of risk clouds their features. The game is won or lost in the smoothness of the touchdown. In a smooth landing, the lucky winner's facial expression is one of tension-relieved satisfaction, pretending all landings were like that. The loser, after a particularly rough arrival, is a bewildering stream of excuses about the gusty wind or difficult airplane.

The concept of flare

The *flare* is named for its characteristic bend, or flare, in the approach glidepath. For the high-performance, short-field landing, the landing flare will be successful only following an effective and accurate approach. If the pilot has carefully arranged all the variables and set the speed, direction, position and altitude properly, the flare will require very little effort and result in the shortest possible landing rollout. The flare is simply a turn in the vertical plane (from descent to level), like the initial pull in the bottom of a gentle loop. The airplane should progress smoothly to maximum angle of attack, dissipate speed and sink rate, and finally roll onto the runway. All excess speed at the end of the approach must be dissipated in the flare, or else the pilot will have to accept a touchdown with undesirable excess energy.

The British have a more accurate term for the landing flare. They call it *holding off*. The concept is simple. The approach is a low-power or power-off descent. During the approach, the airplane will normally have insufficient power to sustain level flight. The pilot maintains adequate flight speed by allowing the airplane to progress in a descent towards the runway. The pilot levels the flight path of the airplane a few feet above the ground. The plane immediately loses speed. Lift dissipates with the airspeed, requiring that progressively larger angle of attack (aft pressure on the elevator controls) be applied by the pilot to maintain level flight above the runway. It doesn't take long before dissipating speed and lift gently places the airplane on the ground.

A common mistake in the flare is to increase angle of attack too aggressively, before the airplane needs it to make up for diminished energy. The result is too much lift, causing the airplane to zoom up-wards from the runway momentarily, only to be left there too high, with too little airspeed. The recovery from that situation requires the pilot to increase power to moderate the subsequent descent and hard landing. It will be tempting for the pilot to quickly lower the nose after this so-called *balloon*, but the result is usually a quick fall and landing best described as a wallop.

During the flight, the pilot's attention should be focused upon keep-ing the airplane in close formation with the runway—not climbing, perhaps even a *very* slow descent—until the attitude and energy are satisfactory for touchdown. For light aircraft, the plane should be al-lowed to stall completely just as it reaches the ground. Airplanes with high wing-loadings are best flared to an ideal pitch attitude and energy condition (as determined to be comfortable and controllable by the pilot) and then allowed to roll on the pavement without fully stalling. A high wing-loading often causes poststall sink rates that are undesirable for meeting a runway. Nevertheless, the ideal landing at-titude selected by the pilot of an airplane with a high wing-loading will be very close to stall, anyway.

The short-field landing

The landing flare for a short-field, high-performance landing is basi-cally the same as for any other, with the exception of the slow ap-proach speeds. The slow speed going into the flare means that the flare happens very quickly, there just is not much speed to dissipate. In other words, the flare happens a little faster. The prettiest landings happen when the pilot executes a perfect approach, has the throttle back, and times the flare so that the airplane stalls just as the wheels touch.

If the pilot did a great job on the approach, the short-field landing is simple. In the Maule, and other STOL airplanes, however, the ap-proach speeds can be so slow that control effectiveness becomes a problem and a little power is needed during the flare. The propwash over the tail makes the flare possible in the first place. The throttle is then closed after the wheels hit the ground.

One really gutsy short-field flare technique is to ride the engine to the landing threshold. I call this gutsy because an engine failure would plant the airplane firmly into the ground right where the fail-ure occurred, but the technique is worth discussing because it results in a spectacularly-short landing. The pilot using this method slows the plane down in the last stages of the final approach segment. It looks from the ground as if the pilot is beginning the landing flare too early. As the speed dissipates, the pilot compensates with big increases in power—remember the drag buildup at low speed can be immense. The airplane strikes the ground at nearly full throttle and right at stall speed. In the Maule (a taildragger) the power-on flare requires an angle of attack that plants the tailwheel into the runway while the mains are still a couple of feet in the air. The pilot closes the throttle as soon as a wheel hits the ground and follows with hard braking. The landing is over about that fast.

A prettier short-field landing procedure is to establish the landing attitude while on short final and use the throttle gingerly to adjust the glidepath. The airplane, already slow, will gently deposit the main gear (or all three wheels at once if it is a taildragger) on the runway and stop a few seconds later. This approach procedure is more stable than the one described above and is the one I recommend. The flare is literally made possible by the throttle. Add power to soften the descent, and cut it completely when the wheels hit the ground. The attitude is nose-high and motionless from short final to touchdown and the landing, believe it or not, is actually very gentle (Fig. 9-1).

9-1 *Power-on short-field landing.*

Failure to cut power quickly at the point of landing is a common mistake. This is not critical to the landing itself, but does extend the landing roll somewhat. It is more critical that the pilot continue to manipulate the flight controls during the landing roll. A bad habit of many pilots is to relax completely at the point of touchdown. Sometimes they actually exhale a big sigh (of relief?) when the wheels start rolling. This can be dangerous; a taildragger left to its own devices on the landing rollout quickly swaps ends. Tri-gear airplanes might yet be producing gobs of lift, still trying to fly. To a lesser degree, some back pressure should be maintained on the controls to prevent the nose-gear strut from compressing too sharply (or the tail from lifting) while braking in the landing roll. The pilot should continue to control the airplane's attitude when it is on the runway. In this manner, crosswinds and gusty conditions have little effect, since the pilot is still actively flying the airplane.

Avoid skidding because it reduces braking effectiveness. If your plane has anti-skid brakes, great. If not, apply the brakes firmly, almost to the point of skidding, but not quite.

Soft-field landings

Although most airplanes can land on nonpaved runways (at least once, anyway), it seems as though the taildraggers are more at home on them. Directional control problems with the tailwheel are lessened on nonpaved surfaces because their reduced friction allows the pilot more time to correct guidance mistakes before the airplane darts off on an undesirable heading. The idea of having the beefy main gear in front to take the bulk of ground abuse also works well for nonpaved runways. Tri-gear aircraft accept greater loads and stresses on their relatively weak nose gear when operating out of soft runways.

You can imagine landing in a body of water with the gear down. The water will grab the tires and deftly flip the plane over. I suppose that such a landing would be impressively short, but taking off again might be a little difficult. The pilot should carefully examine any potential landing surface for its hardness and smoothness. Ideally, you want a golf green. Realistically, anything pretty dry and hard packed will do fine. It is a good idea to walk an intended runway surface on foot, inspecting for potholes, mud and other problems before attempting any ground operations. Also be on the lookout for nearly invisible (from the air) powerlines, fences and other obstacles that could be a threat.

The concept behind a soft-field landing is somewhat analogous to the short-landing procedure. It involves a landing at the slowest possible speed, like the short-field landing, but with an additional margin of control during the landing flare and rollout. This is achieved by carrying power into the landing flare and easing the airplane onto the runway as near to stall as possible. The power in the flare allows the pilot more careful control of the final, momentous descent to the ground, and offers more elevator authority in the event of a sticky runway surface. The object is not so much to hit the mark as it is to hit *gently* and under control—to ease the airplane into the muck. This usually requires a slightly longer runway. As the wheels touch the runway surface, there is a definite tendency for the airplane to imitate a water landing. The pilot will compensate with more back pressure as the plane attempts to pitch over at ground contact. It happens quickly, but most pilots respond to this by reflex anyway. The landing rollout continues quickly from that point and depending on the softness of the ground, it might strongly resemble a splash-down.

Braking effectiveness can be hampered because of the soft ground. Wet grass, for example, might as well be wet leaves or ice and braking friction can be irregular. Wheel ruts left from ground vehicles and other airplanes might pose a directional control problem and should be judiciously avoided. The pilot should do as always, that is, continue flying the airplane throughout the landing roll. If a wheel finds a rut and threatens to take the plane off the runway, the pilot responds with steering, elevator, aileron and perhaps even power, as it becomes necessary to maintain directional control. The landing is not finished until the plane stops completely.

Air braking

During the landing rollout, aerodynamic principles still apply. In crosswinds or gusty conditions the airplane will still be trying to fly while the pilot is applying the brakes. It is important that the pilot continue to manipulate the flight controls and maintain a proper attitude until the airplane comes practically to a stop.

If it is possible to maintain positive control of the plane's pitch attitude during the rollout, keeping the nose high, preferably a stalled attitude, might offer assistance in deceleration because of increased aerodynamic drag. If the airplane is equipped with spoilers or other means of dumping lift, they should be deployed on the ground during heavy braking so as to allow the full weight of the airplane to rest on the wheels, thereby increasing the brakes' effectiveness.

Landing-performance chart

A landing chart is only a performance estimate, a best guess as to how much runway the airplane will need. Your actual results might be better or worse than what is predicted. In my experience, however, manufacturers' performance estimates tend to be quite conservative in the landing department. A skilled pilot can almost always improve upon the manufacturers' claims. The charts take into account practically the same criteria as the takeoff charts discussed in Chapter 3. If you wish, you may refer to those diagrams while reading this section on landing. The landing charts have almost the same appearance. Any distinctions will be noted. With a great deal of practice with a given airplane, you will be able to estimate the landing distance requirement quite accurately from a flight position in the flare. You'll be able to pick your final stopping point with impressive accuracy, more than is possible with a chart.

Density altitude

One of the nice things about landing performance is that it is only marginally affected by density altitude. Inasmuch as the true airspeed of the airplane on approach increases with higher density altitudes, the landing will be longer; but higher density altitudes do not have the drastic effects on landing roll that they do on takeoff. This is because engine power and thrust are practically removed from the problem. For a takeoff, power, thrust, and acceleration were key operators in getting the airplane airborne. Density altitude has a tremendous effect on these, and thus, takeoff performance. A landing, on the other hand, is a condition of low power, much reduced thrust, and deceleration provided by the brakes. Power is not a significant factor, thrust isn't either, and the brakes work quite well regardless of the density altitude. The landing roll is obviously affected at high altitude, but to the extent of only a few percentage points increase over sea-level distance, because of the higher true airspeeds achieved by an approach at high altitudes. For this reason, the density altitude part of the landing performance chart is relatively tight and flat. It looks just like Fig. 3-2, but the slanted pressure altitude lines have less slope and are more closely spaced.

Weight

Weight affects the landing distance in two ways. First, increased weight causes the airplane to stall at a higher speed, thereby increasing the approach speed and generally speeding up the landing. Second, higher weight combines with higher speeds to increase the inertia that must be overcome by the brakes to stop the moving airplane. It is much easier to stop a bicycle than a freight train because of the inertia differences between the two vehicles. In the same way, a heavy airplane is much more difficult to stop than a light-weight one.

Just as with wind, the weight part of the landing chart looks like its counterpart for takeoff as referenced in Fig. 3-3. The effects of weight on takeoff as compared to landing performance are almost identical, with one minor improvement: rolling friction. The drag caused by tires rolling on the ground that is accentuated by higher weights and decreases takeoff performance, is favorable to landing performance. It assists the brakes in slowing the plane.

Wind

Generally, tailwinds are more of a problem than headwinds are a benefit. On performance charts that use a table, wind adjustments are made on a calculator and the detrimental effects of wind are easier to see—something like reducing overall landing distance 7 percent for each 5 knots of headwind and increasing the landing distance 12 percent for every 3 knots of tailwind. The specific numbers are, of course, greatly dependent on the particular airplane.

Crosswinds cause mild increases in landing distance because of the increased approach and touchdown speeds that are necessary for adequate directional control. Most landing performance charts do not take this into account, so the pilot will have to approximate the landing estimate accordingly.

It is groundspeed that must be diminished upon landing. Anything that serves to reduce groundspeed at touchdown will drastically shorten the required landing rollout. I have landed the Maule in stiff winds that nearly equaled the approach speed of the airplane. Consequently, groundspeed at touchdown was ridiculously slow, with the entire rollout occurring on the numbers, maybe 30 feet in length.

Landing with a tailwind increases groundspeed and adversely affects the landing distance, particularly when approaching the runway over an obstacle. Tailwinds make steep approaches very difficult, if not impossible. The wind has the effect of improving the actual glide angle of the airplane causing it to cover more ground for a given loss of altitude. A normal steep approach to the numbers in a tailwind might become an overshoot of the whole runway.

Runway slope

Landing downhill presents a problem to the pilot that is similar to the truck-driver's nightmare of a full load barreling down the side of dead-man's mountain with no brakes. The driver would do anything to find an uphill slope and bring the truck to a stop. With an airplane, landing downhill means that the plane might be very difficult to slow down even while it is still off the ground in the flare. Remember ground effect? The decrease in drag produced by ground effect might be enough to cause the airplane's glide angle to flatten and match that of the slope of the runway indefinitely, floating the airplane the full length of the runway and beyond, smack into any obstacles in the way. Once the plane has actually contacted the ground, braking effectiveness will be minimized because the wings are still trying to fly. The pilot applies brakes, but notices that the tires seem especially willing to skid. Although skids handily destroy tires, they do little to stop an airplane. A runaway truck, indeed.

To make matters worse, the visual picture of the runway from the cockpit is slanted away from the pilot while the plane is on approach. It looks as if the far end of the runway is lower than it should be. The sloped runway gives the illusion of a low approach. The hapless pilot adjusts the approach to present a more favorable sight picture and unknowingly sets the plane up to be high and fast. You can easily visualize this by a small exaggeration: For some insane reason you try to land on the steep downslope of a big mountain side. An ideal approach would be to cross the ridge, land at the top and roll the airplane down the slope. On that approach, the "runway" would be invisible, sloping away on the far side of the mountain. The pilot sees only the touchdown point at the crest of the ridge. On the other hand, if the pilot were positioned high enough to bring the runway into view and make a normal sight of the runway, the plane would be in a near-vertical dive at the ground, hardly the conditions necessary for the shortest landing.

Uphill landings are everything just discussed but in reverse. The plane decelerates much faster, approaches tend to be lower and slower, and the landing ground roll is effectively reduced. One caution: during the landing flare to a steep, upslope runway, the airplane must change direction from an approach descent to a slight climb, to match the runway slope. This requires slightly more speed on the approach to make the bigger flare possible. Failure to do this means the plane will land very hard after an incomplete flare.

The big disadvantage of an uphill landing is the go-around. If you don't like the way the approach looks when you're landing on the uphill side of a mountain, then make the choice early to go around. Often, the best choice is literally a go-around. That is, make a 180-degree turn in the final approach path and fly away from the runway to reposition for the approach. This is often better than trying to out-climb a steep runway slope and hitting it anyway.

As before, the majority of published landing performance charts make little reference to runway slope. This is a variable left to the pilot's eyeball estimates. For obvious reasons, attempt to land uphill whenever possible for the best landing performance.

Technique

Accuracy in the short-field landing is every bit as critical as minimum speed at touchdown. It is imperative that the pilot be able to land on target. Excessive float or a poorly-aimed approach could easily run an airplane into the weeds (or worse) at the far end of the runway. The techniques that follow are variations of the methods discussed above but regard the landing flare and how to develop an *aim*. They are as useful for spot-landing contests at fly-ins as they are for short, unprepared runways.

The carrier landing

To land on an aircraft carrier, the pilot sets up the landing attitude while out on the approach. There is no flare. Attitude is one of the variables stabilized early, along with direction, glidepath and configuration. The pilot adjusts the approach path with subtle variations of the throttle and aims precisely at the point of touchdown. It is important for the pilot to avoid making large corrections late in the approach to avoid overcontrolling; the pilot should simply keep the plane moving in the proper direction and descending at the proper rate, and then let it hit the runway. Watching the process on the deck of an aircraft carrier gives visions of compressed spinal columns and whiplash, or at the least, blown tires and landing struts. Such is the harshness of the landing.

The typical general aviation airplane can safely duplicate the carrier landing with smaller sink rates down final. If obstacles permit, the pilot has only to set up a gentler glide slope to the touchdown point. For airplanes with effective flaps (like Cessnas), large flap extension often causes the airplane to approach with an attitude that is too nose down to permit landing on the mains without a flare. If that is the case, use a milder flap setting, one that will allow the airplane to descend in the approach with the nose slightly high. In some airplanes, ground effect will noticeably flatten the approach automatically just before the tires hit the runway, greatly reducing the landing jolt.

Stepped-flare technique and the X-15

Pilots of the X-15 rocket plane (and also the Space Shuttle) developed flare procedures that were designed for accuracy. They were tasked with the problem of landing a hypersonic glider on various small lake beds in the Nevada desert. If their approach or flare was inaccurate, the plane would miss the lake bed and wipe out into the surrounding desert hills. They could not go around for a second try. Their plane approached at crazy speeds and descended like a streamlined anvil. They typically flew over the landing point at 35,000 feet and 250 to 300 knots indicated airspeed. Making a 180-degree turn in the glide, they had downwind at 18,000 to 20,000 feet and just continued the turn to set up for a 5-mile final. Their average descent rate in this overhead pattern was about 12,000 feet per minute, meaning the whole procedure required just about three minutes to complete. An F-104 Starfighter (tiny wings) with full flaps, gear down, and idle power, diving to 300 knots indicated could make a pretty close approximation.

To get a handle on the procedure, these pilot/astronauts developed a technique in which the landing flare was flown in steps, with a couple of distinct aim points. The plane was literally dived at the first aim point, the target for the approach. Then, at a preplanned altitude, the plane was partially flared to continue on a three-degree glide slope, and a second aim point for the touchdown was picked up by the pilot. From there the landing progressed normally. Later modifications to this procedure, currently used by the Space Shuttle, involved an initial flare to progress on a one-degree glide slope (foregoing the second aim point), during which the airspeed decays, the descent rate is minimized, and landing gear is extended. The flare then continues into the landing.

Students making steep, full-flap approaches in general aviation airplanes have successfully applied a variation of this procedure. Approaching steeply, they initially flare to shallow the approach glide path at which point the airspeed is allowed to decay such that a second and final flare just above the runway can be accomplished accurately with minimum speed. The procedure tends to alleviate the requirement of dissipating excess approach speed in ground effect and with practice is as accurate as it comes.

Flap retraction

This little stunt came directly from an FAA inspector, so if it sounds a little scary, you know the source. Spot landings can be hyperaccurate if the pilot suddenly and completely retracts the flaps when the airplane is still a couple of feet in the air. Yes, the plane will not be in the air any more, once the flaps are taken in. No, it does not work for a soft-field landing.

The flaps need to be actuated quickly. Electric motors or slow hydraulic systems will not work well for this procedure. The best system is the basic Johnson Bar lever used in Pipers and older Cessnas, because of its speed and controllability.

The pilot attempting to use the flaps for a spot landing aims the approach at a normal point in front of the desired landing point. Once the plane is flared, and about to pass over the landing point, the pilot takes the flap lever in hand and retracts them while maintaining a landing attitude with the other hand. In the inspector's words: "You can pick which part of the line you want to land on." From that altitude, flap retraction dumps lift immediately and the plane is on the ground that fast.

The downside of the procedure is that it works about as well from 100 feet as it does in the flare, except that it hurts the airplane and its occupants. Nevertheless, with good judgment and care, dumping flaps can indeed place the plane on the runway with finality if the pilot desires, and can make up somewhat for a misjudged approach to an accuracy landing.

Crosswinds

Of the two primary methods for crosswind landings, the *crab* method of approach allows for slower approach speeds because the airplane is not cross-controlled until late in the landing flare. From a performance standpoint, it would be a little better than flying a slip down final.

During the approach, the pilot corrects wind drift with heading in the same manner used during cross-country flight. It appears as though the airplane is not heading to the runway at all. The pilot carefully watches the ground track and adjusts heading to keep the flight path moving down an extended runway centerline. The plane is flown right into the flare like this, with the nose crabbed off to one side. When sensing that the airplane is about to settle, the pilot uses crossed controls to align the tires with the line of flight just before the plane actually lands. The pilot would use aileron into the wind to get the windward main gear slightly down, and opposite rudder to swing the nose to align with the runway centerline. Crosswind effects on performance can be minimized in this manner; relatively high approach speeds might be avoided in favor of a slightly faster touchdown late in the flare.

Go-around from flare/touchdown

When a go-around is initiated late in the approach or landing flare, rolling the tires on the runway might be inevitable. Once the airplane is flown slow and low enough, it is committed to land. The simple act of reversing a descent and climbing requires a few feet of altitude to accomplish, and if the airplane is low enough, the runway could get in the way. The nice part of the whole thing is this: the runway can actually enhance performance in the go-around transition to climb.

When the airplane is on approach, it has significant inertia toward the runway. This inertia, or momentum, is directed along the airplane's flight path, forward and down. When the pilot elects to abort the approach or landing, the airplane's inertia must be redirected in a climb direction. To do so requires a little time, and quite a bit of energy, as most pilots already understand. When the runway is involved, it affects the go-around two fold. First, the runway puts a definite stop to the airplane's descent. The problem of overcoming the descent is in this way solved. Second, the benefits of ground effect will minimize drag in the critical moments that the airplane needs to accelerate to a climb. The only real disadvantage of the runway is the rolling friction produced by the tires.

When the pilot elects to abort the landing and the airplane is already committed, it is important for the pilot to continue into the landing procedure, even though full throttle has been applied for the go-around. The pilot should simply allow the tires to roll on the runway (don't retract the gear too soon), set flaps for best angle of climb, nail the Vx attitude, and fly away (Fig. 9-2).

9-2 *If you need to go around, make the decision early.*

Compensation for a bounce

Too many pilots are so in love with the ground that they try to plaster the airplane back onto it when a bounce occurs. This usually makes the second bounce worst than the first, the third worse than the second and so on, sometimes crashing the plane. It's a love affair from hell.

A young student pilot nervously soloed to an uncontrolled airport near Salt Lake City. The pilot was concerned about the landing and his face squinted up on final approach, teeth gritted and muscles tensed as the time came—and went—to flare. The plane hit hard on the mains and bounced with rattling wheels about 15 feet in the air. The pilot, at once relieved to have made contact with the ground and alarmed to find himself airborne again, pushed the elevator control forward to hold the airplane to the runway. The plane promptly nosed over, smashed into the runway, collapsed the nose-gear strut, and slid crazily on the asphalt. The prop blades curled up like the tail of a pig, firewall and plane bent into the shape of a banana, and the whole thing took on the appearance of a squashed fruit. The pilot, fortunately, walked away, later to get a job with a foreign airline.

When the airplane bounces during landing, it is imperative that the pilot set and hold the landing attitude. If the bounce is a big one, add a little power to cushion the second touchdown. In no case should the pilot attempt to plant the airplane back on the ground, or hold it there with the elevator controls—that is just begging for a crash.

Skills to practice

The goal of the following exercises is to establish firm and exact control while on the runway or just above it. The benefits of such control should be obvious and are too numerous to mention. Inasmuch as these exercises involve flying very close to the ground, there is no room for error. Get a good instructor to assist you until you are proficient. There are few short-cuts to learning these skills. You have to practice.

The stealth landing

Try flying level formation with the runway, exactly 6 inches or so in the air. Try *not* to physically touch the ground, but to fly just above it: the ultimate buzz job. Do it at approach speed or slower, eventually working your way down to the very minimum speed possible while maintaining positive control. Be sure not to use so much runway that obstacles at the far end become a factor on the go-around. If the wheels touch the runway before you are ready, you will have the beginnings of a beautiful landing, but keep practicing until you can maintain the altitude exactly.

Touchdown and roll on one main

Land the airplane, add a little power, then lift the nose- or tail-wheel and one of the mains from the runway. Maintain directional control as though still flying the airplane. Roll on one main wheel for a while and fly away. Progress to a one-wheel touch and go, landing only one main wheel to the runway. This is crosswind landing practice like no other. It helps if the flaps are not used to their full extent, to maximize aileron authority. The nose wheel is not a player in this game with tri-gear; if the nose wheel strikes the runway first, you are going much too fast.

Short-field landings

Practice several short-field approaches and landings on a good runway, aiming to land on a mark that is not the runway threshold. When you are comfortable and accurate with every approach, move your aim point to the runway threshold and don't miss.

A caution about over-used, over-heated brakes: Several short landings in a row using heavy braking might reduce brake effectiveness. Especially in airplanes where the landing gear is retracted as the plane flies around the pattern. The retracted wheels do not allow the brakes to cool off sufficiently and the result is that the brakes might not work when the pilot needs them. One solution is to leave the gear down and let the slipstream do the work of cooling.

Soft-field landings

Use a little power in the landing flare to control the final settling of your airplane on the runway. See just how gently you can touch down. In the winter, if your airport has a little snow, it is fun to see if you can roll the tires through the snow without actually touching the runway surface. This should not be attempted where the snow is deep enough to present a landing hazard.

When you are comfortable with the soft-field landing flare, attempt it again for an accuracy landing to a specific, preselected point on the runway.

Slow-flight race

Every year in the Midwest, there is a backwards air race. During a season when the wind blows predictably hard, numerous pilots launch into the wind and attempt to get blown backwards to a nearby town. First one to get there while pointed the wrong way, wins. Obviously, the winners are masters of slow flight and do everything possible to improve their groundspeed. If a pilot could get groundspeed reduced to zero, the landing roll would be like that of a helicopter. The pilot could land with the brakes on, because the wheels wouldn't have need of rolling.

With this in mind, it might be interesting to practice groundspeed control techniques at a comfortable altitude, with the hope that some benefit might spill over into a short-field approach, when the opportunity arises.

Pick a short course, laid out by obvious landmarks, such as a short distance between prominent roads. Fly the airplane along the course a couple of times, each time trying to maximize the time en route. You might find that steering into the wind helps greatly. It is considered cheating if you fly in circles or make S-turns. Once you cross the starting line, hold the heading until crossing the finish. Have fun, and don't let the engine temperatures get too hot in the process.

Dead-stick glides to touchdown

It is important that the pilot not become dependent on the throttle in the approach and landing flare. With this in mind, practice short-field approaches and accuracy landings without power, simulating an engine failure. Use glide path and configuration adjustments to control the approach.

Getting your own figures

Since the purpose of this book is to enhance your piloting skills as they affect performance, the actual distance traveled by your airplane on landing is not critical in this section, although it might be fun to actually measure your landing distance. The following procedure is designed to help you, as the pilot, do your best in the landing, so that the next time you use the charts to predict the performance of your airplane, your piloting skills will not be a detriment. In landing especially, superb piloting skills might allow you to substantially exceed the published performance figures for your airplane.

You'll need a friend, a stopwatch, and a stable day. Mark the altimeter for the height of 50 feet above your runway elevation. Make several landings, with your assistant timing the interval between descending through the 50-foot point and coming to a full stop on the runway. Obviously, the shortest interval will occur when the plane is flown straight down into the ground, with a splatter instead of a landing rollout; please do not make a bird-poop simulation. Use

9-3 *A short-field landing.*

caution in every landing, and do your best to keep things safe. When you have nailed down the procedure that results in the shortest time interval, practice and fine-tune it until you can duplicate it every time (Fig. 9-3).

Further reading

Good Takeoffs and Good Landings, Christy/George,McGraw-Hill, 1991
Bush Flying, O'Meara, McGraw-Hill, 1990

10

Emergency procedures

"It's a beautiful, cool morning, a perfect day for a first flight," I assured the nervous computer technician fumbling with her safety belt in the back seat of the T210. In back of her was a few hundred pounds of computer equipment destined for a store in Twin Falls. Bill, the pilot and owner of this small, company plane (and, of course, the company that went with it), had hired me to give him an extended biennial during a routine business trip into Idaho. The technician in back had never flown in a small airplane before and it was written clearly on her face that if she didn't have to be here she wouldn't be coming along for the ride. She revealed the typical "if it ain't Boeing, I ain't going" attitude. However, work is work and so here she was. I chuckled to myself at her unnecessary fear of what would undoubtedly be an easy, uneventful flight.

Bill pushed the throttle to maximum boost and we settled back into the seats as the plane accelerated down the runway. Everything looked good. The nose came up and the plane began to climb. Then, something unusual happened.

The normal growling cadence of the engine missed a beat, then missed again. The engine made a staccato noise, punctuated with short periods of dead silence. Blue smoke poured from the exhaust pipe and the climb rate faded away until the plane was just flying level, and slowing. About 100-feet high, we had just passed the far end of the runway. I quickly scanned the engine gauges in front of me. Manifold pressure was normal, temperatures were fine, fuel flow—where was the fuel flow needle? I saw it on the other side of the dial, sitting by the manifold pressure needle, almost overlapped. The engine was sucking almost 50 gallons per hour. No wonder it ran roughly.

My attention then turned to Bill who was anxiously pulling on the yoke, desperate to make us go a little higher. Airspeed was falling through 100 mph. For an instant, I considered raising the gear, to clean up the airplane for climb, the way you might if this bird had two engines. I thought better of it; we might go down, and we'd need something to land on. The housing complex that was situated off the north end of the runway was getting closer—we couldn't land there. I suggested to Bill that we begin a turn while the engine was still developing a little power. Bill pulled hard on the yoke, and for a moment I resisted his inputs by pushing on the controls from my end. All at once he let go and exclaimed, "You got it!" "Oh boy," I thought, "I get to deal with an emergency on takeoff. Wah-hoo." I really wasn't very grateful.

We got on the radio and announced our intentions to make a one-eighty and land back on the runway. Airspeed diminished slowly but I felt there was sufficient energy for the turn. We were almost around when suddenly the engine made a noise like the last sighing of a whoopee cushion, or a horse blowing its nose, after which we could hear only the propeller blowing in the wind. It was finished. We were going down, but not on the runway as we had hoped.

Powerless from 100 feet, there aren't many options. Thankfully, the neighborhood was no longer in the way. A plowed field lay straight ahead, and luckily the furrows were pretty much aligned with our flight path. All I had to do was flare the plane and make a soft-field landing. Nobody in the plane made a sound, but I was so focused on the landing that I wouldn't have heard them if they were screaming their heads off. A few seconds later we touched down and were slowing to a stop in the field, plane and passengers undamaged.

The engine was still turning about idle speed, with the throttle untouched since the moment we took off. I considered the fuel problem and began to lean the mixture. About a quarter turn of the knob, and the engine promptly quit. I guess that wasn't the problem.

During the next few minutes, the plane safely on the ground, I began to shake with nervousness. I couldn't believe we'd actually made an emergency landing. The magnitude of the whole thing set in as an aftershock. During the short flight, there was absolutely no fear, no time to consider the *what ifs* of the impending crash. I had reacted instinctively to training and practice. But once on the ground again, I was scared, and to make things worse, the FAA was on its way over.

When the officials were finished stomping and muttering around the airplane, they took several pictures, made a report and left. Then we towed the plane back onto the airport grounds and turned it over to a mechanic for inspection and repairs.

Sadly, the computer technician probably will never ride in a little plane again.

Background information

Emergencies come in all shapes and sizes. Things as small as a poorly adjusted screw in a fuel-control unit can pump fuel through an engine with the energy of a fire hose, dousing any hope of internal combustion. Absent cotter pins can leave control surfaces fluttering down from a hapless and shaken airplane. Mosquitoes packing an induction filter can starve an engine for air. Flu viruses in the pilot's internal systems might cause disorientation and vertigo. Corrosion and microscopic cracks in key structures, insidiously-silent vacuum failures, huge, booming thunderstorms, carbon-monoxide poisoning from cracks in the heater system, restricted oxygen flows, tired, overworked air traffic controllers, bad internal filters, bad gas, propeller failures—the list goes on and on and *ON*—could all cause an emergency situation.

The funny thing is, as far as the pilot is concerned, every emergency boils down into a single task: Land right now, or if that's not practical, land as soon as possible. Pretty simple. Going straight to the point, the gist of this chapter is emergency landing skills.

Energy at impact

While the airplane is still flying it has tremendous capacity for damage. The capability to hurt oneself is directly related to the energy of the vehicle. Heavy, fast moving airplanes can do more damage than slow, light-weight ones. The kinetic energy formula looks like Fig. 10-1.

$$\text{Energy at impact} = \frac{1}{2}(\text{mass})(\text{velocity})^2$$

10-1 *Kinetic energy formula.*

Look familiar? The same formula structure applies to lift and dynamic pressure as discussed elsewhere in this book. It's just another way of mathematically describing the energy that might be extracted from the air to make a plane fly. Taken in raw form, the basic kinetic energy formula can be very revealing. Consider a small, bullet-shaped lump of lead. Sitting there on the table by itself, it can do no damage. Yet, take the same lump of lead, accelerate it down a gun barrel to supersonic speeds, and it might be capable of punching a hole in plate steel. Indeed, the killing power of guns is measured in their muzzle velocities and the size of the round, direct indicators of energy.

Apply the energy formula to airplanes, and things get very interesting. You're sitting there in a Boeing 747, flying along at 600 mph. You are part of an 800,000-pound transonic bullet. If your airliner has an emergency and needs to land, it would be easier to stop a freight train rolling at terminal velocity down the steep side of Niagara Falls. The energy contained in a flying 747 is extreme by any standard. When a plane that big crashes, the wreckage knocks over buildings, trees and small hills, scattering debris along a path stretching thousands of feet. As for the passengers inside, they just hope the airplane is able to dissipate its energy gradually, and hopefully on a runway.

By contrast, I saw a sales demonstration video for a prominent ultralight manufacturer. The salesman stood in a field and talked excitedly about the virtues of flight with the birds and the safety features of their latest model of ultralight. With a flourish, he introduced that very model and waved the camera to focus on an ultralight flying by as a mass of wires, tubing, cloth and raspy engine upon which rode a helmeted pilot who enthusiastically waved to the camera. The little flying machine went by about 15 feet high in a pretty bank. As the camera swept to follow the plane, the side of a building came into dreadful view. The ultralight headed right for it . . . and pow! It hit the wall head-on and fell to the ground. Unhurt, the pilot stepped out of the bent conglomeration of tubing and waved again. He was fine and the building didn't have a mark on it. This is an example of a low-energy impact. Lightweight and low speed equal low energy. Low energy means little damage in the crash.

There are two schools of thought in airplane design regarding energy, and they are on opposite sides of the fence. Ultralight designers would claim that light weight and low stall speeds make their machines safe in a crash. Boeing designers argue that four expensive engines, redundant systems and gorgeous design in triplicate reduce the *chance* of ever having a crash in their planes to a bare minimum; you'd have better chances of winning a lottery. You hear the same argument among pilots about the respective virtues of one engine or two. Sure, a single engine might quit, but certification requires a minimum stall speed that keeps the impact forces relatively tolerable. Conversely, the multiengine pilots say that the second engine precludes the possibility of a crash and thus negates the benefit of a slower stall.

In any case, the pilot's task in landing an airplane during an emergency is to minimize energy. The less energy in the landing, the less potential for injury. It's better to crash like a feather than land like a bullet.

Technique

An emergency landing is identical to a short-field landing, which is the epitome of low-energy arrivals. The only differences for the emergency are the occasional lack of power and a runway to land on. With this in mind, the skills needed to execute a successful emergency landing are found in the best short-field landings, with a few differences: namely, control of the approach and landing point without using power, and proper selection of a place to call a runway.

Powerless approach

The specifics of a power-off approach have been ironed out very well, having been used for years by pilots of gliders and rocketplanes. With practice, these pilots can pick and hit their landing point with accuracy every time, and due to the nature of their flying machines they haven't gone around even once.

In addition to the techniques discussed in Chapter 8, regarding the specifics of an accurate approach, the following methods might be helpful during an emergency approach where the pilot's power options are limited.

Configuration

The airplane should be configured for best glide and flown at the correct speed until the landing is a surety. This means that the plane is clean, often with zero or minimum flaps, with landing gear and spoilers/speed brakes retracted and speed at Vglide. As the pilot approaches the desired landing area, the configuration can be used to exercise some control over the plane's glide path. Landing gear, spoilers and speed brakes can be used to steepen the approach, then retracted again if the airplane needs an improved glide. Some pilots like to extend the drag devices part way from the beginning of the approach, then use them like a throttle, retracting them for less drag, extending them farther to increase descent, and so on. In this manner, the approach might be very similar to the normal one with power; i.e., setting the speed and adjusting the glidepath with the throttle; except in this case, the throttle is a configuration change.

Propeller In the absence of spoilers or speed brakes, the propeller-driven airplane still has a wonderful drag-control option. That is the constant-speed propeller itself. When an engine fails, it will usually turn in the slip stream with plenty of revolutions to provide oil pressure to the prop governor. With the engine developing no power, it causes no damage when the pilot pulls the prop control lever back to the lowest RPM setting. This is roughly equivalent to feathered, but not quite. During the approach, the pilot can adjust the drag on the airplane with precision, using the propeller control as a speed brake. The prop produces high drag at the high RPM setting, minimum drag at the low RPM position. It is happily variable at all settings in between.

The pilot may safely practice this method even when the engine is developing power, as long as the throttle is set at idle. Be sure to increase the propeller RPM before advancing the throttle in a go-around, or engine damage could result.

Landing gear If sufficient energy remains in the landing-gear system, the gear itself makes a wonderful speed brake. The only problem is that its position is not optional when the airplane is just about to touch down. Under almost all but the softest of landing surfaces (water), landing gear should be extended for the touchdown.

During the approach, however, the pilot might find the gear useful in adjusting the airplane's glidepath to the runway. If planned carefully, the pilot need only set the approach slightly high, extend the gear once on short final, and land. If, for one reason or another, the plane appears to be low on the approach and far enough from touchdown in the pilot's judgment, it might be beneficial to retract the gear to improve the glide, then extend it again later on.

Flaps Flap extension is a more difficult judgment call. With most airplanes, retracting the flaps again once they have been extended causes momentary losses of altitude that exceed those produced by leaving the flaps down in the first place. Consequently, once the flaps are extended, it is best to leave them there. In the effort to minimize speed and energy in the landing, flaps should be managed so that they are fully extended prior to the airplane meeting the ground.

Under special circumstances, flaps can be effective in extending the glide range of the airplane. This occurs when the flaps are extended while the airplane flies in ground effect. Suppose you are over a large body of water, gliding toward shore. You've kept everything clean in an effort to make land. When the airplane gets low to the surface, you see that you're not going to make it, but you have one last trick up your sleeve.

As you flare the plane to land in the drink, you extend the flaps partially while working to keep the plane as close to the surface as possible. You feel the plane gather itself and float in the air just above the waves. The shore looms closer. As the plane loses speed and lift, you extend the flaps yet farther. Again, as before, the machine seems to gain renewed lift and float a little farther towards shore. Soon, that lift dissipates and you extend the flaps fully. The same thing occurs, but is shorter lived. Never mind, though, you quickly extend the gear and roll up on the beach in the nick of time.

Extending the flaps while the airplane is in ground effect can offer the pilot a momentary reprieve from the sentence of landing. Used carefully, this technique might extend the point of touchdown several thousand feet. It might come in handy when the airplane is just shy of the landing zone and nothing is in the way but a surface that is flat and free of obstacles.

Approach path One of the best excuses for a traffic pattern is the approach-adjustment options it allows the pilot in the event of an emergency landing. During a straight-in approach, the field sits up ahead like a trophy to be attained. If, for some reason, the airplane comes up short, there is little that can be done. But in a pattern around the landing zone, the pilot can adjust the approach path with such accuracy that the landing point can be nailed, even with all the

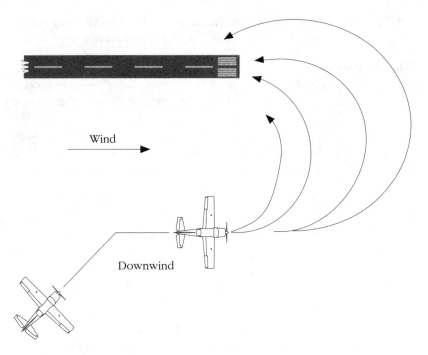

10-2 *For a dead-stick landing, the pilot on downwind has numerous options.*

other tricks left unused. The key lies in the pilot's adjustment of the flight path itself (Fig. 10-2).

Notice that from the airplane's position on downwind, the pilot might adjust the pattern away from the runway to use up excess altitude, or cut the pattern tight if things are low. From the base turn, the same options apply; the pilot might yet turn away or toward the runway and modify the glide path as necessary to nail the landing point every time.

With practice, engine failures in the traffic pattern can result in a spot landing, even when the pilot is forbidden to touch the airplane configuration or power. It is a simple matter of judgment on the approach path but requires a great deal of practice to do consistently.

Selection of a landing site

The landing surfaces upon which most airplanes can touch down are limited because of the plane's relatively small tires, weak landing gear, and high weight. The small tires don't roll very well over rough surfaces, and tend to sink in soft terrain. High landing speeds mean that a rough choice of landing areas might cause the landing-gear system to collapse soon after the plane touches down. For this reason, it is best for the pilot to use care in selecting the best possible landing area during an emergency.

The ideal landing area will be just like the runway, but far away from the FAA and close to the plane when the engine quits. It will be flat, hard, long enough to permit minor misjudgments on approach, and have few obstacles to get in the way of landing. As long as we're wishing, there should also be a telephone nearby, perhaps a nice complimentary hotel or campground, and someone to make repairs. Needless to say, the perfect emergency landing field might be somewhat difficult to find. Nevertheless, most pilots would be surprised at what kind of landing surface their airplanes can handle.

A pilot's first objective is to locate a place that is long enough and flat enough for landing. The field should be as close to the airplane as possible. Resist the temptation to scan the horizon for runways because in most cases you simply can't glide that far. Look below the plane, then scan carefully outward until you find what you're looking for. Once you have picked a field, examine it closely for obstacles, especially the variety that is hard to see, like electrical and telephone wires. Also look for cattle fences, ditches and the cattle themselves, anything that might cause a problem for your landing. Look carefully at the color of the field. Dark-colored soil might indicate a good deal of water and a surface that is undesirably soft, especially if the field is significantly darker than surrounding areas. If it has been plowed, study the direction of the furrows and pick a specific direction and the location on the field where you want to touch down. Watch out for trees.

In the absence of a windsock or control tower, you'll have to determine wind direction based on whatever indicators you can find. Look for nearby smoke, blowing dust, or water surfaces. These are excellent indicators from a distance. Getting closer (and maybe too late to do anything about it) you'll notice that leaves and grass make good wind indicators. Take your best guess and plan your pattern accordingly, to land into the wind.

Of course, during the few moments you have to contemplate your situation, it is wise to attempt to solve the problem and avoid the emergency altogether. Do not extend your restart attempts into the time you need to land. Too many pilots are killed when their airplanes fly into the ground while they are huddled under the panel trying to start a dead engine.

Plan to touch down gently on the spot you picked earlier. Keep in mind that a power loss means you are committed to the landing much earlier than you would be normally because there is no time or power to maneuver for another choice. If you change your mind about the landing place, do it early, don't wait until you're about to touch down.

Emergency takeoff

Although rare, sometimes there is a need to get out of a short field or emergency-landing site if the plane is determined to be flyable. In that case, the need for strong takeoff performance might be extreme.

Airplane modifications

If pilots are really desperate for extra performance, a clean plane is the starting place for a serious taping job. Get some good quality duct tape and cover the inlets for the cabin vents, cover seams in unused doors, baggage hatches, and access panel junctures. Fairing gaps are also good candidates for taping. Be sure not to hinder the operation of critical parts or systems with your tape, such as covering static ports, or oil cooler inlets.

Remove antenna with a simple screwdriver. These performance-enhancing preparations might seem a bit unorthodox or radical for the typical pilot. Many of them are, for normal operations. If anything, some are a bit extreme, but they are all perfectly harmless. Just consider this problem: The pilot has a need to completely maximize the takeoff, or flight, performance of the airplane.

Some time ago, a couple of disoriented pilots mistook the small municipal airport in Salt Lake City for the international one. They were in clouds at the time and landed (I guess) at the first airport they found. The runway at SLC Airport II is a little more than 5000 feet long. These pilots barely stopped, using the full length of the runway. They were flying a Boeing 727. The landing was safely accomplished, but the embarrassed flight crew was then faced with the more difficult prospect of taking off.

They off-loaded all passengers and freight. They removed all the seats and as much of the interior accommodations as possible. After computing the minimum fuel required to safely fly the 8-mile jaunt to the international airport, they reduced fuel quantity to that minimum. New decision and rotation speeds were calculated, and finally, after much deliberation and removal of all unnecessary items and waiting for a cool day, the plane was successfully flown away.

Obviously these methods would be unnecessary on a long runway, but they might be very useful after a forced landing, or even for the pilot's own entertainment. Consider yourself in the same position as the hapless 727 pilots. The available runway might be a smidgen too short and maybe covered with mud. What can you do to improve your takeoff safety margin?

Survival gear

What kind of survival gear would enhance pilot or airplane performance? Ever consider carrying a few select tools? What about a big roll of duct tape? I was teaching aerobatics in an old Citabria one day when the cowling came loose and started flapping violently on the nose. It was frightening. The metal began to tear loose and it was apparent that soon it would fly off the plane, perhaps hitting the windshield in the process. Fortunately, we were directly over a runway at the time. If there had not been a runway down there, I would have seriously considered landing in a field. A hard slip helped lose altitude and kept the cowling from flapping at the same time. After landing, we called a mechanic over from the main airport and he brought a single tool; you guessed it—a roll of duct tape. With tape plastered all over the nose of the airplane and the cowling buttoned down beyond hope of coming loose again, we flew back home.

After a precautionary landing in a field somewhere, duct tape and a few tools might be extremely handy. Consider packing a small tool kit with your survival gear that might include a knife, pliers, an adjustable wrench, a multiheaded screwdriver, tape, a little wire and some rope. If you can't fix the plane with that stuff, the items might be very handy for making a camp.

Skills to practice

Simulate an emergency landing at every opportunity. Obviously, you don't want to actually make an emergency of your own, but *safely* simulate its conditions. Use the techniques described above to control the descent and landing. Practice until your eye becomes trained in what an emergency approach should look like.

When you're flying cross-country, entertain yourself with the task of picking suitable emergency landing fields. As far as possible, look for enough detail to help you pick the precise landing point and direction you would use. Identify an approach path to get there. Someday, you might actually have to do it.

Speaking of using a field, it is wise to get some experience by actually landing in one. Find a good instructor with a suitable airplane and go play. Some of the most enjoyable flying I have ever done involved a simple airplane and some mountain-side *runways*. The skills to be learned and the experience to be gained doing this kind of flying are invaluable.

Further reading

Design for Safety, David Thurston, McGraw-Hill, 1994
I Learned About Flying From That, Flying Magazine, McGraw-Hill, 1993
Aftermath, Flying Magazine, McGraw-Hill, 1994

A

Abbreviations

AFM	Aircraft flight manual
agl	Above ground level
AoA	Angle of attack
ARNAV	Area Navigation
ASI	Airspeed indicator
ATIS	Automatic Terminal Information Service
ATC	Air Traffic Control
C	Centigrade/Celsius
CFI	Certificated Flight Instructor
CG	Center of gravity
DEN	Denver, Colorado
EGT	Exhaust gas temperature
FBO	Fixed Base Operation—airport business
G	Load factor
H	High pressure
hp	Horsepower
IAS	Indicated air speed
IFR	Instrument Flight Rules
kts	Nautical miles, miles/hr
L	Low pressure
L/D	Lift to drag ratio, glide ratio
LAX	Los Angeles, California
lbs	Pounds—unit of weight
mph	Statute miles per hour
msl	Mean sea level
N1	Rotational speed (%) of primary turbine
OAT	Outside air temperature
p	Air density, slugs/cubic feet
PIH	Pocatello, Idaho

RPM	Revolutions per minute
SLC	Salt Lake City, Utah
STOL	Short takeoff and landing
T	Temperature
TAS	True airspeed
TBO	Time between overhauls
V1	Takeoff decision speed
V2	Takeoff safety speed
Va	Maneuvering speed
VFR	Visual Flight Rules
Vfs	Flaps-up climb speed
Vglide	Best glide speed
Vl/d	Best glide speed
Vne	Never exceed speed
Vr	Rotation speed
Vs	Stall speed, clean
VSI	Vertical speed indicator
Vso	Stall speed, landing configuration
VW	Volkswagen (car)
Vx	Best angle of climb speed
Vxse	Best angle climb speed, one-engine out
Vy	Best rate of climb speed

B

Aircraft

Many aircraft models come with various horsepower, seating, and other options. The following descriptions represent typical configurations.

Aero Commander: 500 hp, high-wing twin, 7 seats

B-52: Heavy bomber, eight-jet

B-727: Medium range, tri-jet airliner

B-737: Medium range/capacity airliner, twin-jet

B-747: Heavy, wide-body airliner, four-jet

B-767: Wide-body airliner, twin-jet

Beech Baron: 600 hp low-wing twin, 6 seats

Beech C-23/Sundowner: 180 hp single, low-wing, 4 seats

C-152: 115 hp single, 2 seats, trainer

C-T210/Turbo Centurion: 300 hp single, 6 seat, retract

Cessna 182: 235 hp high-wing single, 4 seats

Cessna 310: 420-600 hp low-wing twin, 6 seats

Cessna 172: 145-160 hp high-wing single, 4 seats

Cessna 206: 285-300 hp high-wing single, 6 seats

Citabria: 118-150 hp high-wing single, tailwheel

Concorde: Supersonic long-range airliner, four-jet

Convair 580: Turboprop airliner

E-35 Bonanza: 225 hp low-wing single, 4 seats, retract

EMB-120 Brasilia: Regional twin-turboprop, 30 seats

Ercoupe: 65 hp, 2 seat plane for every garage

Extra 300: 300 hp, unlimited aerobatic monoplane

F-104/Starfighter: Supersonic fighter, single-jet

F-16: Supersonic modern fighter, single-jet

Helio Courier: 250-400 hp high-wing STOL, 6 seat

Lancair IV: 350 hp low-wing single, 4 seats, retract

Learjet: Twin-jet, business plane
Maule MX7-235: 235 hp high-wing STOL, 4 seat, tailwheel
MC15 Cricri: 30 hp low-wing aerobatic twin, 1 seat
Mig 15: Subsonic single-jet fighter, Russian
Mitsubishi MU-2: Turboprop twin, corporate transport
Mooney: 200 hp low-wing single, 4 seats, retract
Piper Arrow: 200 hp low-wing single, 4 seats, retract
Piper Cherokee 140: 150 hp low-wing single, 4 seats
Piper Cub: 150 hp high-wing STOL, 2 seat, tailwheel
Piper Lance: 300 hp low-wing single, 6 seats, retract
Piper Cherokee 180: 180 hp low-wing single, 4 seats
Pitts Special: 260 hp aerobatic biplane, 2 seats
SR-71: Mach 3+, twin-jet, spy-plane, 2 seats
Suhkoi: 360 hp, unlimited aerobatic monoplane
SX-300: 300 hp low-wing single, 2 seats, retract
T-38: Supersonic, twin-jet, advanced trainer
U-2: High flying jet spy-plane, long wings
Waco Biplane: 225 hp biplane, 3 seats, tailwheel
X-15: Mach 6+ experimental rocket plane

Index

Boldface numbers indicate illustrations

About the author

Lewis Bjork graduated from Westminster College with a B.S. in air operations. He has logged more than 2500 hours of flight instruction at all levels and is presently teaching off-airport, emergency landings in a Maule and aerobatics in a Pitts S-2B.

Lewis's methods for instrument flying make difficult concepts easy to understand and simple to execute. Many other flight instructors have adopted his methods successfully. His locally published aircraft performance guide is presently being used by Maule as a training aid for buyers.